Substance Use and Family Violence

Substance Use and Family Violence

Margaret Campe, Kathi Harp, and Carrie Oser, Editors

Cognella Series on Family and Gender-Based Violence

Series edited by Claire Renzetti

❖ cognella®
SAN DIEGO

Bassim Hamadeh, CEO and Publisher
Amy Smith, Senior Project Editor
Casey Hands, Production Editor
Jess Estrella, Senior Graphic Designer
Alexa Lucido, Licensing Manager
Natalie Piccotti, Director of Marketing
Kassie Graves, Senior Vice President, Editorial
Jamie Giganti, Director of Academic Publishing

Cover image: Cover image copyright © 2019 iStockphoto LP/Vizerskaya.

Printed in the United States of America.

cognella | ACADEMIC PUBLISHING
3970 Sorrento Valley Blvd., Ste. 500, San Diego, CA 92121

This book is dedicated to all the people who have experienced family violence intersected with substance use. Our hope is that this textbook serves as an important resource for training the next generation of scholars and practitioners to help alleviate the burdens associated with substance use and various types of familial violence.

Brief Contents

Detailed Contents

Chapter 3   Substance Use and Intimate Partner Violence   61

Yu Lu, PhD and Jeff R. Temple, PhD

Preface

Substance use and family violence have implications for a wide range of disciplines and affect the lives of countless individuals. Whether you plan to work in research or education, in policy or criminal justice, in social work or public health, or in some other field affected by these issues, it is hoped that awareness and knowledge of the concepts discussed in this textbook will be an important tool.

As researchers of substance use and the negative effects it has not only on individuals, but also their families and communities, we found that there were no up-to-date textbooks available that delve into the relationship between substance use and violence within families. So, we decided to write one. The purpose of this text is to provide readers with a better understanding of how and why substance use and violent behavior can co-occur, and specifically, how the relationship between the two play out across a range of familial relationships. Providing both historical context and contemporary evidence, this volume uses peer-reviewed literature, theories, and perspectives from numerous fields, including sociology, criminology, psychology, social work, public health, gerontology, and gender and women's studies, to provide a comprehensive understanding of the scope of the problem, who it impacts, and effective strategies for both preventing violent behavior and intervening to stop its spread.

This book is intended to serve as a core text in both upper-level undergraduate and graduate courses. We focus specifically on four principal domains in which substance use and violence affect families: *substance use and interpersonal violence, substance use and intimate partner violence, substance use and child neglect and abuse, and substance use and elder neglect and abuse.* Following each of the four content chapters is a discussion and analysis of contemporary issues in practice. These supplemental discussions aid the reader in applying substantive chapter content to real-world quandaries practitioners face in the field and provide perspective related to the disparate effects of substance use and family violence on specific marginalized populations. Each topical content chapter covers the following:

- key definitions
- the scope of the problem

- historical and current perspectives
- risk and protective factors
- data on prevalence rates across demographic groups
- an overview of prominent theories across disciplines
- summaries of relevant policies, programs, or interventions

The goal of this pedagogical and organizational structure is to facilitate students' understanding of the relationship between substance use and violence in four family context domains, as well as equip them with the knowledge related to the real-world effects and challenges of addressing substance use and family violence. Additionally, we think instructors will find that the supplemental discussions, key words and definitions, discussion questions, and other features in this book allow for the assessment of a variety of student learning outcomes throughout their course(s).

The first chapter, written by Martha Tillson, is an introduction. It outlines definitions of both family violence and substance use, overviews the scope of the problem, and provides a brief historical contextual overview. This chapter also introduces theoretical perspectives and addresses risk and protective factors, as well as presents the concepts of prevention, intervention, and treatment. The second chapter, written by Callie Rennison and Carlos Cuevas, discusses substance use and *interpersonal violence*, or violence that occurs between family members (e.g., spouses, sibling-to-sibling violence, parental violence, child-to-parent violence, and violence among other relatives). Jeff Temple and Yu Lu authored Chapter 3, which covers substance use and *intimate partner violence (IPV)*. IPV is defined as physical, sexual, or psychological aggression by a current or former partner or spouse that can occur in a heterosexual or same-sex relationship. Chapter 4, by Samantha Brown and Jennifer Bellamy, describes substance use and *child maltreatment*, which includes emotional and physical abuse, neglect, and sexual abuse. In the final chapter, Georgia Anetzberger focuses on substance use and *elder abuse and neglect*, which encompasses elder mistreatment, self-neglect, and fraud. The chapters include a variety of vignettes, contemporary data, activities, and examples from news media to aid in comprehension of terms, types of violence, and substantive themes. Following each chapter there is an additional discussion of a specific matter or issue related to the preceding chapter topic.

CHAPTER ONE

Substance Use and Family Violence

An Introduction and Overview

Martha Tillson, BSW, MA

Introduction

For most people, being a member of a family is one of the few lifelong constants: it is the first environment, the first people we come to know and relate to and interact with, and often the people that we know for the longest length of time. As children, we begin our lives within families; as spouses, partners, or parents, we join new families and create families of our own. Families can guide our growth, dispense advice, support us in our vulnerable times, celebrate our achievements, and provide purpose and meaning to our lives.

Although families have the potential to be a constant, nurturing structure in an individual's life, this is not always the case. The vulnerability of family relationships—particularly with children, older adults, and women in intimate partnerships—creates an opportunity for neglect, exploitation, or abuse (physical, sexual, or emotional). Too often, such maltreatment is kept "within the family," reflecting a widespread and harmful belief that family matters need not involve outsiders, such as law enforcement, adult and child protective services, community members, or friends. This belief has maintained a prolonged silence around family violence. To this day, it is still a difficult and sensitive topic, often associated with shame, guilt, trauma, or broken trust, but also with incredible resiliency, as victims navigate and negotiate their safety.

The connection of substance use to violence within families is complex and often misunderstood. Stories of husbands drinking and physically abusing wives, or of parents using drugs (and occasionally overdosing) in the presence of children, may lead to the conclusion that substance use is a *cause* of violence, abuse, and neglect. However, both substance use and violence may be more strongly related to other factors (including stress, comorbid mental health problems, or a perpetrator's history of experiencing violence themselves). Victims may also engage in substance use, which can increase vulnerability and dependence within a violent relationship, even as it may also serve as a coping mechanism. While substance use may exacerbate violence, and often co-occurs with it, understanding and acknowledging the true nature of this relationship is no small task.

Within this book, the term **family violence** is used broadly to refer to the use of power or force with the intention of causing deprivation or physical, psychological, or developmental harm to a family member. *Power or force* may be actual physical violence, or the plausible threat thereof. The type of harm committed may vary depending on the relationship between family members, as well as victim and perpetrator characteristics. For example, older adults may be physically, sexually, or emotionally abused by family members, but they may also be victims of financial exploitation, or engage in self-neglect behaviors. Specifically, this book will discuss interpersonal violence within families, intimate partner violence, child maltreatment, and elder abuse and neglect, all in the context of substance use.

The term **substance use** should also be carefully defined. It is the broadest term, describing use of any intoxicant, regardless of the substance's legality or an individual's patterns of use. Many people use substances safely in a purely recreational or experimental capacity without developing a **substance use disorder,** the current terminology used by the *Diagnostic and Statistical Manual of Mental Disorders* (5th ed.; DSM-5; APA, 2013) to describe "a cluster of cognitive, behavioral, and physiological symptoms indicating that the individual continues using the substance despite significant substance-related problems" (p. 483). Without meeting the specific diagnostic criteria of a disorder, as determined by a qualified clinical professional, an individual may still be described as engaging in **substance misuse** or *problematic substance use*. Terms such as "substance abuse" or "substance dependence" refer to diagnostic categories from a prior version of the *DSM* and are being phased out of widespread usage.

The purpose of this introduction is to provide a broad overview of types of family violence in the context of substance use. It is not intended to be comprehensive, as the remaining chapters of the book will describe specific topics in greater detail, but should offer a preliminary understanding of relevant issues. We begin by describing the scope of the problem at hand.

Scope of the Problem

Family violence is, unfortunately, not an uncommon occurrence. Global estimates provided by the World Health Organization (WHO, 2021a) indicate that 30% of women worldwide have been physically or sexually victimized by an intimate partner or have experienced sexual violence from a non-partner. Furthermore, approximately 58% of women murdered around the world are killed at the hands of intimate partners or other family members (UNODC, 2019). Elder mistreatment, by comparison, occurs at a global rate of approximately 16% (Yon et al., 2017, 2019). Finally, global data suggest that approximately 54% of all children have experienced past-year bullying or physical, emotional, or sexual violence, or have witnessed violence in the past year (Hillis et al., 2016). Furthermore, 75% of young children worldwide (ages 2–4) have experienced past-month violent physical or psychological discipline, and 176 million children under 5 years old live with a mother who has experienced past-year intimate partner violence (UNICEF, 2017).

Statistics related to the prevalence of family violence should be interpreted with caution, however, due to frequent underreporting. For example, global data indicate that only 4% of elder abuse incidences are reported (WHO, 2016). Community-based studies have found that approximately 5% to 9% of child physical and sexual abuse cases result in protective services involvement (Afifi et al., 2015; MacMillan et al., 2003), and only 1% of adolescent girls who have experienced forced sex have reached out for professional help (UNICEF, 2017). Child, partner, or older adult fatalities may be difficult to attribute directly to family violence, maltreatment, or neglect situations. Phrasing of questions on self-report surveys may produce different responses, depending on terms used or behaviors described. Finally, fear, shame, and perceived stigma may further prevent victims from accurately reporting experiences of violence, whether to law enforcement, protective services, health providers, confidantes, or researchers.

Particularly when substance use is involved, victims may worry about criminal justice involvement, consequences for child custody, or forced substance use treatment attendance, further reducing the likelihood of reporting. Globally, approximately 275 million people (or 5.5% of the global population 15 to 64 years old) used illicit drugs in 2019, with the most common drugs used being cannabis (200 million people), opioids (62 million people), amphetamines (27 million people), and cocaine (20 million people; WHO, 2021b). Although more than half of the global population abstained from drinking alcohol in 2016, drinking rates in the United States were considerably higher, with only 28.3% of individuals over 15 reporting not drinking in the past 12 months (WHO, 2018). Approximately 14.5% of the United States population aged 12 and over (40.3 million people) had a past-year substance use disorder in 2020, according to data from the National Survey on Drug Use and Health (SAMHSA, 2021).

Both substance use and family violence have myriad consequences across a variety of life domains. Beyond injuries such as cuts, bruises, and broken bones, negative consequences to physical health—including long-term and chronic conditions—are a common consequence of all types of interpersonal violence (Bick & Nelson, 2016; Campbell et al., 2002; CWIG, 2019; Podnieks & Thomas, 2017; Widom et al., 2012), as are mental health problems, including depression, anxiety, and posttraumatic stress disorder (Begle et al., 2011; Mechanic et al., 2008; Mills et al., 2013; Sugaya et al., 2012). Consequences to physical health resulting from substance use vary considerably by type of substance, frequency of use, and route of administration: for example, excessive, prolonged alcohol consumption may lead to liver problems (such as cirrhosis or steatosis), heart problems, or pancreatitis (NIAAA, n.d.), whereas injection drug use is associated with risk of transmission of blood-borne illnesses (such as HIV or hepatitis C), abscesses, deep vein thrombosis, and increased chances of overdose (O'Donnell & Lawson, 2016; Roy et al., 2016). However, although mental health problems and substance use disorder very often co-occur, the direction of influence is less clear: substance use may contribute to mental illness, mental illness may contribute to substance use, or both may arise from a common etiology (NIDA, 2020).

Beyond physical and mental health, family violence and substance use are also associated with billions of dollars of costs to society in medical costs, lost productivity, criminal justice costs, property damage, and financial fraud and abuse (DeVooght et al., 2014; NDIC, 2011; Peterson et al., 2018; Sacks et al., 2015; True Link Financial, 2015). Much research has also supported the finding that both violence (Black et al., 2010; Ehrensaft et al., 2003; McTavish et al., 2016; Menard et al., 2014; Stuart et al., 2014a, 2014b) and substance use (Bailey et al., 2006; Hedges, 2012; Henry et al., 2018; Knight et al., 2014) are perpetuated through generations within families, which involves contributions from both genetic factors and social learning. Traumatic or violent experiences can also set the stage for later victimization, as evidenced by the strong association between a history of childhood sexual abuse and sexual exploitation or trafficking (Franchino-Olsen, 2021; Laird et al., 2020).

Finally, both issues can result in involvement with criminal justice or social service systems. In many instances, such involvement leads to ultimately positive results, such as the arrest of a violent domestic partner, or increased monitoring of an older adult exhibiting signs of self-neglect. However, positive outcomes resulting from systemic involvement are contingent on appropriate services and resources being available and accessible. Without such services, systemic involvement may worsen a family's situation by creating or exacerbating trauma (Harp & Oser, 2018; Kenny et al., 2015) and stigma (Hartwell, 2004; Moore & Tangney, 2017).

Historical Context

Over time, the evolution of legal and policy responses to family violence has largely centered around discussion of the **public/private dichotomy**. Historically, violence and maltreatment within families—including spouses, children, or older adults—has been viewed as a private matter: the rearing and discipline of children was viewed as the responsibility of the parents, as treatment of wives was left to the discretion of husbands. To this day, many cultures still struggle to implement effective responses to family violence due to the predominance of this perspective, including in some North African and Middle Eastern Islamic societies (Salhi, 2013), India (Rao et al., 2017), and South Africa (Mogstad et al., 2016). Patriarchal norms and reluctance to involve law enforcement also contribute to the silence surrounding violence within the family. However, such cultural differences should be carefully considered when designing treatment or prevention programs.

Much legislation has aimed to address aspects of family violence. The **Victims of Crime Act (VOCA)**, an early piece of critical legislation passed in 1984, marked an important turning point in public policy response. According to *West's Encyclopedia of American Law*, VOCA "was an attempt by the federal government to help the victims of criminal actions through means other than punishment of the criminal" (Phelps & Lehman, 2007, p. 222). The Crime Victim's Fund created by VOCA, which is funded by fines and forfeited bonds from convicted individuals, provides both direct and indirect support for victims (OVC, n.d.). Also passed in 1984, the **Family Violence Prevention and Services Act (FVPSA)** provides further monetary support by earmarking federal funding for aid to victims of domestic violence, including both children and adults. The majority of funding annually supports shelters, programs, and supportive services for victims, while lesser amounts are spent to fund prevention or education programs, as well as the National Domestic Violence Hotline. In fiscal year 2021, enacted funding for FVPSA totaled over $650 million, including $250 million in new funding for grant programs to support culturally specific populations and survivors of sexual assault (CRS, 2021a).

Ten years later, the **Violence Against Women Act (VAWA)** of 1994 authorized additional grant funding for programs addressing domestic violence, dating violence, sexual assault, stalking, or other violent crimes against women; allowed for enhanced prosecution of repeat sex offenders; and mandated restitution to some victims of sex offenses. Although men may certainly be victims of any of the abovementioned crimes, the naming of the act and the inclusion of "women" in its title reflected a growing awareness of women's disproportionate risk of victimization. VAWA's reauthorizations (most recently in 2013) have expanded grant purpose areas to include sex trafficking and established nondiscrimination provisions for funded programs, which have received over $8 billion through the Office on Violence Against Women since 1995 (CRS, 2019). As of 2021, a reauthorization bill has passed the U.S. House of Representatives (H.R. 1620), but a partner bill has yet to be introduced in the Senate (CRS, 2021b).

The year of VAWA's passage also marked the point at which all 50 states had adopted some form of civil restraining or protective order legislation (Ko, 2002). Although such legislation still varies considerably from state to state in terms of types of protective orders offered, limitations, and definitions, the existence of such legal protections for victims of family violence has been an important shift. Typically, the **protective order** process begins with an *emergency protective order (EPO)*, which usually lasts for a brief period (often a few days) and serves to insure a victim's immediate safety. Victims may then seek a *preliminary (PPO)* or *temporary protective order (TPO)*, which maintain protective conditions until a full hearing. At the hearing, a judge will decide whether a full protective order may be granted, which allows restrictions to be extended, usually for a finite period of a few years. Such orders may include coverage for victims of domestic violence, stalking, harassment, or sexual assault, depending on state law, and can require the perpetrator to refrain from certain behaviors (like contacting the victim) or comply with conditions (such as obtaining a formal assessment).

The most recent piece of legislation marking a shift in policy related to family violence has been the **Elder Justice Act (EJA)**, passed in 2010 as part of the Patient Protection and Affordable Care Act (ACA). Although the Act did not include provisions for a targeted criminal justice response to abuse of older persons, the EJA did authorize state-level funding to support adult protective services, as well as ombudsmen and surveyors of long-term care facilities, to enhance protection of older adults. Furthermore, the EJA requires crimes occurring in federally funded long-term care facilities to be reported, and has established federal bodies (the Elder Justice Coordinating

Council and Advisory Board on Elder Abuse, Neglect, and Exploitation) to make strategic plans and recommendations to promote development in the field of elder justice (CRS, 2017).

Alongside these shifts in legislation related to family violence has been a change in the legal response to substance use, reflecting shifts in public understanding of substance use as a medical, rather than a moral, problem. Although federal laws controlling or restricting distribution, manufacture, or possession of substances had begun in the United States during the 1900s, local criminal justice and international military responses escalated with the "War on Drugs" declared by President Richard Nixon in 1971. Legislation such as the Controlled Substances Act (1970) and the Anti-Drug Abuse Act (1988) created the modern system of criminal penalties for illicit drugs, based upon potential for abuse, accepted medical use, and potential for addiction. In recent years, however, legislation such as the Comprehensive Addiction and Recovery Act (2016), 21st Century Cures Act (2016), and Substance Use-Disorder Prevention that Promotes Opioid Recovery and Treatment (SUPPORT) for Patients and Communities Act (2018) have prioritized treatment for substance use disorders, rather than punishment through incarceration, as the most effective public response. This shift reflects a changing understanding of disordered substance use as a chronic and relapsing disease, affected by diverse biological, social, and environmental factors, rather than a voluntary behavior to be corrected through punishment.

In the chapters that follow, these historical and contemporary factors will be discussed in greater detail as they pertain to specific types of family violence and the relationship between violence and substance use. Theoretical perspectives will also be presented as models through which to understand this complex relationship. One such model, describing the role of power and control in family violence, will be presented next.

Theoretical Perspectives

Numerous models and tools have been designed to frame our understanding of violent victimization. One such model, the **Power and Control Wheel** (Figure 1.1), was created in 1984 by the Minnesota Domestic Abuse Intervention Programs (DAIP, 2017) of Duluth, Minnesota, as a means of describing women's experiences of intimate partner violence. Based on focus group discussions with local victims, clinicians developed a diagram depicting common tactics and patterns of behaviors used by male perpetrators to control female victims in domestic violence contexts. The

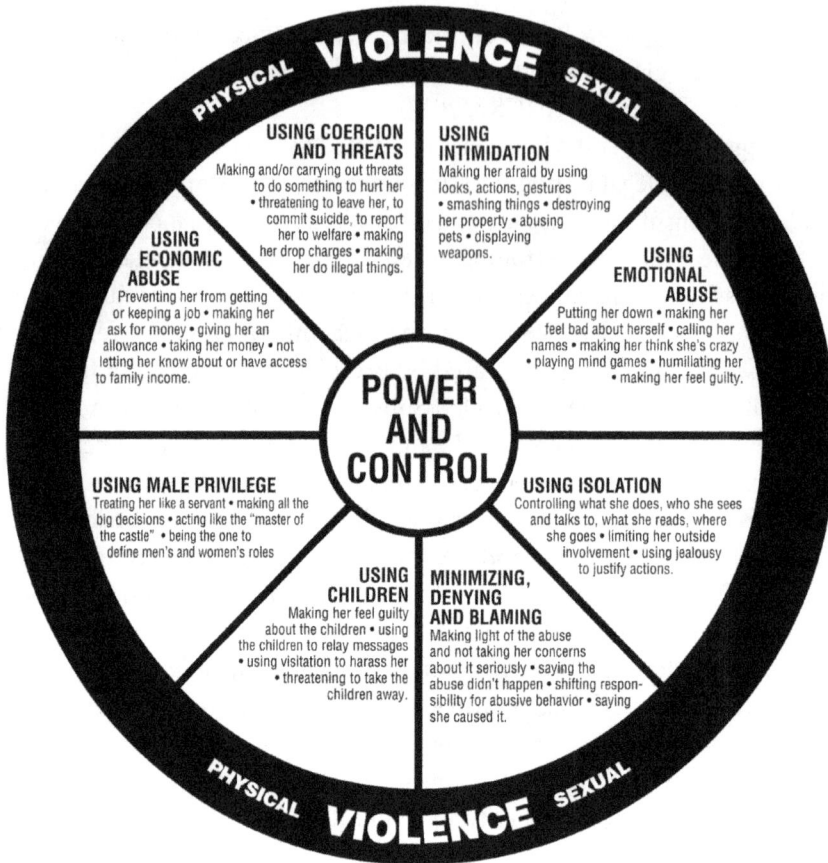

PHYSICAL VIOLENCE SEXUAL

USING COERCION AND THREATS
Making and/or carrying out threats to do something to hurt her • threatening to leave her, to commit suicide, to report her to welfare • making her drop charges • making her do illegal things.

USING INTIMIDATION
Making her afraid by using looks, actions, gestures • smashing things • destroying her property • abusing pets • displaying weapons.

USING ECONOMIC ABUSE
Preventing her from getting or keeping a job • making her ask for money • giving her an allowance • taking her money • not letting her know about or have access to family income.

USING EMOTIONAL ABUSE
Putting her down • making her feel bad about herself • calling her names • making her think she's crazy • playing mind games • humiliating her • making her feel guilty.

POWER AND CONTROL

USING MALE PRIVILEGE
Treating her like a servant • making all the big decisions • acting like the "master of the castle" • being the one to define men's and women's roles

USING ISOLATION
Controlling what she does, who she sees and talks to, what she reads, where she goes • limiting her outside involvement • using jealousy to justify actions.

USING CHILDREN
Making her feel guilty about the children • using the children to relay messages • using visitation to harass her • threatening to take the children away.

MINIMIZING, DENYING AND BLAMING
Making light of the abuse and not taking her concerns about it seriously • saying the abuse didn't happen • shifting responsibility for abusive behavior • saying she caused it.

PHYSICAL VIOLENCE SEXUAL

FIGURE 1.1 Power and Control Wheel

Copyright © by Domestic Abuse Intervention Programs.

Wheel has been used for counseling and education for both victims and perpetrators, as well as to inform practitioners and the general public.

The concepts of *power* and *control* lie at the centermost point of the Wheel, representing their central position in the experience of domestic violence. Surrounding *power* and *control* are specific behaviors or tactics that reinforce these concepts, such as *intimidation*, *isolation*, and *emotional abuse*. Encompassing these tactics, outlining the Wheel as a whole, are *physical and sexual violence*. This violence, as well as the plausible threat of it, strengthens the efficacy of the perpetrator's tactics and thereby supports their power and control in the relational context.

Another important aspect of the Power and Control Wheel as a model for intimate partner violence is the way in which it reflects how abusive behaviors are recognized or acknowledged. At the outside of the wheel, *physical and sexual violence* are more readily identified as abusive behaviors.

The specific tactics within the Wheel, however, are not always as easily recognizable as abuse, from the perspective of outsiders and victims alike. These behaviors rather represent a broader pattern of **coercive control**, a term coined by Dr. Evan Stark (2007) to describe how perpetrators of abuse "use various means to hurt, humiliate, intimidate, exploit, isolate, and dominate their victims" through use of threatened or actualized physical abuse in combination with psychological, emotional, or political tactics (p. 5). Once again, the central themes of power and control frequently underly the dynamics of such relationships.

The Power and Control Wheel has been criticized in the past, in part for a lack of cultural appropriateness for marginalized groups, an important consideration given that the model was designed based on a population that was over 90% White (Paymar & Barnes, 2007). However, the Wheel's framework may be adapted to reflect the unique experiences of diverse populations (Pope & Ferraro, 2006). Such adaptations may incorporate multiple intersecting identities of victims (including sexual orientation, age, race or ethnicity, physical or mental disability, religion, and class) to more accurately describe how these factors shape individuals' experience of, and response to, violence (Chavis & Hill, 2008). In particular, it is important to recognize that abusive tactics are often adapted and tailored by perpetrators to inflict greater harm upon victims, depending on a victim's individual needs, characteristics, and values.

Such adaptations can create the opportunity for distinct patterns of abuse. For example, the rise of digital media (e.g., use of smartphones or social media websites) has resulted in increasing occurrence of **digital abuse** (also known as cyber abuse), including monitoring victims' online behaviors, location, or social networks; posting incriminating photos or spreading harmful rumors about victims; and sending unwanted sexual images or messages to victims (Reed et al., 2016; Reyner, 2017). **Religious** or **spiritual abuse**, another specific pattern, may occur when a perpetrator uses their own or a victim's religious beliefs to rationalize or justify abuse, to shame or manipulate a victim, or control the victim's religious practices.

Substance use may further shape abusive or violent behaviors, whether it is present in the victim, the perpetrator, or both parties. A perpetrator using substances may use their intoxication as an excuse for violence, or may threaten to use a substance as a controlling tactic if the victim knows their use to be associated with violence. A victim using substances may become more vulnerable to abuse while intoxicated; if they are dependent (physically or psychologically) on a substance, the perpetrator may also withhold or limit access to the substance to maintain control. Substance use may furthermore be a coping mechanism for victims seeking to dissociate, forget, or manage physical pain, though it may have the unfortunate effect of aiding victims' tolerance for a violent situation rather than leaving. These scenarios also align with victims' experiences of sexual exploitation or sex trafficking, whether as children, youth, or adults; substance use often co-occurs in exploitative situations, but may be used as a means of reducing victims' resistance, of manipulation, or as a coping tool among victims themselves (Barnert et al., 2017; Le et al., 2018). Particularly when both victim and perpetrator are engaging in problematic substance use, the perpetrator may discourage or prevent the victim from seeking treatment in order to keep them entrapped in an abusive, exploitative situation. In many ways, substance use affects the nature of violence in families and determines tactics by which an abuser may obtain and maintain power and control.

Considering the complex and intertwined nature of both substance use and family violence, it is all the more important to understand risk and protective factors—for both issues separately and as co-occurring conditions—as will be discussed in the following section.

Risk and Protective Factors

A **risk factor** is any characteristic (physiological, psychological, or social) associated with an increased likelihood of an undesirable outcome, including disease, injury, or harmful behaviors. Conversely, a **protective factor** is any characteristic associated with a *decreased* likelihood of such an outcome. Understanding risk and protective factors associated with a given phenomenon allows for clinicians, researchers, policymakers, and other professionals in the field to more easily detect when the phenomenon is occurring, to predict which individuals are most likely to experience it, to take preventive measures against it, and to more effectively respond with evidence-based treatment. It is important to remember that risk factors are by no means deterministic: in other words, individuals with such factors in their past or present environments are not guaranteed to experience substance use or violence, just as not all individuals experiencing violence or substance use will present with each risk factor indicated by the research. Similarly, the presence of protective factors does not guarantee immunity from these issues. However, in the cases of substance use and victimization or perpetration of family violence, understanding associated risk and protective factors provides a more complete and holistic awareness of the connections and common causes within this complex relationship.

First and foremost, gender is implicated as a risk factor for experiencing family violence, particularly in context of intimate partnerships. Although men are not immune to experiencing violence, the fact remains that most domestic violence incidents in the United States are perpetrated against women (Truman & Morgan, 2014). Furthermore, transgender individuals (both male-to-female and female-to-male) experience sexual and physical violence at high rates, although prevalence varies between studies (Stotzer, 2009). Research on gender nonbinary individuals is limited, yet evidence suggests that the transgender and gender nonconforming population experiences physical and sexual intimate partner violence at rates even higher than cisgender women, a group already at increased risk (Valentine et al., 2017). Similarly, sexual orientation can be associated with additional risks. Research has shown that intimate partner violence occurs at equal or greater rates among gay and lesbian couples compared to heterosexual couples (Rollè et al., 2018). Lesbian, gay, and bisexual individuals may also be at higher risk for substance use compared to their heterosexual counterparts (King et al., 2008; Marshal et al., 2008).

In and of itself, substance use may be considered a risk factor for many types of family violence. Maternal misuse of substances has been associated with child abuse and neglect (Clément et al., 2016). Substance misuse has also been found to correlate with perpetration of financial exploitation and physical or emotional abuse against older adults (Conrad et al., 2016). Finally, substance misuse is strongly associated with perpetration of intimate partner violence (Stith et al., 2004) as well as victimization, though this latter relationship appears stronger for illicit drugs than for alcohol, and for women than for men (Cafferky et al., 2018; Capaldi et al., 2012).

However, the relationship between family violence and substance use appears more complex when other contextual or developmental risk factors are considered. Many factors indicating risk for substance use are similar, or closely related, to those which indicate a risk for both perpetration or victimization of violence. As early as adolescence, risk factors associated with substance use include childhood physical, emotional, or sexual abuse and neglect, parental substance use, co-occurring mental disorders (e.g., depression or anxiety), and association with deviant peers (Whitesell et al., 2013). Other sociodemographic factors associated with risk of substance involvement appear to vary depending on history of use and stage of progression towards problematic use, suggesting an interactive effect with environmental or contextual factors (Swendsen et al., 2009). It becomes ever more difficult to tease apart causal elements when one considers, for example, that childhood abuse is associated with substance use, which is in turn associated with violence in adulthood, while both substance use and violence correlate strongly with mental health problems.

Additional risk factors have been associated with both substance use and violence. For example, membership to a minority race or ethnicity (especially African American), younger age, and low socioeconomic status have all been associated with experiences of domestic violence (Capaldi et al., 2012). Although research into risk factors for elder mistreatment is limited, poverty, physical or mental impairment, and separated or divorced marital status have all been associated with experiencing violence, while results surrounding race and ethnicity are mixed (Burnes et al., 2015). Finally, low family socioeconomic status and family cohesion, as well as high parental anger or hyper-reactivity, have been observed as prominent risks for child abuse and neglect, while demographic factors (e.g., gender, age, and race of child) may be less important (Stith et al., 2009). Stress, perhaps associated with many of the above factors, is also strongly associated with all types of family violence (Clément et al., 2016; Capaldi et al., 2012; Bonnie & Wallace, 2003).

Prevention and Intervention

Numerous strategies have been proposed to address family violence and substance use. These strategies differ greatly, depending on the target of the program (i.e., victim of violence or perpetrator; individual using substances or their surrounding networks), the duration and severity of behaviors being addressed, and whether the program addresses violence, substance use, or the two issues jointly. Programs specific to interpersonal violence, elder maltreatment, intimate partner violence, and child abuse and neglect will be discussed in greater detail throughout this book; however, this section will offer a brief overview of types of programs, important differences, and current limitations. All programs discussed are examples of **evidence-based practices (EBPs)**, meaning they are supported by research demonstrating the program's efficacy to address a given issue with a particular population, rather than relying on tradition, personal experience, or advice from colleagues (McKibbon, 1998).

Programs designed to address issues such as family violence or substance use exist along a continuum of care, depending on how far the issue has progressed in duration or severity. At one end of the continuum, **prevention** programs aim to deter or reduce the likelihood of behaviors before those behaviors have occurred or progressed. According to guidelines offered by the Institute of Medicine (1994), prevention programs may be *selective* (targeting high-risk individuals), *indicated* (targeting high-risk individuals who have demonstrated the behavior), or *universal* (targeting all individuals, regardless of risk or pre-existing behaviors). **Intervention** programs are more broadly defined, in that they aim to create behavioral changes; interventions may be implemented to forestall unwanted behaviors (similar to prevention programs), or to interrupt established behaviors (similar to treatments). Most commonly, the term intervention refers to *early intervention* programs, which seek to detect problematic behaviors at an early stage and prevent them from progressing to more harmful outcomes. Finally, **treatment** programs utilize individual and group counseling, medications, and other supportive services through inpatient or outpatient modalities to change established behaviors and support long-term positive outcomes.

One arm of prevention, intervention, and treatment programs seeks to address individuals who have been, or are at risk of becoming, victims of family violence. Immediate safety is a first priority of such programs. Often, state agencies—including child welfare services, adult protective services, or law enforcement—may assist in removing victims from harmful situations and placing them in foster care, group homes, or shelters, providing legal protection against perpetrator contact when necessary. Once safety is established, many programs aim to address the negative consequences of maltreatment or abuse to the victim's physical and mental health, and to prevent or mitigate future harm.

For victims with co-occurring substance use disorders, programs may be designed to address both issues simultaneously, thus producing more sustainable positive outcomes. *Seeking Safety*, for example, is an evidence-based counseling model designed to establish coping skills related to safety in relationships, recovery from substance use, and trauma resulting from violent victimization (Najavits, 2002). Prevention programs, such as the school-based Fourth R [Reading, w(R)iting, a(R)ithmetic, and Relationships], may similarly address substance use and violence in relationships as interrelated risky behaviors (Wolfe et al., 2009).

Treating or intervening with perpetrators of violence, particularly when substance use is also occurring, presents additional issues. However, many integrated models are available that address both substance use and partner violence (including cognitive behavioral therapies and couples counseling models), with some programs tailored for unique populations, such as fathers or veterans (Easton & Crane, 2016). Research has consistently demonstrated the importance of addressing substance use disorders among perpetrators of intimate partner violence (Stuart et al., 2009). Similarly, among parents who have substance use issues, integrated programs may address substance use in conjunction with deficits in parenting knowledge or coping with psychosocial stressors, in outpatient, residential, or home-based settings (Neger & Prinz, 2015). Such programs may be implemented as treatment for existing behaviors, or as prevention in cases where substance use is present, creating risk for child maltreatment.

Although evidence-based solutions exist for parents, children, and couples with co-occurring issues of violence and substance use, less is known about appropriate strategies for addressing such issues in the context of elder maltreatment. Although substance use by both victims and perpetrators has been implicated in instances of elder abuse (Flores et al., 2015) and acknowledged as a theoretical cause of elder maltreatment, particularly in relation to caregiver stress (Jones et al., 1997), research related to treatment and prevention of elder maltreatment and substance use simultaneously is extremely limited. Integrated programs to address the co-occurrence of elder abuse or neglect, as well as the co-occurrence of multiple types of family violence (e.g., intimate partner victimization and child maltreatment) with substance use, will continue to be an important area for future research.

Conclusion

Both substance use and family violence are prevalent concerns, impacting millions of individuals globally, and contributing to serious short- and long-term consequences for physical and mental health, costs to society, and intergenerational transmission. Historically, although these issues have been often treated as private matters, legislation enacted over the past 50 years in the United States has advanced opportunities for evidence-based prevention, intervention, and treatment programs to reach affected individuals, whether victims, perpetrators, people with substance use disorders, or family members. These systemic responses, along with theoretical frameworks such as the Power and Control Wheel, have helped to raise awareness about coercive control and various patterns of abuse. Along with research, they have also emphasized the importance of understanding risk and protective factors to prevent future violence and substance misuse, to more efficiently identify and intervene when needed, and to provide more effective treatment services. Following this general overview of the complex relationship between substance use and family violence, the next chapters will offer more in-depth examinations of specific types of violence in family relationships, as well as ways in which substance use may shape or impact these experiences.

Discussion Questions

1. The relationship between family violence and substance use is a complex one.
   a. In what ways can substance use contribute to family violence?
   b. In what ways can experiences of family violence contribute to substance use?
   c. Discuss how and why substance use is an important issue for *both* perpetrators and victims of family violence.
2. Name at least one other factor that can contribute to *both* family violence and substance use. In what ways does this factor relate to both issues?
   a. Why are these types of factors important to consider from a prevention or treatment perspective?

Key Terms

Coercive control: A term coined by Dr. Evan Stark (2007) to describe how perpetrators of abuse "use various means to hurt, humiliate, intimidate, exploit, isolate, and dominate their victims" through use of threatened or actualized physical abuse in combination with psychological, emotional, or political tactics.

Digital abuse: Also known as cyber abuse, a form of abuse which may include monitoring victims' online behaviors, location, or social networks; posting incriminating photos or spreading harmful rumors about victims; and sending unwanted sexual images or messages to victims.

Elder Justice Act (EJA): Passed in 2010 as part of the Patient Protection and Affordable Care Act (ACA), the EJA authorized funding to support adult protective services, required ombudsmen and surveyors of long-term care facilities, improved mandated reporting of crimes in federally funded long-term care facilities, and established federal bodies to support plans and development in the field of elder justice.

Evidence-based practices (EBPs): Practices (e.g., programs or interventions) supported by research demonstrating their efficacy to address a given issue with a particular population.

Family violence: The use of power or force (through physical violence, or the plausible threat thereof) with the intention of causing deprivation or physical, psychological, or developmental harm to a family member.

Family Violence Prevention and Services Act (FVPSA): Passed in 1984, this Act earmarks federal funding for aid to victims of domestic violence, and supports shelters, programs, and supportive services for victims, as well as (to a lesser extent) prevention or education programs (through Domestic Violence Prevention Enhancement and Leadership Through Alliance, or DELTA) and the National Domestic Violence Hotline.

Intervention: Programs implemented to forestall unwanted behaviors or to interrupt established behaviors; often refers to *early intervention* programs, which seek to detect problematic behaviors at an early stage and prevent them from progressing to more harmful outcomes.

Power and Control Wheel: A diagram depicting common tactics and patterns of behaviors used by male perpetrators to control female victims in domestic violence contexts, originally created in 1984 by the Minnesota Domestic Abuse Intervention Programs (DAIP, 2017) of Duluth, Minnesota.

Prevention: Programs which aim to deter or reduce the likelihood of behaviors before they have occurred or progressed (including selective, indicated, and universal prevention programs).

Protective factor: Any characteristic (physiological, psychological, or social) associated with a decreased likelihood of an undesirable outcome, including disease, injury, or harmful behaviors.

Protective order: A legal order, decided by a judge (usually after an *emergency protective order* and *preliminary or temporary protective order* have been granted), usually lasting for a finite period of a few years. Such orders may include coverage for victims of domestic violence, stalking, harassment, or sexual assault, depending on state law, and can require the perpetrator to refrain from certain behaviors (like contacting the victim) or comply with conditions (such as obtaining a formal assessment).

Public/private dichotomy: Tension between historical perspectives, which often view family violence or maltreatment as a private matter, and modern efforts to implement effective legal and social responses.

Religious or spiritual abuse: A specific pattern of abuse that may occur when a perpetrator uses their own or a victim's religious beliefs to rationalize or justify abuse, to shame or manipulate a victim, or to control the victim's religious practices.

Risk factor: Any characteristic (physiological, psychological, or social) associated with an increased likelihood of an undesirable outcome, including disease, injury, or harmful behaviors.

Substance misuse: Use of a substance in greater frequency or amounts, for a longer duration, or by a route of administration other than intended or recommended; commonly used to describe *problematic substance use*, or use of a substance resulting in harm, distress, dysfunction, or reduced quality of life.

Substance use: A phrase used to broadly describe use of any intoxicant, regardless of the substance's legal status or an individual's patterns of use.

Substance use disorder: A diagnosis determined by a qualified clinical professional, based on specific criteria, describing continued use of a substance despite significant problems.

Treatment: Programs that involve individual and group counseling, medications, and other supportive services through inpatient or outpatient modalities to change established behaviors and support long-term positive outcomes.

Victims of Crime Act (VOCA): Passed in 1984, VOCA established the Crime Victim's Fund, funded by fines and forfeited bonds from convicted individuals, to provide both direct and indirect support for victims. Individuals may apply for victim compensation at the state level, but programs providing services to victims of crime may also apply for grants to support operations.

Violence Against Women Act (VAWA): Passed in 1994, VAWA authorized additional grant funding for programs addressing domestic violence, dating violence, sexual assault, stalking, or other violent crimes against women; allowed for enhanced prosecution of repeat sex offenders; and mandated restitution to some victims of sex offenses. VAWA's reauthorizations (most recently in 2013) have expanded grant purpose areas to include sex trafficking and established nondiscrimination provisions for funded programs.

References

Afifi, T. O., MacMillan, H. L., Taillieu, T., Cheung, K., Turner, S., Tonmyr, L., & Hovdestad, W. (2015). Relationship between child abuse exposure and reported contact with child protection organizations: Results from the Canadian Community Health Survey. *Child Abuse & Neglect, 46*, 198–206. https://doi.org/10.1016/j.chiabu.2015.05.001

[APA] American Psychiatric Association. (2013). *Diagnostic and statistical manual of mental disorders* (5th ed.). https://doi.org/10.1176/appi.books.9780890425596

Bailey, J. A., Hill, K. G., Oesterle, S., & Hawkins, J. D. (2006). Linking substance use and problem behavior across three generations. *Journal of Abnormal Child Psychology, 34*(3), 273–292. https://doi.org/10.1007/s10802-006-9033-z

Barnert, E., Iqbal, Z., Bruce, J., Anoshiravani, A., Kolhatkar, G., & Greenbaum, J. (2017). Commercial sexual exploitation and sex trafficking of children and adolescents: A narrative review. *Academic Pediatrics, 17*(8), 825–829. https://doi.org/10.1016/j.acap.2017.07.009

Begle, A. M., Strachan, M., Cisler, J. M., Amstadter, A. B., Hernandez, M., & Acierno, R. (2011). Elder mistreatment and emotional symptoms among older adults in a largely rural population: The South Carolina Elder Mistreatment Study. *Journal of Interpersonal Violence, 26*, 2321–2332. https://doi.org/10.1177/0886260510383037

Bick, J., & Nelson, C. A. (2016). Early adverse experiences and the developing brain. *Neuropsychopharmacology, 41*, 177–196. https://doi.org/10.1038/npp.2015.252

Black, D. S., Sussman, S., & Ungar, J. B. (2010). A further look at the intergenerational transmission of violence: Witnessing interparental violence in emerging adulthood. *Journal of Interpersonal Violence, 25*, 1022–1042. https://doi.org/10.1177/0886260509340539

Bonnie, R. J., & Wallace, R. B. (Eds.). (2003). *Elder mistreatment: Abuse, neglect, and exploitation in an aging America.* National Academies Press.

Burnes, D., Pillemer, K., Caccamise, P. L., Mason, A., Henderson, C. R., Berman, J., Cook, A. M., Shukoff, D., Brownell, P., Powell, M., Salamone, A., & Lachs, M. S. (2015). Prevalence of and risk factors for elder abuse and neglect in the community: A population-based study. *Journal of the American Geriatrics Society, 63*, 1906–1912. https://doi.org/10.1111/jgs.13601

Cafferky, B. M., Mendez, M., Anderson, J. R., & Stith, S. M. (2018). Substance use and intimate partner violence: A meta-analytic review. *Psychology of Violence, 8*(1), 110. https://doi.org/10.1037/vio0000074

Campbell, J., Jones, A. S., Dienemann, J., Kub, J., Schollenberger, J., O'Campo, P., Gielen, A. C., & Wynne, C. (2002). Intimate partner violence and physical health consequences. *JAMA Internal Medicine, 162*, 1157–1163. https://doi.org/10.1001/archinte.162.10.1157

Capaldi, D. M., Knoble, N. B., Shortt, J. W., & Kim, H. K. (2012). A systematic review of risk factors for intimate partner violence. *Partner Abuse, 3*(2), 231–280. https://doi.org/10.1891/1946-6560.3.2.231

Chavis, A. Z., & Hill, M. S. (2008). Integrating multiple intersecting identities: A multicultural conceptualization of the Power and Control Wheel. *Women & Therapy, 32*, 121–149. https://doi.org/10.1080/02703140802384552

Clément, M. E., Bérubé, A., & Chamberland, C. (2016). Prevalence and risk factors of child neglect in the general population. *Public Health, 138*, 86–92. https://doi.org/10.1016/j.puhe.2016.03.018

Conrad, K. J., Liu, P-J., & Iris, M. (2016). Examining the role of substance abuse in elder mistreatment: Results from mistreatment investigations. *Journal of Interpersonal Violence, 34*(2), 366–391. https://doi.org/10.1177/0886260516640782

[CRS] Congressional Research Service. (2017). The Elder Justice Act: Background and issues for Congress [R43707]. https://fas.org/sgp/crs/misc/R43707.pdf

[CRS] Congressional Research Service. (2019). The Violence Against Women Act (VAWA): Historical overview, funding, and reauthorization [R45410]. https://fas.org/sgp/crs/misc/R45410.pdf

[CRS] Congressional Research Service. (2021a). Family Violence Prevention and Services Act (FVPSA) [IF11170]. https://crsreports.congress.gov/product/pdf/IF/IF11170

[CRS] Congressional Research Service. (2021b). The Violence Against Women Act (VAWA) reauthorization: Issues for Congress [R46742]. https://sgp.fas.org/crs/misc/R46742.pdf

[CWIG] Child Welfare Information Gateway. (2019). Long-term consequences of child abuse and neglect [Factsheet]. https://www.childwelfare.gov/pubpdfs/long_term_consequences.pdf

[DAIP] Domestic Abuse Intervention Programs. (2017). Understanding the Power and Control Wheel. https://www.theduluthmodel.org/wheels/

DeVooght, K., Fletcher, M., & Cooper, H. (2014). *Federal, state, and local spending to address child abuse and neglect in SFY 2012*. Child Trends, The Annie E. Casey Foundation, and Casey Family Programs. https://www.childtrends.org/wp-content/uploads/2014/09/SFY-2012-Report-for-Posting-July2015.pdf

Easton, C. J., & Crane, C. A. (2016). Interventions to reduce intimate partner violence perpetration among people with substance use disorders. *International Review of Psychiatry, 28*, 533–543. https://doi.org/10.1080/09540261.2016.1227307

Ehrensaft, M. K., Cohen, P., Brown, J., Smailes, E., Chen, H., & Johnson, J. G. (2003). Intergenerational transmission of partner violence: A 20-year prospective study. *Journal of Consulting and Clinical Psychology, 71*, 741–753. https://doi.org/10.1037/0022-006X.71.4.741

Franchino-Olsen, H. (2021). Vulnerabilities relevant for commercial sexual exploitation of children/domestic minor sex trafficking: A systematic review of risk factors. *Trauma, Violence, & Abuse, 22*(1), 99–111. https://doi.org/10.1177/1524838018821956

Flores, D. V., Burnett, J., Booker, J., & Dyer, C. B. (2015). Uncomfortably numb: Substance use associated with elder mistreatment. *Drug and Alcohol Dependence, 146*, e279. https://doi.org/10.1016/j.drugalcdep.2014.09.225

Harp, K. L. H., & Oser, C. B. (2018). A longitudinal analysis of the impact of child custody loss on drug use and crime among a sample of African American mothers. *Child Abuse & Neglect, 77*, 1–12. https://doi.org/10.1016/j.chiabu.2017.12.017

Hartwell, S. (2004). Triple stigma: Persons with mental illness and substance abuse problems in the criminal justice system. *Criminal Justice Policy Review, 15*(1), 84–99. https://doi.org/10.1177/0887403403255064

Hedges, K. E. (2012). A family affair: Contextual accounts from addicted youth growing up in substance using families. *Journal of Youth Studies, 15*(3), 257–272. https://doi.org/10.1080/13676261.2011.635194

Henry, K. L., Fulco, C. J., Agbeke, D. V., & Ratcliff, A. M. (2018). Intergenerational continuity in substance abuse: Does offspring's friendship network make a difference? *Journal of Adolescent Health, 63*, 205–212. https://doi.org/10.1016/j.jadohealth.2018.02.014

Hillis, S., Mercy, J., Amobi, A., & Kress, H. (2016). Global prevalence of past-year violence against children: A systematic review and minimum estimates. *Pediatrics, 137*(3), e20154079. https://doi.org/10.1542/peds.2015-4079

Institute of Medicine. (1994). *Reducing risks for mental disorders: Frontiers for preventive intervention research*. P. J. Mrazek & R. J. Haggerty (Eds.). National Academies Press.

Jones, J. S., Holstege, C., & Holstege, H. (1997). Elder abuse and neglect: Understanding the causes and potential risk factors. *American Journal of Emergency Medicine, 15*(6), 579–583. https://doi.org/10.1016/S0735-6757(97)90162-5

Kenny, K. S., Barringon, C., & Green, S. L. (2015). "I felt for a long time like everything beautiful in me had been taken out": Women's suffering, remembering, and survival following the loss of child custody. *International Journal of Drug Policy, 26*, 1158–1166. https://doi.org/10.1016/j.drugpo.2015.05.024

King, M., Semlyen, J., Tai, S. S., Killaspy, H., Osborn, D., Popelyuk, D., & Nazareth, I. (2008). A systematic review of mental disorder, suicide, and deliberate self harm in lesbian, gay and bisexual people. *BMC Psychiatry, 8*(70). https://doi.org/10.1186/1471-244X-8-70

Knight, K. E., Menard, S., & Simmons, S. B. (2014). Intergenerational continuity of substance use. *Substance Use & Misuse, 49*, 221–233. https://doi.org/10.3109/10826084.2013.824478

Ko, C. N. (2002). Civil restraining orders for domestic violence: The unresolved question of "efficacy." *Southern California Interdisciplinary Law Journal, 11*, 361–390.

Laird, J. J., Klettke, B., Hall, K., Clancy, E., & Hallford, D. (2020). Demographic and psychosocial factors associated with child sexual exploitation: A systematic review and meta-analysis. *JAMA Network Open, 3*(9), e2017682. doi:10.1001/jamanetworkopen.2020.17682

Le, P. D., Ryan, N., Rosenstock, Y., & Goldmann, E. (2018). Health issues associated with commercial sexual exploitation and sex trafficking of children in the United States: A systematic review. *Behavioral Medicine, 44*(3), 219–233. https://doi.org/10.1080/08964289.2018.1432554

MacMillan, H. L., Jamieson, E., & Walsh, C. A. (2003). Reported contact with child protection services among those reporting child physical and sexual abuse: Results from a community survey. *Child Abuse & Neglect, 27*, 1397–1408. https://doi.org/10.1016/j.chiabu.2003.06.003

Marshal, M. P., Friedman, M. S., Stall, R., King, K. M., Miles, J., Gold, M. A., Bukstein, O. G., & Morse, J. Q. (2008). Sexual orientation and adolescent substance use: A meta-analysis and methodological review. *Addiction, 103*(4), 546–556. https://doi.org/10.1111/j.1360-0443.2008.02149.x

McKibbon, K. A. (1998). Evidence-based practice. *Bulletin of the Medical Library Association, 86*(3), 396–401.

Mechanic, M. B., Weaver, T. L., & Resick, P. A. (2008). Mental health consequences of intimate partner abuse: A multidimensional assessment of four different forms of abuse. *Violence Against Women, 14*(6), 634–654. https://doi.org/10.1177/1077801208319283

Mills, R., Scott, J., Alati, R., O'Callaghan, M., Najman, J., & Strathearn, L. (2013). Child maltreatment and adolescent mental health problems in a large birth cohort. *Child Abuse & Neglect, 37*(5), 292–302. https://doi.org/10.1016/j.chiabu.2012.11.008

Mogstad, H., Dryding, D., & Fiorotto, O. (2016). Policing the private: Social barriers to the effective policing of domestic violence. *South African Crime Quarterly, 56*. https://doi.org/10.17159/2413-3108/2016/v0n56a414

Moore, K. E., & Tangney, J. P. (2017). Managing the concealable stigma of criminal justice system involvement: A longitudinal examination of anticipated stigma, social withdrawal, and post-release adjustment. *Journal of Social Issues, 73*(2), 322–340. https://doi.org/10.1111/josi.12219

Najavits, L. M. (2002). *Seeking safety: A treatment manual for PTSD and substance abuse.* The Guilford Press.

[NDIC] National Drug Intelligence Center. (2011). *The economic impact of illicit drug use on American society.* United States Department of Justice.

Neger, E. N., & Prinz, R. J. (2015). Interventions to address parenting and parental substance abuse: Conceptual and methodological considerations. *Clinical Psychology Review, 39*, 71–82. https://doi.org/10.1016/j.cpr.2015.04.004

[NIAAA] National Institute on Alcohol Abuse and Alcoholism. (n.d.). Alcohol's effects on the body. https://www.niaaa.nih.gov/alcohols-effects-body

[NIDA] National Institute on Drug Abuse. (2020). Common comorbidities with substance use disorders [Research report]. https://www.drugabuse.gov/publications/research-reports/common-comorbidities-substance-use-disorders

O'Donnell, P., & Lawson, E. (2016). Managing physical health problems in people who inject drugs. *British Journal of General Practice, 66*, 48–49. https://doi.org/10.3399/bjgp16X683365

[OVC] Office for Victims of Crime. (n.d.). About OVC: Crime Victims Fund. Retrieved December 27, 2021, from https://www.ovc.gov/about/victimsfund.html

Paymar, M., & Barnes, G. (2007). *Countering confusion about the Duluth Model.* Domestic Abuse Intervention Programs. https://www.theduluthmodel.org/wp-content/uploads/2017/03/CounteringConfusion.pdf

Peterson, C., Kearns, M. C., McIntosh, W. L., Estefan, L. F., Nicolaidis, C., McCollister, K. E., Gordon, A., & Florence, C. (2018). Lifetime economic burden of intimate partner violence among U.S. adults. *American Journal of Preventive Medicine, 55*(4), 433–444. https://doi.org/10.1016/j.amepre.2018.04.049

Phelps, S., & Lehman, J. (Eds.). (2007). Victims of Crime Act of 1984. In *West's Encyclopedia of American Law* (Vol. 10, 2nd ed., pp. 222–223). Gale Virtual Reference Library.

Podnieks, E., & Thomas, C. (2017). The consequences of elder abuse. In X. Dong (Ed.), *Elder abuse: Research, practice and policy* (pp. 109–123). Springer International Publishing.

Pope, L., & Ferraro, K. (2006). *Considerations when adapting the Power and Control Wheel.* http://www.oneinthreewomen.com/ckfinder/userfiles/files/adaptingwheel.pdf

Rao, K., Sharma, K. S., Kumar, S. U., Bhat, K. V., & Babu, S. G. (2017). The trailing trials of humiliation: Legal, social, and medical perspectives of women facing domestic violence in India. *Indian Journal of Social Psychiatry, 33*(3), 274–279. https://doi.org/10.4103/ijsp.ijsp_53_16

Reed, L. A., Tolman, R. M., & Ward, L. M. (2016). Snooping and sexting: Digital media as a context for dating aggression and abuse among college students. *Violence Against Women, 22*, 1556–1576. https://doi.org/10.1177/1077801216630143

Reyner, J. C. (2017). *Partner aggression in a digital age: Prevalence and predictors of cyber psychological abuse* [Doctoral dissertation, University of Maryland, Baltimore County]. Retrieved from ProQuest [10266729].

Rollè, L., Giardina, G., Caldarera, A. M., Gerino, E., & Brustia, P. (2018). When intimate partner violence meets same sex couples: A review of same sex intimate partner violence. *Frontiers in Psychology, 9*, 1506. https://doi.org/10.3389/fpsyg.2018.01506

Roy, E., Arruda, N., Bruneau, J., & Jutras-Aswad, D. (2016). Epidemiology of injection drug use: New trends and prominent issues. *The Canadian Journal of Psychiatry, 61*(3), 136–144. https://doi.org/10.1177/0706743716632503

Sacks, J. J., Gonzales, K. R., Bouchery, E. E., Tomedi, L. E., & Brewer, R. D. (2015). 2010 national and state costs of excessive alcohol consumption. *American Journal of Preventive Medicine, 49*(5), e73–e79. https://doi.org/10.1016/j.amepre.2015.05.031

Salhi, Z. S. (Ed.). (2013). *Gender and violence in Islamic societies: Patriarchy, Islamism and politics in the Middle East and North Africa.* I.B. Tauris.

[SAMHSA] Substance Abuse and Mental Health Services Administration. (2021). *Key substance use and mental health indicators in the United States: Results from the 2020 National Survey on Drug Use and Health* (HHS Publication No. PEP21-07-01-003, NSDUH Series H-56). Center for Behavioral Health Statistics and Quality, Substance Abuse and Mental Health Services Administration.

Stark, E. (2007). *Coercive control: How men entrap women in personal life.* Oxford University Press.

Stith, S. M., Liu, T., Davies, C., Boykin, E. L., Alder, M. C., Harris, J. M., Som, A., McPherson, M., & Dees, J. E. M. E. G. (2009). Risk factors in child maltreatment: A meta-analytic review of the literature. *Aggression and Violent Behavior, 14*, 13–29. https://doi.org/10.1016/j.avb.2006.03.006

Stith, S. M., Smith, D. B., Penn, C. E., Ward, D. B., & Tritt, D. (2004). Intimate partner physical abuse perpetration and victimization risk factors: A meta-analytic review. *Aggression and Violent Behavior, 10*, 65–98. https://doi.org/10.1016/j.avb.2003.09.001

Stotzer, R. L. (2009). Violence against transgender people: A review of United States data. *Aggression and Violent Behavior, 14*, 170–179. https://doi.org/10.1016/j.avb.2009.01.006

Stuart, G. L., McGeary, J., Shorey, R. C., & Knopik, V. (2014a). Further investigation of genetics and intimate partner violence. *Violence Against Women, 20*, 420–426. https://doi.org/10.1177/1077801214528586

Stuart, G. L., McGeary, J., Shorey, R. C., Knopike, V., Beaucage, K., & Temple, J. R. (2014b). Genetic associations with intimate partner violence in a sample of hazardous drinking men in batterer intervention programs. *Violence Against Women, 20*, 385–400. https://doi.org/10.1177/1077801214528587

Stuart, G. L., O'Farrell, T. J. & Temple, J. R. (2009). Review of the association between treatment for substance misuse and reductions in intimate partner violence. *Substance Use & Misuse, 44*(9), 1298–1317. https://doi.org/10.1080/10826080902961385

Sugaya, L., Hasin, D. S., Olfson, M., Lin, K-H., Grant, B. F., & Blanco, C. (2012). Child physical abuse and adult mental health: A national study. *Journal of Traumatic Stress, 25*(4), 384–392. https://doi.org/10.1002/jts.21719

Swendsen, J., Conway, K. P., Degenhardt, L., Dierker, L., Glantz, M., Jin, R., Merikangas, K. R., Sampson, N., & Kessler, R. C. (2009). Socio-demographic risk factors for alcohol and drug dependence: The 10-year follow-up of the national comorbidity survey. *Addiction, 104*, 1346–1355. https://doi.org/10.1111/j.1360-0443.2009.02622.x

True Link Financial. (2015). *The True Link report on elder financial abuse 2015*. https://www.truelinkfinancial.com/research

Truman, J. L., & Morgan, R. E. (2014). *Nonfatal domestic violence, 2003-2012*. U.S. Department of Justice, Office of Justice Programs, Bureau of Justice Statistics. https://www.bjs.gov/content/pub/pdf/ndv0312.pdf

[UNICEF] United Nations Children's Fund. (2017). *A familiar face: Violence in the lives of children and adolescents*. https://data.unicef.org/resources/a-familiar-face/

[UNODC] United Nations Office on Drugs and Crime. (2019). *Global study on homicide: Gender-related killing of women and girls*. https://www.unodc.org/documents/data-and-analysis/gsh/Booklet_5.pdf

Valentine, S. E., Peitzmeier, S. M., King, D. S., O'Cleirigh, C., Marquez, S. M., Presley, C., & Potter, J. (2017). Disparities in exposure to intimate partner violence among transgender/gender nonconforming and sexual minority primary care patients. *LGBT Health, 4*(4), 260–267. https://doi.org/10.1089/lgbt.2016.0113

Whitesell, M., Bachand, A., Peel, J., & Brown, M. (2013). Familial, social, and individual factors contributing to risk for adolescent substance use. *Journal of Addiction*. Retrieved from https://www.hindawi.com/journals/jad/2013/579310/

[WHO] World Health Organization. (2016). Elder abuse: The health sector role in prevention and response. https://www.who.int/violence_injury_prevention/violence/elder_abuse/WHO_EA_ENGLISH_2017-06-13.pdf?ua=1

[WHO] World Health Organization. (2018). *Global status report on alcohol and health, 2018*. World Health Organization.

[WHO] World Health Organization. (2021a). *Violence against women prevalence estimates, 2018*. World Health Organization.

[WHO] World Health Organization. (2021b). *World Drug Report 2021: Executive summary: Conclusions and policy implications*. United Nations Office on Drugs and Crime.

Widom, C. S., Czaja, S. J., Bentley, T., & Johnson, M. S. (2012). A prospective investigation of physical health outcomes in abused and neglected children: New findings from a 30-year follow-up. *American Journal of Public Health, 102*, 1135–1144. https://doi.org/10.2105/AJPH.2011.300636

Wolfe, D. A., Crooks, C., Jaffe, P., Chiodo, D., Hughes, R., Ellis, W., Stitt, L., & Donner, A. (2009). A school-based program to prevent adolescent dating violence: A cluster randomized trial. *Archives of Pediatrics & Adolescent Medicine, 163*(8), 692–699. https://doi.org/10.1001/archpediatrics.2009.69

Yon, Y., Mikton, C. R., Gassoumis, Z. D., & Wilber, K. H. (2017). Elder abuse prevalence in community settings: A systematic review and meta-analysis. *The Lancet Global Health, 5*(2), e147–e156. https://doi.org/10.1016/S2214-109X(17)30006-2

Yon, Y., Mikton, C., Gassoumis, Z. D., & Wilber, K. H. (2019). The prevalence of self-reported elder abuse among older women in community settings: A systematic review and meta-analysis. *Trauma, Violence, & Abuse, 20*(2), 245–259. https://doi.org/10.1177/1524838017697308

CHAPTER TWO

Substance Use and Interpersonal Violence

Callie Marie Rennison, PhD, and Carlos A. Cuevas, PhD

Introduction

The literature on family violence has largely focused on three important domains: intimate partner violence (IPV), **child** maltreatment/child abuse, and sexual violence/sexual abuse. This means that the vast majority of the scholarly work centers on violence perpetrated by current and former **spouses**, boy/girlfriends, child maltreatment at the hands of caretakers, and sexual abuse, which is significantly perpetrated by family members and other known individuals to the victim. While sexual abuse is not exclusive to family violence (Briere & Elliott, 2003; Finkelhor et al., 2008), it has been a central area of focus within this literature. While not as central, another area of research has focused on elder abuse, although the literature suggests that the dynamics associated with this form of abuse are different than those of the other three areas of study (Barboza, 2016). What has gone largely unexamined is an investigation of **familial violence** as a whole and outside the scope of these areas of focus. This essentially leaves us to center our efforts on incidents of violence that include **sibling**-to-sibling violence, and child-to-parent violence, and violence perpetrated by "other" relatives. In an effort to further understanding of these forms of violence, the purpose of this chapter is twofold. First, we provide an overview of the current scholarly work on these understudied areas of violence. Second, we offer contemporary nonfatal estimates of the extent and nature of these types of understudied familial violent victimization. For purposes of this chapter, we define nonfatal familial violent victimization as violence between current family members which includes spouses, children, parents, siblings, and **other relatives** but falls outside the domains of IPV, child maltreatment, and elder abuse.

Prior Research on Family Violence

In examining the research on family violence more broadly, we center our efforts on work that has been done outside the mainstream lines of research. One of the challenges in focusing on these under-studied areas in the context of family violence is the dearth of research. In some cases, no literature was located. Limited attention has been paid to these areas of violence, and as a result, little research is available to provide information about the scope and dynamics of this form of family violence. Consideration of this violence is important, as it can constitute a source of considerable trauma over the life course.

The purpose of this chapter is to examine nonfatal family violence, which includes violence perpetrated by current spouses, siblings, **parents**, children, and other relatives. To accomplish this, we first present a brief literature review that discusses some of the work in this arena and provide some background. From this we offer contemporary estimates of these types of violence, with an emphasis on victim, offender, and incident characteristics. In total, the chapter should offer a foundational background for others to delve more deeply into what is an understudied type of violence.

Scope of the Problem

Violence Perpetrated by Current Spouses

While the field of partner violence has continued to grow over the recent years, the focus has expanded from its origins in spousal violence (Straus et al., 1980). The growth has come to include non-spousal partners, former spouses, boyfriends/girlfriends, and the larger arena of adolescent dating violence and dating aggression. Beyond this, the challenges of measurement and how to best capture partner violence has been an ongoing discussion in the field (Hamby, 2016, 2017; National Institute of Justice, 2015) and continues to be debated. However, the focus of our piece centers on violence within the family, and as such, requires us to focus on the "original roots" of the field, spousal violence.

An example of this is provided by Toni Tails (2020) who described the first (and last) time her husband violently attacked her. She was trying to walk away from an argument when her husband grabbed her hair and started punching her. She fell to the ground, where he bit and scratched her as he continued yanking out her hair.

Most recent research now centers on gathering estimates of partner violence, regardless of who the partner is. For example, the National Intimate Partner and Sexual Violence Survey (Black et al., 2011) gives a lifetime intimate partner violence (IPV) rate of 35.6%; however, it is not separated by spouses versus other non-spousal partners. However, they do report that 21.9% experienced victimization at the hands of a current partner (as opposed to 23.1% by a former partner). Similarly, the National Violence Against Women Survey found a lifetime IPV rate of 25.5% for women and 7.9% for men, but does not distinguish between current or former partners nor between spouses and other intimate partners (Tjaden & Thoennes, 2000). As such, while much of the current research has expanded our knowledge of IPV, the focus on spousal abuse (also referred to as marital abuse or domestic violence) has diminished. This shift is not without consequences. While our understanding of violence in intimate relationships has expanded and allowed inclusion of other types of intimate relationships (e.g., adolescent dating couples), groups (e.g., LGBTQ), and the temporal shifts in relationships (e.g., break up and reunite), the emphasis on the unique components associated with spousal relationships, and their impact on the characteristics of an abusive relationship, have diminished.

A key component, and central to why it is important to maintain some attention to violence among spousal couples, is that there are dynamics in these relationships that play a role in the manifestation of partner violence, often absent from non-spousal relationships. For example, there are a number of controlling tactics that are unique to spouses, such as manipulation of economic resources, ease of access/contact with the victim, and the presence of children in the relationship. As an example, economic dependence or perceived economic dependence is a key factor in why victims do not leave abusive relationships or return if they have left in the past (Conner, 2014). Those violence-relevant characteristics are likely absent in dating or non-spousal relationships, even in cases where couples may cohabitate.

Sibling-to-Sibling Violence

Violence research has generally found that sibling-to-sibling (STS) violence is a relatively common occurrence. Rates from national surveys show that approximately 30% of youth report being victimized by a sibling, with rates peaking between the ages of 6 and 9 years and being relatively evenly split between boys and girls (Finkelhor, Ormrod, et al., 2005; Finkelhor et al., 2009). As a point of comparison, this was the third most frequent form of victimization in these surveys, exceeded only by any physical assaults and non-weapon physical assaults. The common occurrence of this form of victimization suggests that this form of violence merits greater scholarly attention. Sexual abuse of children has historically received extensive research, interventions, and prevention efforts, but has rates of approximately one fifth that of sibling violence (Finkelhor & Turner, 2009). This is not to say that sexual violence does not merit the attention it has received, but it speaks to the void that needs to be filled in the area of sibling violence.

Beyond the frequency of sibling violence, the perception of the problem has also impacted the degree to which it is an arena of emphasis within violence research. As many have argued, sibling violence has been normalized and thought of as less severe than other forms of violence (Caspi & Barrios, 2016). This comes across in both how it is described (Kettrey & Emery, 2006) and the degree to which it is considered problematic or worthy of intervention (Khan & Rogers, 2015; Tucker & Kazura, 2013). Collectively, these factors are likely to perpetuate sibling violence and decrease the likelihood that it will be a focus of intervention or prevention efforts.

Examples of minimizing sibling violence are present in the media noting that brothers fight, sisters fight, and that this is normal. Yet, violence by siblings against siblings is still violence. One individual in an online forum related how he punched his brother in the face (while both were adults) because he felt his brother is a "drunk asshole" and he was "sick of his shit." In another anonymous online account, a woman describes kicking her "annoying" brother in the head because he would not stop bothering her. Many accounts describe the presence of alcohol, which is used to minimize the accountability of the perpetrator.

Where there has been growth and scholarly progress has been in examining and conceptualizing the severity of sibling aggression. Work by Caspi (2012, 2016) has brought about a conceptualization of sibling violence severity that presents four dimensions of sibling violence. The dimensions—competition, conflict, violence, and abuse—allow for both what may be considered developmentally normative sibling behavior as well as behavior that can potentially be abusive or damaging to a family member. This conceptualization provides context for this form of violence and a framework for both research and intervention.

Contrary to the opportunity presented by his conceptualization, Caspi (2016) notes a lack of intervention or prevention efforts that target this form of violence. There are no programs targeted to this form of aggression, it is absent from the forms of violence that are the focus of school-based intervention programs, and it is not an area of central focus in many clinical training programs for practitioners. Work going forward should not only bring attention to this form of family violence, but also present it in the context of other forms of violence, so as to better understand how it is experienced within the family system.

Parental Violence

The substantial body of literature that exists on child abuse has given us a good overview of the scope of the problem of child victimization and abuse within the home and the family. Recent work with the National Survey on Children's Exposure to Violence (Finkelhor & Turner, 2009) has provided detailed estimates of maltreatment across a number of domains within the home. This, along with other data sources, such as the National Child Abuse and Neglect Data System (U.S. Department of Health and Human Services, 2019) and the National Incidence Studies (Sedlak et al., 2010), provide comprehensive figures of both officially reported and unreported child abuse and neglect. While detailing rates here across the various studies would be too expansive an endeavor, the degree to which we can still pinpoint victimization that occurs in the home has remained relatively intact. While scholarly work has expanded the domains of victimization experienced by children (Finkelhor, Hamby, et al., 2005), the core concerns surrounding the victimization of children continue to be central in this line of research.

Accounts of parental violence are common. A quick online search finds examples of individuals seeking information about how to handle a parent who violently victimizes them. One young man pled with online followers for ways to make his father stop physically and verbally abusing him. He describes the beatings as involving strikes to his skull so that his hair will cover the bruising. His offense? Watching YouTube during the week. In this particular case, the young man pleads for ways to make his father stop hitting him, and instead focus only on verbally abusing him, since, as he states, the verbal abuse is easily endurable.

Less formally evaluated is the degree to which victimization of children continues as they become older and age into adulthood (including when they are no longer considered dependents of their parents). The lack of attention to this line of research is likely centered on a number of issues, but most likely is that once children are adults, violence directed at them is no longer considered child abuse. Arguably, this enters a "no man's land" of family violence. They are too old to be included in the child abuse literature, but not typically what falls within the scope of domestic violence.

As a result, this has become a neglected component of violence within the family. The only way to explore this is to examine victimization in adulthood perpetrated by a parent, an endeavor infrequently taken. The reasons for this are unclear, although the lack of concern about serious harm following this form of violence and potential limitations of existing data (e.g., no perpetrator information) are likely culprits. The data presented in this chapter aim to provide some insight into this form of victimization within the family and help bring attention to a neglected area of study.

Child-to-Parent Violence

Child-perpetrated aggression toward parents is also an understudied area in violence research, though it has received more attention than many other familial relationships.[1] To some degree, this is a result of the fact that it is more infrequently occurring than other forms of violence.

A woman, identifying only as "Jennifer," describes how her son began hitting her when he was 14 years old. She endured his beatings because she did not want to call the police and did not want to see her son arrested. She even hid what her son was doing to her from family for fear they would call the police. Still, she struggled trying to find ways to make his attacks stop. She describes living this way as being in a car with no brakes.

Rates have generally been found to be below 10% for a three-year period (Fischer & Kidwell, 1985). More recent work has found that rates tend to be in the mid-teens, with frequency generally being higher during preschool-age years (Margolin & Baucom, 2014; Ulman & Straus, 2003). The rate for school-age children hovers around 10% through adolescence (Ulman & Straus, 2003). While the overall rate is part of an argument for the emphasis in a particular area of study, the broader picture of how child-to-parent (CTP) violence manifests provides context that suggests this form of aggression needs additional attention as a way of understanding violence within the family system.

A key component of much of the research on CTP violence emphasizes the importance of understanding that form of aggression within the context of family violence overall. Particular emphasis has also been on adolescent-perpetrated aggression, as one could argue that pre-school age children's aggression is unlikely to be severe or traumatic to the parent, and likely to be considered developmentally appropriate (ask any parent who has been on the receiving end of a 3-year-old's tantrum). Work by various researchers has noted that CTP violence is best understood in the context of other forms of violence within the family. For example, work by Ulman and Straus (2003) noted that CTP violence is more likely to happen in homes where there is evidence of intimate partner violence (IPV), specifically aggression directed toward mothers. As such, our efforts in the data we present aim to provide the context for violence in the family generally, while allowing us to have information about some of these specific forms of violence.

---

1   Child-to-parent violence includes stepchildren, adopted children, and those born to the parent.

An additional key component of CTP violence is understanding how this occurs as children become older. As we mention above, aggressive behavior early in childhood is not uncommon, and to a certain degree, developmentally appropriate. However, aggression towards parents by adolescents is likely more severe and behaviorally problematic. Generally, the research suggests that much of this form of aggression peaks between the ages of 14 and 17 and is most commonly perpetrated by male youth (Condry & Miles, 2013; Ulman & Straus, 2003). Furthermore, some have conceptualized that this form of aggression is either the lagged effect of a reaction to parent-perpetrated violence, or a manifestation of mutual violence between children and parents (Gallego et al., 2019). With many other forms of violence, there is a high frequency of CTP violence co-occurring with other forms of aggressive behavior (Margolin & Baucom, 2014).

Other Relatives

An area receiving no research attention that we could locate is violence perpetrated by some "other" relative. That is, violence perpetrated by a non-parent, child, spouse, or sibling. This violence may be committed by grandparents, cousins, aunts, and uncles, for example. This is also an important area deserving of attention that has lacked any sort of significant empirical inquiry. The reality that many homes consist of blended and extended families has not been a central focus of family violence research, and as such, leaves unanswered questions about additional familial violence dynamics that may exist outside of the more traditional expected family roles or relationships.

Wil Hylton (2019) shared in *New York Times Magazine* how his cousin was his hero, until the day his cousin tried to kill him. In short, his cousin developed homicidal rage in a workshop that prompted him to attack. When people ask Wil why this happened, he responds that he doesn't think he had a reason, although he suspects toxic masculinity played a role.

In the next section, we present some historical context before moving on the theoretical perspectives and then contemporary estimates to enhance our understanding of nonfatal familial violence. To do this, we discuss the methods used, and then present estimates for victim, offender, and incident characteristics of these types of violence.

Historical Context

The field of violence research has experienced a number of shifts over the years in terms of the areas of focus and emphasis. Early on, seminal work by Straus, Gelles, and Steinmetz (1980) brought attention to the issue of spousal violence, which centered on interpersonal violence among married couples. That work highlighted the notion that research could identify behaviors that were usually hidden from the public and considered private. Most often in parallel, the focus on sexual violence also began to develop, with emphasis on child sexual abuse, and the understanding of the dynamics and motivations for perpetration. That work first noted on the experience of victims and an understanding of how they are impacted by sexual victimization (Summit, 1983; Finkelhor, 1984, 1990). This arena of study brought forth a number of crucial questions surrounding issues of revictimization (Classen et al., 2005) and debates on the issues of false and recovered memories (Dalenberg, 2006; Dallam, 2001). When focusing on offenders, sexual abuse scholars embarked on a failed attempt at identifying offender profiles (Murphy & Smith, 1996). More fruitful work resulted in research that identified typologies (Groth & Oliveri, 1989; Prentkey et al., 1989), varying theories of offending (Ward et al., 2006), and a focus on factors impacting recidivism risk (Hanson & Morton-Bourgon, 2009).

In more recent years, research has begun to steer away from primarily focusing on a singular form of abuse, into the understanding of the cumulative impact of violence. Much of this has centered on the topic of poly-victimization and how multiple different forms of victimization account for deleterious outcomes beyond the impact of any singular form of victimization (Finkelhor et al., 2007). Additionally, work has begun to better grasp the importance of understanding the impact of violence among more diverse communities. Much of this work has not only centered on studying violence in different ethnic and racial populations, but also among the LGBTQ+ community, and understanding factors unique to those groups in terms of their risk and experience of violence (Pfeffer & Cuevas, 2016).

Theoretical Perspectives

In the field of violence research, there are four primary theories of victimization that are discussed: victim precipitation theory (Wolfgang, 1957), lifestyle activities theory (Hindelang et al., 1978), deviant place theory (Stark, 1987), and routine activity theory (Cohen & Felson, 1979). While these theories have been used broadly in the literature, they are not well developed across multiple individual-level contexts. These four approaches are underdeveloped and do not account for many of the forms of victimization that individuals experience, and have limited empirical support that provides any robust evidence of their validity. One hopes that the use of the following estimates can assist in additional theory construction that is able to adequately explain familial victimization.

Risk and Protective Factors

In an effort to move forward the research knowledge on these understudied forms of violence, we examine the rates and demographic correlates of family violence. While our emphasis is to highlight STS and CTP violence, the presentation across perpetrators provides comparative context. Furthermore, and largely absent from much of the scholarly work, examining demographic and incident information allows for additional knowledge regarding the circumstances under which this form of violence presents itself.

Data

The estimates presented below are calculated using National Crime Victimization Survey (NCVS) data that are collected using a stratified, multistage cluster design from a sample of housing units and group quarters in the United States and the District of Columbia. All individuals aged 12 or older in each sampled household are interviewed, either in person or on the phone, at 6-month intervals for a 3-year period. The first year of data, 2007, was selected because variables identifying offenders as siblings and children were added. Prior to this time, these categories were aggregated into "other relative." The final year of data used is 2020 because it is the most recent data available. On average, from 2007 to 2020, 178,870 individuals (age 12+) were interviewed in 105,3820 households annually for the survey. The average household response rate from 2007 to 2020 was 83% (varying from 67% to 92% annually), and the average person response rate was 86% (varying from 82% to 89% annually). Given these criteria, estimates provided in this chapter are based on 22,273 unweighted violent victimizations committed by family members, which corresponds to 9,080,870 weighted nonfatal familial violent victimizations. These estimates are generalizable to the population age 12 or older living in housing units in the United States. NCVS data are publicly available through the National Archive of Criminal Justice Data (Hubble, 1995; Rennison, & Rand, 2007).

A problem inherent with investigating violence is how to handle series victimizations. A series victimization is when a respondent sustains a series of victimizations that are so similar in nature or occur so often that respondents are unable to provide details of each individual event. Because details of the victimizations are required to classify an event as a crime or non-crime, and to classify crimes into types of crime in the NCVS, this presents special problems in estimation. The literature offers a few ways to deal with this challenge (e.g., Rand & Rennison, 2005) although all are imperfect. The most recent approach, and the one we employ, is to enumerate series victimizations based on the victim's estimate of the number of times the victimizations occurred during the six-month reference period, with a maximum of 10 victimizations per interview (see Lauritsen et al., 2012).

The NCVS is ideal for examining the extent and nature of less studied nonfatal familial violence for several reasons. First, the NCVS offers a large sample size, enabling investigation into specific groups of victims, and specific types of violence. Second, NCVS data include an extensive range of incident characteristics, including specific types of violence, weapon presence, injuries sustained, and police reporting. Third, because the NCVS includes both reported and unreported violent victimizations, the dark figure of crime issue, which refers to the absence of unreported crimes in official crime data, thus raising concerns about its accuracy, is minimized. Fourth, it includes information on perpetrators. Like all data, the NCVS is subject to limitations. First, the NCVS covers a limited set of violence, including threatened, attempted, and completed **rape/sexual assault**, **robbery**, and **aggravated assault**, as well as **simple assault**. Other types of violence, such as homicide, kidnapping, emotional or psychological terror, coercive control, and stalking, are not included in these analyses. Second, though the data includes relational information between victim and offender, it is not as granular as would be ideal. For example, identification of violence by aunts/uncles or cousins is not available, although it is included in an "other relative" category. Third, because the population of interest includes those 12 or older in housing units, the NCVS data do not capture the experiences of individuals younger than 12 years of age, or those who are homeless, incarcerated, or otherwise in non-housing unit situations (e.g., military barracks, jails/prisons). Finally, familial violence is likely prone to be series in nature, making it difficult for victims to identify discrete events if they are ongoing. As a result, it is clear that estimates presented here are conservative. While imperfect, the NCVS provides an excellent opportunity to examine nonfatal familial violence in the United States.

Analytic Approach

To estimate the extent and nature of nonfatal familial violence, we use descriptive statistics such as percentages and rates, using weighted data to account for non-response and other aspects of the data collection.[2]

Risk and Protective Factor Estimates

Before focusing exclusively on only nonfatal familial violent victimization, we first place nonfatal family violence in context of all violent victimization. While it receives little attention, nonfatal familial violence is the third most common type of violence, when considering the victim and offender relationship, committed in the United States (see Table 2.1). In total, from 2007 to 2020, family members perpetrated approximately 9,060,868 nonfatal violent victimizations, which corresponds to 11.6% of all violence. Only stranger violence (37.8%), and violence by friends or acquaintances (31.1%) occurred at higher percentages. Nonfatal violent victimizations committed by family members occur at a percentage almost twice that of violence by a current or former boy/girlfriend, and more than five times that of violence by an ex-spouse. These estimates demonstrate that while largely understudied, family member–perpetrated violence is responsible for a large amount of violent victimization in the United States.

Nonfatal Familial Violence in Context

Nonfatal familial violence includes violence perpetrated by a current spouse, sibling, parent, child, or other relative. Family-perpetrated violence

TABLE 2.1 Nonfatal Familial Victimization in a Larger Context, 2007–2020, NCVS

Perpetrator	Frequency	Percent
Total nonfatal violent victimization	78,230,398	100.0
Familial	9,060,868	11.6
Ex-spouse	1,466,534	1.9
Current or former boy/girlfriend	6,016,982	7.7
Friends/acquaintances	24,359,056	31.1
Strangers	29,580,626	37.8
Don't know	6,424,291	8.2
Missing data	1,322,041	1.7

2   Data weights are found on the NCVS data files. These weights are described in the accompanying codebook. Both the NCVS data and the codebook are available at the ICPSR website at https://www.icpsr.umich.edu/icpsrweb/NACJD/series/95/studies.

TABLE 2.2 Overview of Nonfatal Familial Victimization, 2007–2020, NCVS

Perpetrator	Frequency	Percent
Total nonfatal familial violent victimization	9,060,868	100.0
Spouse	3,193,513	35.2
Sibling/step-sibling	480,607	5.3
Parent/step-parent	1,048,341	11.6
Child/step-child	1,638,948	18.1
Other relative	2,699,460	29.8

is not randomly distributed among family members. As shown in Table 2.2, from 2007 to 2020, the person most likely to commit violence against a family member is a current spouse, who is responsible for 35.2% of nonfatal familial violence. About one in three nonfatal familial violent victimizations is committed by some "other relative" (29.8%). A child/stepchild (18.1%), and a parent (11.6%) commit a significant portion of familial violence. Siblings least often perpetrate nonfatal familial violence, although it still accounted for 5.3% of all familial violence, and more than 480,607 violent victimizations from 2007 to 2020.

Types of Nonfatal Familial Violence

The majority of nonfatal familial violence (65.3%) was categorized as a simple assault, which is defined as a threatened or attempted attack by an unarmed offender, from which no injury or a minor injury (i.e., involves bruises, black eyes, cuts, scratches or swelling; see Table 2.3). In addition, a simple assault is defined as involving an unspecified injury that results in less than two days of hospitalization (Bureau of Justice Statistics, 2011). Simple assault is the most common type of violence perpetrated, regardless of the victim and offender relationship considered. For example, 60.0% of spousal violence and 63.7% of sibling violence took the form of simple assault. Simple assault was also most common among "other" relative violence (70.3%), parental violence (65.1%), and violence committed by one's child (68.0%).

From 2007 to 2020, 1,481,796 nonfatal familial violent victimizations took the form of aggravated assault. Aggravated assault includes attempted and completed violence that involves a weapon, regardless of whether an injury occurred. It also includes instances in which the offender was unarmed, but the victim was seriously injured. Serious injuries include harm such as broken bones, stab wounds, gunshot wounds, lost teeth, internal injuries, loss of consciousness, and any unspecified injury that required the victim to be hospitalized for two or more days (Bureau of

TABLE 2.3 Counts, and Percentages, Nonfatal Familial Violence by Type of Violence, 2007–2020, NCVS

| Type of Violence | Relationship of Perpetrator | | | | | |
	Spouse	Sibling	Parent	Own Child	Other Relative	Total
Rape & sexual assault						
Count	496,416	0	59,946	33,555	52,721	642,638
Percentage	15.5%	0.0%	5.7%	2.0%	2.0%	7.1%
Robbery						
Count	198,149	111,372	152,151	257,513	300,901	1,020,086
Percentage	6.2%	23.2%	14.5%	15.7%	11.1%	11.3%
Aggravated assault						
Count	582,389	63,207	153,684	233,465	449,051	1,481,796
Percentage	18.2%	13.2%	14.7%	14.2%	16.6%	16.4%
Simple assault						
Count	1,916,559	306,027	682,560	1,114,415	1,896,787	5,916,348
Percentage	60.0%	63.7%	65.1%	68.0%	70.3%	65.3%
Total						
Count	3,193,513	480,606	1,048,341	1,638,948	2,699,460	9,060,868
Percentage	100.0%	100.0%	100.0%	100.0%	100.0%	100.0%

Justice Statistics, 2011). Spouses committed aggravated assault in the highest percentage (18.2%). Siblings committed aggravated assault at the lowest percentage (13.2%).

Individuals are not immune from being robbed by a family member. Robbery includes attempted or completed theft, directly from a person, of cash or property, by force or threat of force, regardless of whether a weapon was used, or an injury occurred (Bureau of Justice Statistics, 2011). Between 2007 and 2020, more than 1.02 million robberies were committed by a family member. Robberies were committed in the highest percentages by siblings, and one's own child (23.2% and 15.7%, respectively).

Finally, estimates in Table 2.3 demonstrate that sexual violence between family members occurs in distressing numbers: there were 642,638 rapes/sexual assaults that occurred among family members from 2007 to 2020. In the NCVS data, rape is defined as attempted or completed forced vaginal, anal, or oral penetration (using a body part or an object) using psychological coercion and/or physical force, regardless of the victim or offender's sex. Sexual assault differs from rape and accounts for a broad range of victimizations that include attempted or completed attacks involving unwanted sexual contact (e.g., grabbing or fondling), regardless of force used. Among familial violence, spousal violence involved sexual violence at the highest percentage: 15.5% of rapes/sexual assaults were committed by a spouse. An additional 5.7%, or 59,946, rapes/sexual assaults were perpetrated by one's parent.

Victim Sex

Findings show that women experience family violence at higher percentages and rates than men (see Table 2.4). From 2007 to 2020, women experienced 72.9% of all family violence, which corresponds to 3.5 victimizations per 1,000 women. Findings also indicate that women are the victim by every category of family member at higher rates, and in greater

TABLE 2.4 Victim Demographics, Nonfatal Familial Victimization, 2007–2020 NCVS

Demographic	Frequency	Percent	Rates per 1,000
Total	9,060,868	100.0	2.4
Sex			
Male	2,452,836	27.1	1.4
Female	6,608,031	72.9	3.5
Race/Hispanic origin			
Non-Hispanic White	6,483,434	71.6	2.7
Non-Hispanic Black	892,899	9.9	2.0
Non-Hispanic American Indian/Alaskan Native	147,840	1.6	7.6
Non-Hispanic Asian/ Pacific Islander	131,843	1.5	0.6
Non-Hispanic, multiple races	431,750	4.8	9.5
Hispanic, any race	973,101	10.7	1.7
Age			
12–15	630,146	7.0	2.7
16–19	560,927	6.2	2.4
20–24	874,493	9.7	2.9
25–34	1,840,843	20.3	3.1
35–49	2,780,131	30.7	3.2
50–64	1,997,185	22.0	2.4
65 or older	377,142	4.2	0.6

numbers than are men.[3] Women are victims of 88.9% of spousal violence, 59.7% of parental violence, 76.3% of violence committed by a child, and 60.7% of violence perpetrated by some other relative. These findings are in direct contrast to non-familial violence in the population, where men are violently victimized at rates higher than women, with the exception of sexual violence and IPV.

Victim Race/Hispanic Origin

Findings also demonstrate tremendous variation in familial victimization by the race/Hispanic origin of the victim. During this period, American Indians/Alaskan Natives and individuals who self-identify as multi-race were victimized by family members at relatively high rates (7.6 and 9.5 violent victimizations per 1,000, respectively). Non-Hispanic Whites (2.7 per 1,000), non-Hispanic Blacks (2.0 per 1,000), and Hispanics (1.7 per 1,000) were victims of family violence at a fraction of the rates characterizing violence against American Indians/Alaskan Natives, and those self-describing as multiple race. The lowest rates measured were found for Asian/Pacific Islanders, as 0.6 violent victimizations (per 1,000) by a family member is estimated from 2007 to 2020.

Victim Age

In the general victimization literature, violent victimization increases to late adolescence and emerging adulthood, after which it declines (see Table 2.5). A somewhat similar pattern is evident when considering overall familial violence. Family violence rates are estimated to be 27.3 (per 10,000) among 12- to 15-year-olds. The rate decreases among 16- to 19-year-olds (23.7 per 10,000), but increases among ages 20 to 24, remaining similar among 25- to 29-year-olds (29.2 and 30.6 per 10,000). At that point, victimization rates decline.

However, the story changes when considering the victim/offender relationship (see Figure 2.1). Over one's life course, violence perpetrated by a spouse peaks from ages 25 to 34 (17.2 per 10,000), and declines after that. In contrast, sibling-perpetrated violence peaks at age 12 to 15 (5.1 per 10,000), and then declines over the life course. Parent-perpetrated violence is highest among victims age 12 to 15 (12.0 per 10,000) and 16 to 19 (11.0 per 10,000), and declines thereafter. In contrast, violence committed by one's own child peaks at age 50 to 64 (9.4 per 10,000).

---

3   These values are not shown in the table, but are available upon request.

TABLE 2.5 **Rates per 10,000, Familial Nonfatal Violent Victimization by Victim's Age, 2007–2020, NCVS**

Victim's Age	Spouse	Siblings	Parent	Child	Other Relative	Total
Total	8.6	1.3	2.8	4.4	7.3	24.4
12–15	0.0	5.1	12.0	0.0	10.2	27.3
16–19	0.2	3.8	11.0	0.0	8.7	23.7
20–24	6.5	2.6	6.3	0.2	13.6	29.2
25–34	17.2	1.4	1.7	0.9	9.4	30.6
35–49	15.5	0.7	1.9	7.1	6.7	31.9
50–64	6.7	0.7	0.5	9.4	6.4	23.6
65 or older	0.7	0.0	0.1	2.6	2.6	6.1

Note. Relationships listed refer to the perpetrator.

Victim Annual Household Income

Nonfatal familial violence rates and annual household income are inversely related. As illustrated in Figure 2.2, and shown in Table 2.6, as a victim's annual household income increases, rates of familial violent victimization decrease. Among those with the lowest annual household income (less than $15,000 annually), there are an estimated 6.9 family-perpetrated victimizations (per 1,000). In contrast, those with the highest incomes are victimized by a family member at a rate of 1.4 per 1,000.

Familial violence is a serious issue, and the estimated rates of violence differ greatly across victim characteristics (e.g., sex, race, Hispanic origin and race) and annual household income. We next turn to examining the perpetrators of nonfatal familial violence to investigate and describe family violence associated with the offender's perceived gender, race, age, and their use of drugs/alcohol.

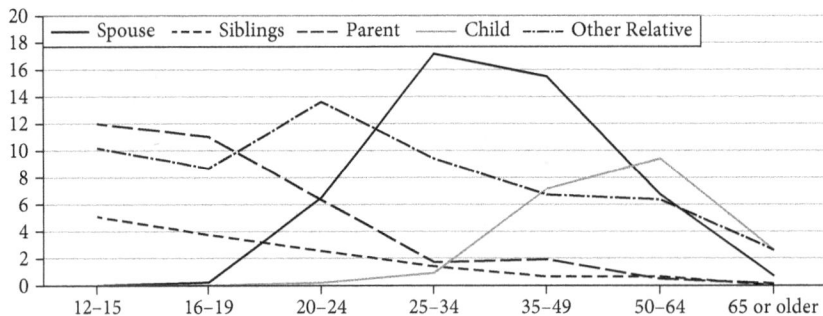

FIGURE 2.1 **Rates per 10,000, Nonfatal Familial Violence by Age of Victim, 2007–2020**

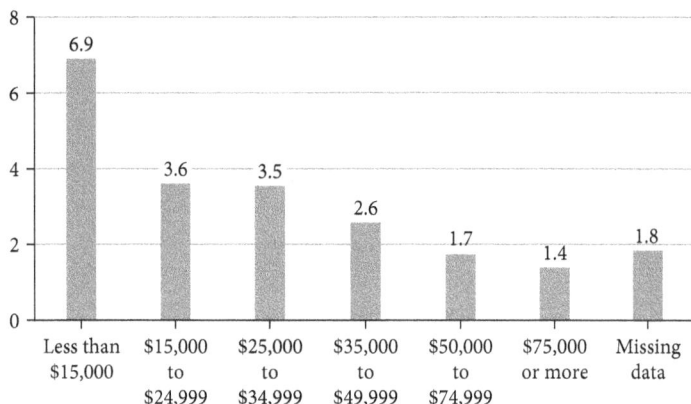

FIGURE 2.2 Rates per 1,000, Familial Nonfatal Violence Victimization by Annual Household Income, 2007–2020

TABLE 2.6 Annual Household Income and Familial Violence, 2007–2020, NCVS

Annual Household Income	Count	Percentage	Rate per 1,000
Total	9,060,868	100.0	2.4
Less than $15,000	1,794,153	19.8	6.9
$15,000 to $24,999	920,520	10.2	3.6
$25,000 to $34,999	1,056,532	11.7	3.5
$35,000 to $49,999	1,076,902	11.9	2.6
$50,000 to $74,999	850,244	9.4	1.7
$75,000 or more	872,314	9.6	1.4
Missing data	2,490,204	27.5	1.8

Offender's Gender

Most people who commit family violence are male, whether acting alone or with other males (72.2%; see Table 2.7). This is especially the case when examining spousal violence, where 88.4% of victimizations were perpetrated by male offenders. While male offenders dominate family victimization regardless of the victim/offender relationship, female offenders perpetrate a substantial portion of violence against other relatives, and their own children (35.3% and 29.7%, respectively).

Offender's Race

When asked to identify the race of the offender of family violence, victims were unable (or unwilling) to do so in large percentages. For example, 63.0% of all perpetrators were not identified by race by the victim. In two-thirds (71.5%) of violence committed by one's own child, the victim did not

TABLE 2.7 Offender Characteristics, Nonfatal Familial Violence, 2007–2020, NCVS

	Spouse	Sibling	Parent	Own Child	Other Relative	Total
			Offender's Relationship to the Victim			
Total familial violence	3,193,514	480,607	1,048,341	1,638,948	2,699,460	9,060,870
Percent	100.0	100.0	100.0	100.0	100.0	100.0
Perceived gender of all offender(s)						
Male						
Count	2,824,277	341,576	626,076	1,115,328	1,632,761	6,540,018
Percentage	88.4	71.1	59.7	68.1	60.5	72.2
Female						
Count	337,459	139,031	335,018	486,016	951,985	2,249,509
Percentage	10.6	28.9	32.0	29.7	35.3	24.8
Both male and female						
Count	30,077	0	66,791	37,604	87,900	222,372
Percentage	0.9	0.0	6.4	2.3	3.3	2.5
Offender(s) gender unknown						
Count	1,701	0	20,456	0	26,814	48,971
Percentage						
Perceived race of all offender(s)*						
White						
Count	1,085,212	194,118	252,293	357,126	693,338	2,582,087
Percentage	34.0	40.4	24.1	21.8	25.7	28.5

	Spouse	Sibling	Offender's Relationship to the Victim Parent	Own Child	Other Relative	Total
Black						
Count	111,578	0	33,758	40,080	114,583	299,999
Percentage	3.5	0.0	3.2	2.4	4.2	3.3
Other						
Count	46,505	57,450	0	21,620	68,984	194,559
Percentage	1.5	12.0	0.0	1.3	2.6	2.1
Group of different races						
Count	0	0	0	5,403	3,574	8,977
Percentage	0.0	0.0	0.0	0.3	0.1	0.1
Race/Number unknown						
Count	1,938,997	218,381	689,541	1,171,192	1,688,592	5,706,703
Percentage	60.7	45.4	65.8	71.5	62.6	63.0
Perceived age of all offender(s)*						
All younger than 18						
Count	0	142,856	0	695,075	293,333	1,131,264
Percentage	0.0	29.7	0.0	42.4	10.9	12.5
All 18 to 29						
Count	538,159	195,100	21,556	533,806	753,628	2,042,249
Percentage	16.9	40.6	2.1	32.6	27.9	22.5

(*Continued*)

TABLE 2.7 Offender Characteristics, Nonfatal Familial Violence, 2007–2020, NCVS   (Continued)

	Spouse	Sibling	Offender's Relationship to the Victim Parent	Own Child	Other Relative	Total
All 30 or older						
Count	2,560,014	131,993	980,298	357,744	1,410,255	5,440,304
Percentage	80.2	27.5	93.5	21.8	52.2	60.0
Mixed age group						
Count	19,239	10,658	11,206	14,889	96,223	152,215
Percentage	0.6	2.2	1.1	0.9	3.6	1.7
Perceived use of drugs/alcohol*						
Used alcohol and/or drugs						
Count	1,408,269	144,697	405,996	650,526	1,020,909	3,630,397
Percentage	44.1	30.1	38.7	39.7	37.8	40.1
Did not use alcohol and/or drugs						
Count	1,286,392	185,416	448,770	731,319	1,089,154	3,741,051
Percentage	40.3	38.6	42.8	44.6	40.3	41.3
Do not know						
Count	391,855	150,494	180,633	239,179	509,161	1,471,322
Percentage	12.3	31.3	17.2	14.6	18.9	16.2

Missing data values are not shown

share the race of the perpetrator. In contrast, when a sibling committed the violence, race was identified in 45.4% of the cases.

Offender's Age

Contrary to the notion that violence is perpetrated primarily by younger individuals, when it comes to family violence, older people commit the most violence. The majority of perpetrators were older than 30 years according to those victimized (60.0%). When considering spousal violence, 80.2% of perpetrators were older than 30. Young adults are most often engaged in sibling violence. For example, 40.6% of sibling violence is committed by a person age 18 to 29, and 29.7% is committed by someone younger than 18.

Offender's Use of Drugs/Alcohol

The use of drugs and/or alcohol among perpetrators of family violence was common. A total of 40.1% of all family victimizations were committed by a perpetrator thought to be under the influence of drugs and/or alcohol. Yet, even more family violence was perpetrated by a sober offender. For example, 41.3% of spousal violence was committed by a sober offender. About 4 in 10 sibling violence and parental victimizations were perpetrated by a sober perpetrator (38.6%, and 42.8%, respectively).

Where the Family Violence Occurred

The majority of familial violence occurs in the victim's home (71.6%; see Table 2.8). The degree to which the violence occurs in the victim's home differs by the relationship between the victim and offender. More than 8 in 10 instances of spousal (83.1%) and sibling (86.4%) violence, and 9 in 10 (90.3%) instances of violence perpetrated by one's own child, occurred in the victim's home.

Other relatives also perpetrate violence against family members near the victim's home (15.1%) or in/near/at their own, the victim's friend, or neighbor's home (24.9%). Very small percentages of family violence occurred in other locations. Findings show that familial violence rarely occurs in other locations, such as public areas like schools, parking lots, gas stations, or other commercial or open areas.

Weapon Presence

Most familial violence did not involve an armed perpetrator. In total, 79.6% of familial violence included an armed family member. The family violence least often involving an armed offender is that committed by a sibling (15.5%). A somewhat higher percentage of victimizations (18.9%) by a parent involved an armed perpetrator.

TABLE 2.8 Incident Characteristics, Nonfatal Familial Violence, 2007–2020, NCVS

	Spouse	Sibling	Parent	Own Child	Other Relative	Total
Total familial violence	3,193,514	480,607	1,048,341	1,638,948	2,669,460	9,060,870
	100.0	100.0	100.0	100.0	100.0	100.0
Location of victimization						
Victim's home or lodging						
Count	2,655,272	415,050	689,452	1,480,615	1,243,116	6,483,505
Percentage	83.1	86.4	65.8	90.3	46.1	71.6
Near victim's home						
Count	266,023	0	45,461	65,006	408,064	784,554
Percentage	8.3	0.0	4.3	4.0	15.1	8.7
In/at/near friend's/neighbor's/ relative's home						
Count	91,754	46,325	277,037	45,190	671,307	1,131,613
Percentage	2.9	9.6	26.4	2.8	24.9	12.5
Commercial place						
Count	10,916	19,232	3,937	8,255	85,651	127,991
Percentage	0.3	4.0	0.4	0.5	3.2	1.4
Parking lot/garage						
Count	63,273	0	13,552	16,650	39,656	133,131
Percentage	2.0	0.0	1.3	1.0	1.5	1.5

	Spouse	Sibling	Parent	Own Child	Other Relative	Total
School						
Count	0	0	0	0	32,775	32,775
Percentage	0.0	0.0	0.0	0.0	1.2	0.4
Open area/on street/public transportation						
Count	83,448	0	10,913	19,719	100,515	214,595
Percentage	2.6	0.0	1.0	1.2	3.7	2.4
Other location						
Count	22,827	0	7,989	3,513	118,375	152,704
Percentage	0.7	0.0	0.8	0.2	4.4	1.7
Was offender armed?						
Unarmed offender						
Count	2,529,989	405,886	832,253	1,299,741	2,148,868	7,216,737
Percentage	79.2	84.5	79.4	79.3	79.6	79.6
Armed offender						
Count	537,745	74,721	197,944	301,136	436,018	1,547,564
Percentage	16.8	15.5	18.9	18.4	16.2	17.1
Don't know						
Count	125,778	0	18,143	38,072	114,574	296,567
Percentage	3.9	0.0	1.7	2.3	4.2	3.3

(Continued)

TABLE 2.8 Incident Characteristics, Nonfatal Familial Violence, 2007–2020, NCVS   (Continued)

	Spouse	Sibling	Parent	Own Child	Other Relative	Total
Victim injury*						
Victim not injured						
Count	1,510,978	312,306	663,731	1,021,857	1,853,584	5,362,456
Percentage	47.3	65.0	63.3	62.3	68.7	59.2
Victim injured						
Count	1,682,535	168,301	384,609	617,091	845,875	3,698,411
Percentage	52.7	35.0	36.7	37.7	31.3	40.8
Medical treatment of injured victim						
Not treated						
Count	1,510,978	312,306	663,731	1,021,857	1,853,584	5,362,456
Percentage	47.3	65.0	63.3	62.3	68.7	59.2
Treated at scene, home, neighbor's or friend's						
Count	259,982	0	52,332	94,535	209,572	616,421
Percentage	8.1	0.0	5.0	5.8	7.8	6.8
Treated at MD office, clinic or hospital						
Count	84,321	0	21,308	56,339	30,065	192,033
Percentage	2.6	0.0	2.0	3.4	1.1	2.1

	Spouse	Sibling	Parent	Own Child	Other Relative	Total
Treated at other location						
Count	216,643	57,997	53,746	74,879	144,102	547,364
Percentage	6.8	12.1	5.1	4.6	5.3	6.0
Do not know if treated						
Count	36,947	0	0	2,849	0	39,796
Percentage	1.2	0.0	0.0	4.6	0.0	0.4
Were the police notified?*						
Yes, police notified						
Count	1,701,151	174,990	510,974	1,039,842	1,407,396	4,834,353
Percentage	53.3	36.4	48.7	63.4	52.1	53.4
No, police not notified						
Count	1,450,529	305,617	523,012	592,656	1,267,345	4,139,159
Percentage	45.4	63.6	49.9	36.2	46.9	45.7
Do not know						
Count	25,826	0	14,355	6,450	22,097	68,728
Percentage	0.8	0.0	1.4	0.4	0.8	0.8

Missing data values not shown

Injuries and Medical Treatment

About 4 in 10 victims of nonfatal familial violence were injured as a result of the incident (40.8%). Spousal violence was most often associated with injury, as 52.7% of victims were injured. When one's sibling is the offender, the victim is injured during 35.0% of incidents. Medical treatment for injuries was *not* obtained for a majority of victims, regardless of the victim/offender relationship.

Police Reporting

In total, 53.4% of familial violence was reported to the police. However, percentages of victimization reported varied by the victim/offender relationship. More than 6 in 10 victimizations by one's own child were reported to the police (63.4%). About half of violence by a spouse (53.3%), a parent (48.7%), and some other relative (53.4%) were reported.

Prevention and Intervention

These findings point to the need for intervention and prevention for family violence outside of the traditional IPV realm. While current spouses are responsible for a large amount of family violence, other family members are active perpetrators as well. Further, findings indicate that the type of intervention and prevention measures taken must focus on and be adapted to particular groups. For example, among older victims, understanding that their children are most often perpetrators is key. Among younger adult victims, a focus on current spousal abuse is imperative. The very high rates of family violence experienced by American Indians is alarming and demonstrates the need to develop and implement culturally specific intervention and prevention programs. This includes the need to recognize the diversification of the populous and how to best meet the needs of victims. Adaptation of programs to both address linguistic needs (e.g., translation of materials) as well as culturally specific components is essential. In addition, training of those in the criminal justice system and in the medical care field must recognize the degree to which this violence affects these particular groups. In addition, given the degree to which offenders are under the influence of drugs and/or alcohol, attention must be paid to this, and should inform programs designed to assist offenders of family violence. For example, a more holistic approach to service delivery should address many of the associated challenges that accompany family violence, such as mental health needs, recovery and substance abuse interventions, as well as medical needs connected to victimization experiences. Programs designed to encourage police reporting remain important, but they must be tied to social services and support for victims—something that does not appear to be readily accessible or well-integrated into the extant criminal justice system.

Conclusion

While generally understudied, family-perpetrated violence is responsible for a substantial amount of violence in the United States. As described, family violence occurs at high rates. Certain perpetrators, such as current spouses, stand out as particularly violent. This demonstrates the need to consider current spouses alone (versus aggregated with ex-spouses and boy/girlfriends). This subset of intimates commits a staggering amount of violence.

While anyone can be a victim of family violence, findings demonstrate that some groups of victims are particularly vulnerable. For example, women are most likely to be victims of family-perpetrated violence by all family members, and experience a range of types of violence. In addition, American Indians suffer at the hands of family members at very high rates. Unlike other types of violence, family-perpetrated violence continues as one ages, although the primary perpetrator changes over time. At younger ages, victims are most likely to be victimized by parents, other relatives, and siblings. As one ages, the primary perpetrator shifts to current spouses. And at older ages, the perpetrator becomes one's children. In fact, the findings shown here indicate different dynamics associated with elder abuse, which requires more attention.

An unexpected finding is that women and men were victimized by their own child at similar and unexpectedly high rates. In total, 18.2% of women and 15.5% of men were victimized by their own child. These estimates run counter to existing literature and underscores the need to further examine violence perpetrated by one's own children.

Considering offenders' characteristics, it is clear that men, and especially men age 30 and older, are the primary perpetrators of family violence. As well, White men constitute the majority of perpetrators of family violence. Further, data reveal that while most family violence is committed by a sober perpetrator, the use of drugs and/or alcohol by these perpetrators is common.

Results presented demonstrate that familial violence is a private act committed mostly in homes, and rarely in public spaces. The use of weapons in family-perpetrated violence is uncommon, although 17.0% of this violence does include an armed offender. Nonetheless, 41.5% of victims are injured. More than half of those victimized by a current spouse are injured (53.2%). Injury or not, 61.6% of injured victims did not seek medical attention. While medical attention was not often sought, the police were notified 55.2% of the time.

As with all results, this work has limitations. The NCVS gathers data on those living in housing units, meaning that it does not collect information from the homeless or those in other institutions, such as prisons or military barracks. This is an important limitation to acknowledge, as many end up homeless as a way to flee from violence. This suggests it is reasonable to conclude these family violence estimates are conservative and the problem is larger than shown here. Further, the NCVS gathers information from people age 12 and older. As a result, the estimates here do not include violence experienced by those under age 12. When considering sibling, parental, and other relative violence, this certainly means NCVS-based estimates are significantly limited. This points to the need for multiple measures, samples, and research methodologies to comprehensively study this issue.

Discussion Questions

1. Why is it important to understand rates and trends of nonfatal familial violence?
2. The information presented here is focused on the United States only. What would be the benefits of comparing these rates/trends to those from other countries? What more could be gained by understanding relative differences?
3. Given the information presented in this chapter, what are some policy recommendations you would give to policy makers?
4. Given the information offered in this chapter, what education or training could be implemented, and to whom would this training be offered? To policing agencies? To advocacy groups? To the general public? Others?

Key Terms

Aggravated assault: Includes attempted and completed violence that involves a weapon, regardless of whether an injury occurred. It also includes instances in which the offender was unarmed, but the victim was seriously injured. Serious injuries include harm such as broken bones, stab wounds, gunshot wounds, lost teeth, internal injuries, loss of consciousness, and any unspecified injury that required the victim to be hospitalized for two or more days (Bureau of Justice Statistics, 2011).

Child: One's own child or step-child.

Familial violence: Violence between current family members, which includes spouses, children, parents, siblings, and other relatives, but which falls outside the domains of IPV, child maltreatment, and elder abuse by nonfamily members.

Other relative: Includes perpetrators such as cousins, aunts, uncles, and grandparents.

Parent: Includes one's parents and/or step-parents.

Rape/sexual assault: Rape is defined as attempted or completed forced vaginal, anal, or oral penetration (using a body part or an object) using psychological coercion and/or physical force, regardless of the victim or offender's sex. Sexual assault differs from rape and accounts for a broad range of victimizations that include attempted or completed attacks involving unwanted sexual contact (e.g., grabbing or fondling), regardless of force used.

Robbery: Includes attempted or completed theft, directly from a person, of cash or property, by force or threat of force, regardless of whether a weapon was used, or an injury occurred (Bureau of Justice Statistics, 2011).

Sibling: Includes one's siblings and step-siblings.

Simple assault: Defined as a threatened or attempted attack by an unarmed offender, from which no injury or a minor injury (i.e., involves bruises, black eyes, cuts, scratches or swelling). In addition, a simple assault is defined as a involving an unspecified injury is experienced that results in less than two days of hospitalization (Bureau of Justice Statistics, 2011).

Spouse: Includes current spouses and excludes ex-spouses.

References

Barboza, G. E. (2016). Elder maltreatment: The theory and practice of elder-abuse prevention. In C. A. Cuevas & C. M. Rennison (Eds.), *The Wiley handbook on the psychology of violence* (pp. 324–352). Wiley-Blackwell.

Black, M. C., Basile, K. C., Breiding, M. J., Smith, S. G., Walters, M. L., Merrick, M. T., ... Stevens, M. R. (2011). *The national intimate partner and sexual violence survey:*

2010 summary report. National Center for Injury Prevention and Control, Centers for Disease Control and Prevention.

Briere, J., & Elliott, D. M. (2003). Prevalence and psychological sequelae of self-reported childhood physical and sexual abuse in a general population sample of men and women. *Child Abuse & Neglect, 27,* 1205–1222.

Bureau of Justice Statistics. (2011). Criminal victimization in the United States—Statistical tables, 2008. http://bjs.ojp.usdoj.gov/content/pub/pdf/cvus/cvus08mt.pdf

Caspi, J. (2012). *Sibling aggression: Assessment and treatment.* Springer Publishing Co.

Caspi, J., & Barrios, V. R. (2016). Destructive sibling aggression. In C. A. Cuevas & C. M. Rennison (Eds.), *The Wiley handbook on the psychology of violence* (pp. 297–323). Wiley-Blackwell.

Classen, C. C., Palesh, O. G., & Aggarwal, R. (2005). Sexual revictimization: A review of the empirical literature. *Trauma, Violence, & Abuse, 6,* 103–129.

Cohen, L. E., & Felson, M. (1979). Social change and crime rate trends: A routine activity approach. *American Sociological Review, 44,* 588–608.

Condry, R., & Miles, C. (2013). Adolescent to parent violence: Framing and mapping a hidden problem. *Criminology & Criminal Justice, 14*(3), 257–275. doi:10.1177/1748895813500155

Conner, D. H. (2014). Financial freedom: Women, money, and domestic abuse. *William & Mary Journal of Race, Gender, and Social Justice, 20*(2), 339–420. https://scholarship.law.wm.edu/wmjowl/vol20/iss2/4

Dalenberg, C. (2006). Recovered memory and the Daubert criteria: Recovered memory as professionally tested, peer reviewed, and accepted in the relevant scientific community. *Trauma, Violence, & Abuse, 7*(4), 274–310.

Dallam, S. J. (2001). Crisis or creation? A systematic examination of False Memory Syndrome. *Journal of Child Sexual Abuse, 9*(3/4), 9–36.

Finkelhor, D. (1984). *Child sexual abuse: New theory and research.* The Free Press.

Finkelhor, D. (1990). Early and long-term effects of child sexual abuse: An update. *Professional Psychology Research and Practice, 21,* 325–330.

Finkelhor, D., Hamby, S. L., Ormrod, R. K., & Turner, H. A. (2005). The Juvenile Victimization Questionnaire: Reliability, validity, and national norms. *Child Abuse & Neglect, 29,* 383–412.

Finkelhor, D., Hammer, H., & Sedlak, A. J. (2008). *Sexually assaulted children: National estimates and characteristics* (National Incidence Studies of Missing, Abducted, Runaway, and Thrownaway Children). U.S. Department of Justice.

Finkelhor, D., Ormrod, R. K., & Turner, H. A. (2007). Poly-victimization: A neglected component in child victimization. *Child Abuse & Neglect, 31*(1), 7–26.

Finkelhor, D., Ormrod, R. K., Turner, H. A., & Hamby, S. L. (2005). The victimization of children and youth: A comprehensive, national survey. *Child Maltreatment, 10,* 5–25.

Finkelhor, D., & Turner, H. (2009). *National Survey on Children's Exposure to Violence: A survey of parents and children age 0–17: Methods Report.* Abt. SRBI, Inc.

Finkelhor, D., Turner, H., Ormrod, R., & Hamby, S. L. (2009). Violence, abuse, and crime exposure in a national sample of children and youth. *Pediatrics, 124,* 1411–1423.

Gallego, R., Novo, M., Fariña, F., & Arce, R. (2019). Child-to-parent violence and parent-to-child violence: A meta-analytic review. *The European Journal of Psychology Applied to Legal Context, 11*(2), 51–59. doi:10.5093/ejpalc2019a4

Groth, N. A., & Oliveri, F. J. (1989). Understanding sexual offense behavior and differentiating among sexual abusers: Basic conceptual issues. In E. Suzanne & M. Sgroi (Ed.), *Vulnerable populations: Sexual abuse treatment for children, adult survivors, offenders, and persons with mental retardation, Vol. 2.* (pp. 309–327). Lexington Books/D. C. Heath and Company.

Hamby, S. (2016). Self-report measures that do not produce gender parity in intimate partner violence: A multi-study investigation. *Psychology of Violence, 6*(2), 323–335. doi:10.1037/a0038207

Hamby, S. L. (2017). A scientific answer to a scientific question: The gender debate on intimate partner violence. *Trauma, Violence & Abuse, 18*(2), 145–154. doi:10.1177/1524838015596963

Hanson, R. K., & Morton-Bourgon, K. E. (2009). The accuracy of recidivism risk assessments for sexual offenders: A meta-analysis of 118 prediction studies. *Psychological Assessment, 21*, 1–21.

Hindelang, M. J., Gottfredson, M. R., & Garofalo, J. (1978). *Victims of personal crime: An empirical foundation for a theory of personal victimization.* Ballinger.

Hubble, D. L. (1995). *The National Crime Victimization Survey redesign: New questionnaire and procedures development and phase-in methodology.* Paper presented at the Joint Statistical Meetings, August 13–17, Orlando, FL.

Hylton, W. S. (2019, May 8). My cousin was my hero. Until the day he tried to kill me. *The New York Times.* https://www.nytimes.com/2019/05/08/magazine/cousin-kill-me-male-violence.html

Kettrey, H. H., & Emery, B. C. (2006). The discourse of sibling violence. *Journal of Family Violence, 21*(6), 407–416. doi:10.1007/s10896-006-9036-0

Khan, R., & Rogers, P. (2015). The normalization of sibling violence: Does gender and personal experience of violence influence perceptions of physical assault against siblings? *Journal of Interpersonal Violence, 30*(3), 437–458. doi:10.1177/0886260514535095

Lauritsen, J. L., Owens, J., Planty, M. G., Rand, M. R., & Truman, J. L. (2012). Methods for counting high-frequency repeat victimizations in the national crime victimization survey (NCJ 237308). Bureau of Justice Statistics.

Margolin, G., & Baucom, B. R. (2014). Adolescents' aggression to parents: Longitudinal links with parents' physical aggression. *Journal of Adolescent Health, 55*(5), 645–651. doi:10.1016/j.jadohealth.2014.05.008

Murphy, W. D., & Smith, T. A. (1996). Sex offenders against children: Empirical and clinical issues. In J. Briere, L. Berliner, J. A. Bulkley, C. Jenny, & T. Reid (Eds.), *The APSAC handbook on child maltreatment* (pp. 175–192). Sage Publications.

National Institute of Justice. (2015). *Teen dating violence measurement meeting summary* (NCJ 249015).

Peek, C. W., Fischer, J. L., & Kidwell, J. S. (1985). Teenage violence toward parents: A neglected dimension of family violence. *Journal of Marriage and Family, 47*(4), 1051–1058. doi:10.2307/352350

Pfeffer, R., & Cuevas, C. A. (2016). Research on the victimization of understudied populations: Current issues and future directions. In C. A. Cuevas & C. M. Rennison (Eds.), *The Wiley handbook on the psychology of violence* (pp. 715–726). Wiley-Blackwell.

Prentky, R. A., Knight, R. A., Rosenberg, R., & Lee, A. (1989). A path analytic approach to the validation of a taxonomic system for classifying child molesters. *Journal of Quantitative Criminology, 5*(3), 231–257.

Rand, M. R., & Rennison, C. M. (2005). Bigger is not necessarily better: An analysis of violence against women estimates from the National Crime Victimization Survey and the National Violence Against Women Survey. *Journal of Quantitative Criminology, 21*, 267–291. doi:10.1007/s10940-005-4272-7

Rennison, C. M., & Rand, M. (2007). Introduction to the National Crime Victimization Survey. In J. P. Lynch & L. A. Addington (Eds.), *Understanding crime statistics: Revisiting the divergence of the NCVS and the UCR* (pp. 17–54). Cambridge University Press.

Sedlak, A. J., Mettenburg, J., Basena, M., Petta, I., McPherson, K., Greene, A., & Li, S. (2010). *Fourth national incidence study of child abuse and neglect (NIS - 4): Report to congress.* U.S. Department of Health and Human Services, Administration for Children and Families.

Stark, R. (1987). Deviant places: A theory of the ecology of crime. *Criminology, 25*(4), 893–910.

Straus, M. A., Gelles, R. J., & Steinmetz, S. K. (1980). *Behind closed doors: Violence in the American family.* Sage.

Summit, R. C. (1983). The child sexual abuse accommodation syndrome. *Child Abuse & Neglect, 7,* 177–193.

Tails, T. (2020, December 27). This is the first & last time my husband hit me. *Medium.* https://tonitails.medium.com/this-is-the-first-last-time-my-husband-hit-me-893ebe915ced

Tjaden, P., & Thoennes, N. (2000). *Full report of the prevalence, incidence, and consequences of violence against women* (NCJ 183781). U.S. Department of Justice, Office of Justice Programs.

Tucker, C. J., & Kazura, K. (2013). Parental responses to school-aged children's sibling conflict. *Journal of Child and Family Studies, 22*(5), 737–745. doi:10.1007/s10826-013-9741-2

Ulman, A., & Straus, M. A. (2003). Violence by children against mothers in relation to violence between parents and corporal punishment by parents. *Journal of Comparative Family Studies, 34*(1), 41–6.

U.S. Department of Health and Human Services. (2019). *Child maltreatment 2017.*

Ward, T., Polaschek, D., & Beech, A. R. (2006). *Theories of sexual offending.* Wiley.

Wolfgang, M. (1957). Victim precipitated criminal homicide. *Journal of Criminal Law and Criminology, 48*(1), 1–11.

Spotlight on Special Issues

Immigrants, Interpersonal Violence, and Substance Use

Brenda M. Hernandez, BS

The previous chapter gives a comprehensive overview of familial violence from 2007 to 2020, including racial demographic characteristics; however, one area not covered that deserves attention is the relationship between immigration status, interpersonal violence, and substance use. There are more immigrants in the United States than any other country in the world, accounting for about one-fifth of the world's migrants (Budiman, 2020). The majority of immigrants are authorized to live in the United States as naturalized citizens (45%) or lawful permanent residents (27%; Budiman, 2020). An authorized status increases access to fundamental resources that support families who struggle with substance use disorders and family violence. However, there are 10.5 million undocumented and DACAmented[1] immigrants who experience systemic barriers that limit their access to mental health and substance use disorder resources. Moreover, even when undocumented or DACAmented immigrants may have access to mental health and substance use disorder (SUD) resources, involvement in government assistance programs could potentially cause more harm to families due to deportation laws (Budiman, 2020). Additionally, both legally residing immigrant families and those who are undocumented experience distinct impediments, such as acculturation, discrimination, and institutional racism barriers that need be taken into consideration when examining the nexus of family violence and substance use.

The association between acculturation and the likelihood of engaging with substance use has been explored in the literature and continues to be a topic of discussion in relation to the immigrant experience. Rebhun (1998) defines acculturation as "the process by which immigrants and their U.S.-born children change their ideas and behaviors in response

---

1   DACAmented is a term that describes a person who is residing in the United States and falls under the category of Deferred Action for Childhood Arrivals (DACA). DACA provides some protections for immigrants who were brought to the United States as children, but is not a substitute for citizenship. For more information on DACA, visit the National Immigration Law Center (NILC) at www.nilc.org/issues/daca.

to the host culture" (pp. 493–494). Research by Borges et al. (2007) suggests that the longer immigrants reside in the United States, the higher they are at risk for experiencing substance use disorders. In addition, acculturation may heighten substance use, when protective factors such as external support from family members are removed. The "acculturative stress" model of substance use is a reaction to the disorienting, isolated, impoverished, and discriminatory experiences of immigrants that increases their tendency to use substances that can offer immediate comfort to the stress of being an immigrant in an unwelcoming environment (Rebhun,1998). Over time, the association between acculturation and substance use can have detrimental effects on the health and well-being of immigrant families and may increase risk of substance use and interpersonal family violence. For example, studies have shown that as adaptation to culture in the United States progresses, both fatal and nonfatal spousal violence from male to female increases at disproportionate rates for Latina immigrant women (Zarza & Adler, 2008).

Another important factor that can influence increased rates of substance use among immigrant populations is discrimination. According to Tran et al. (2010), race, color, ethnicity, or country of origin are ranked as one of the most frequently cited reasons for discrimination. For African-born Black immigrants, discrimination while dealing with the police was particularly high, and Latino immigrants reported higher rates of discrimination in the workplace, specifically when applying for a job. The number of discriminatory experiences was positively related to the number of drinking days, and the number of years in the United States was significantly related to engaging in binge drinking (Tran et al., 2010). The discriminatory experiences of immigrants, over time, can have lasting impact on family dynamics, and coping mechanisms like substance use, particularly for men, can create stressors for their wives, children, and other family members, which may increase the likelihood of interpersonal familial violence.

Despite the cultural and economic contributions immigrants offer, the United States has systematically created an unwelcoming environment that limits access to vital resources. Undocumented and DACAmented immigrants experience the most inequalities, and growing research suggests the federal government has implemented a wide range of harmful policies that enhance immigration law enforcement and limit use of public assistance programs (Kaiser Family Foundation, 2020). Furthermore, many immigrants fear that any report of interpersonal violence can lead to deportation and family separation. As stated in the Kaiser Family Foundation report Health Coverage of Immigrants (2020), "noncitizens, including lawfully present and undocumented immigrants, were significantly more likely to be uninsured than citizens," which can have important implications for the health and well-being of families and the health care system. Additionally, other factors like language barriers discourage immigrants from inquiring about resources available to them (Ku, 2006).

Bearing in mind these factors, any efforts to address substance use and interpersonal familial violence should consider translating effective clinical interventions to community-based interventions, particularly for immigrants with limited access to health care. Interventions that utilize promotores de salud are recognized as culturally appropriate and effective approaches to provide health education and counseling in community-based settings (Ornelas et al., 2015). Promotores are highly trained community experts and they use their insights and knowledge of cultural norms to provide relevant health information. Promotores can provide support to work through the barriers immigrant communities face when addressing complex issues such as SUD, family violence, and navigating the immigration and health care systems. Although few studies have focused on interventions that address the issue of limited health care access, incorporating promotores de salud and adapting the setting of the intervention is consistent with theory and recommendations (Ornelas et al., 2015).

Health insurance is important for enabling families to access needed care; it offers protection from unaffordable medical care costs, and plays a significant role in the health and well-being of families. States like California have adapted their health insurance policies to include undocumented and DACAmented immigrants, giving them option to enroll in free or low cost Medi-Cal, or they can purchase a health plan privately (Covered California, n.d.). Other states should consider implementing policies that make health insurance available and accessible to immigrants regardless of documentation status. Moreover, other public benefits, such as food support or childcare assistance, should be made accessible to immigrants, with policies in place to assure that those who are undocumented or DACAmented will not face repercussions, particularly those related to deportation or immigration status. Nonprofits and government agencies that serve clients who are immigrants should make materials available in multiple languages, and ensure interpreter services are available as needed for clients with access issues related to literacy. Transparency in what, if any, repercussions an undocumented or DACAmented person may face when accessing services is needed, such that immigrants have an informed choice regarding what services may be available to them, and the risks involved with accessing these services. All things considered, the unique barriers that immigrants experience should be considered when developing policies, interventions, and treatment initiatives aimed at immigrant communities.

References

Borges, G., Medina-Mora, M. E., Breslau, J., & Aguilar-Gaxiola, S. (2007). The effect of migration to the United States on substance use disorders among returned Mexican migrants and families of migrants. *American Journal of Public Health, 97*(10), 1847–1851. https://doi.org/10.2105/AJPH.2006.097915

Budiman, A. (2020). *Key findings about U.S. immigrants | Pew Research Center.* https://www.pewresearch.org/fact-tank/2020/08/20/key-findings-about-u-s-immigrants/

Covered California Eligibility Requirements | Health for CA. (n.d.). Retrieved September 30, 2020, from https://www.healthforcalifornia.com/covered-california/eligibility

Kaiser Family Foundation. (2020). *Health coverage of immigrants.* https://www.kff.org/racial-equity-and-health-policy/fact-sheet/health-coverage-of-immigrants/

Matthews, A., Li, C.-C., Aranda, F., Torres, L., Vargas, M., & Conrad, M. (2014). The influence of acculturation on substance use behaviors among Latina sexual minority women: The mediating role of discrimination. *Substance Use & Misuse, 49*(14), 1888–1898. https://doi.org/10.3109/10826084.2014.913632

Ornelas, I. J., Allen, C., Vaughan, C., Williams, E. C., & Negi, N. (2015). Vida PURA: A cultural adaptation of screening and brief intervention to reduce unhealthy drinking among Latino day laborers. *Substance Abuse, 36*(3), 264–271. https://doi.org/10.1080/08897077.2014.955900

Rebhun, L. A. (1998). Substance use among immigrants to the United States. In S. Loue (Ed.), *Handbook of immigrant health* (pp. 493–519). Springer US. https://doi.org/10.1007/978-1-4899-1936-6_24

Thai, N. D., Connell, C. M., & Tebes, J. K. (2010). Substance use among Asian American adolescents: Influence of race, ethnicity, and acculturation in the context of key risk and protective factors. *Asian American Journal of Psychology, 1*(4), 261–274. https://doi.org/10.1037/a0021703

Tran, A. G. T. T., Lee, R. M., & Burgess, D. J. (2010). Perceived discrimination and substance use in Hispanic/Latino, African-born Black, and Southeast Asian immigrants. *Cultural Diversity and Ethnic Minority Psychology, 16*(2), 226–236. https://doi.org/10.1037/a0016344

Why immigrants lack adequate access to health care and health insurance | migrationpolicy.org. (n.d.). Retrieved September 30, 2020, from https://www.migrationpolicy.org/article/why-immigrants-lack-adequate-access-health-care-and-health-insurance

Zarza, M. J., & Adler, R. H. (2008). Latina immigrant victims of interpersonal violence in New Jersey: A needs assessment study. *Journal of Aggression, Maltreatment & Trauma, 16*(1), 22–39. https://doi.org/10.1080/10926770801920453

CHAPTER THREE

Substance Use and Intimate Partner Violence

Yu Lu, PhD and Jeff R. Temple, PhD

Introduction

Intimate partner violence (IPV) is a prevalent public health problem with significant negative consequences. A number of risk factors have been identified for IPV, such as age, gender, race/ethnicity, family relationships, developmental psychopathology, and relationship (dis)satisfaction (Calpaldi et al., 2012). Substance use, including alcohol and illicit drug use, were identified as one of the most salient risk factors for IPV, both perpetration and victimization (Stith et al., 2004). This chapter focuses on the relationship between IPV and substance use. We first describe the scope of the problem by providing definitions of various types of IPV and summarize the link between substance use and IPV. We then describe the history of substance use and IPV research and provide an overview of the theoretical perspectives that explain the link between these public health problems. We further discuss the shared risk and protective factors in the link between substance use and IPV. The chapter concludes with a description of and suggestions for interventions/preventions, as well as policy recommendations.

Scope of the Problem

By definition, IPV encompasses physical violence, psychological violence, sexual abuse, and stalking toward a current or former romantic partner or spouse (Capaldi et al., 2012; CDC, 2018). According to CDC (2019), physical abuse is when one person hurts or tries to hurt a partner (or ex-partner) by hitting, kicking, or using any type of physical force. **Psychological intimate**

partner violence or emotional abuse refers to acting in an offensive or degrading manner toward another, verbally or nonverbally, with the intent to harm another mentally or emotionally and to exert control over another person (e.g., social isolation, financial control; O'Leary & Maiuro, 2001). **Sexual intimate partner violence** is coercive behaviors to force a partner to take part in a sex act, sexual touching, or a nonphysical sexual event (e.g., sexting) without consent. **Stalking** is a pattern of repeated, unwanted attention and contact by a partner that causes fear or concern for the safety of oneself or someone close to the victim.

Prevalence of IPV varies by IPV type. A recent National Intimate Partner and Sexual Violence Survey indicates that about 1 in 4 women and 1 in 10 men in the United States experience sexual violence, physical violence, and/or stalking from an intimate partner in their lifetime (CDC, 2021a). Specifically, about 1 in 4 adult women and approximately 1 in 7 adult men report having experienced severe physical violence from an intimate partner in their lifetime. About 20% of women and 8% of men have experienced contact sexual violence from an intimate partner, including rape, being made to penetrate someone else, sexual coercion, and/or unwanted sexual contact, and 10% of women and 2% of men report having been stalked by an intimate partner. Over one-third of women and men experience psychological aggression by an intimate partner during their lifetime (Smith et al., 2018). Some degree of psychological abuse, at least at a minor or occasional level, is very common (Shortt, 2011).

IPV perpetrated by both genders can lead to physical conditions (e.g., headache, chronic pain, difficult sleeping), injury, fear, depression, post-traumatic stress disorder symptomatology, suicide, and homicide (CDC, 2021a; Hines & Malley-Morrison, 2001; Schumacher et al., 2001; Smith et al., 2017). Worldwide, 13.5% of homicides were committed by an intimate partner, and the proportion is six times higher for female homicides than for male homicides (Stöckl et al., 2013). Although women were slightly more likely than men to use at least one act of physical aggression and to utilize such behaviors with greater frequency (Archer, 2000; Herrera et al., 2008; Schluter et al., 2008), men were more likely to inflict injury, and the majority of IPV victims that were injured were women (Ehrensaft et al., 2004).

Dating Violence

Dating violence, a type of IPV, is defined as "the threat or actual use of physical, sexual, or verbal abuse by one member of an unmarried couple on the other member within the context of a dating relationship" (Anderson & Danis, 2007, p. 88). Dating violence is differentiated from marital violence in that marital relationships are likely characterized by greater familial and economic attachment, making investment and enmeshment in the relationship greater. Married partners are often economically bound to each other, may have children, and are more likely to be involved in each other's families of origin (Carlson, 1987), whereas dating relationships do not involve a legal binding relationship, making alternative relationships more accessible to dating couples than to married individuals. Dating violence research has primarily focused on high school and college aged adolescents (Shorey et al., 2008).

Teen dating violence (TDV)—dating violence among adolescents—has increasingly gained the interest of the public and researchers. About 26% of women and 15% of men experience IPV for the first time before age 18 (CDC, 2021b). The prevalence of TDV is 60%–90% for any type of psychological abuse (20%–50% for severe forms), 20%–37% for physical abuse, and 10%–20% for sexual abuse (Bell & Naugle, 2007; Choi & Temple, 2016; Garthe et al., 2016; Sears et al., 2007; Shorey et al., 2008; Silverman et al., 2001). With the exception of sexual TDV, which is more frequently perpetrated by males, the prevalence of TDV is similar for both genders (Shorey et al., 2008). Although the severity of TDV is often lower than IPV, youth in violent relationships, relative to their non-victimized counterparts, exhibit higher rates of depression, anxiety, suicidal ideation, substance use, posttraumatic stress disorder, sexually transmitted infections and risky sexual behavior, teen pregnancy, and eating disorders (Exner-Cortens et al., 2013; Nahapetyan et al., 2014; Parker et al., 2016; Shorey et al., 2015; Vagi et al., 2015). They are also more likely to perform poorly in school and to experience difficulties in future relationships (Holt et al., 2007). Moreover, TDV victimization and perpetration in adolescence predicts violence in adulthood. A 5-year longitudinal study of adverse health outcomes found that TDV victimization predicted adult partner violence victimization, as well as heavy episodic drinking, depression, suicidality, smoking, marijuana use, and antisocial behaviors (Exner-Cortens et al., 2013).

Cyber dating abuse (CDA) is a relatively new phenomenon that followed the advent and near ubiquity of smartphones. Cyber dating abuse refers to the control, harassment, stalking, and abuse of one's dating partner via technology and social media (Zweig et al., 2014). CDA can be conceptualized as a type of psychological abuse, but it is unique because it presents an opportunity for perpetrators to have continuous access and publicly degrade and humiliate victims to an extent that is not possible with in-person abuse. Consequently, victims can be continuously targeted, and might, therefore, feel unable to escape the abuse. Moreover, perpetrators might experience fewer inhibitions to engage in abusive behaviors, as their actions are more removed, potentially anonymous, and less likely to be immediately confronted with the consequences of their behaviors. Recent studies have reported 12%–20% CDA perpetration and 26%–60% CDA victimization among adolescents (Lu et al., 2018; Peskin et al., 2017; Van Ouytsel et al., 2016; Zweig et al., 2013).

IPV and Substance Use Consequences and Effects

Various types of substance use have been examined in relation to IPV. The association of substance use with IPV and TDV are mostly consistent, although married samples showed larger effects compared to dating samples. In addition, samples aged 18 to 40 showed larger effects than adolescents (Moore et al., 2008). In the review below, we summarize findings in both IPV and TDV. We first describe the association between partner violence and alcohol use, then turn to drug use (inclusive of various drug types). We also provide an overview of the association between substance use and CDA.

IPV and Alcohol Use

An extensive number of studies have examined the relationships between IPV and alcohol use (Bennett, Tolman, Rogalski, & Srinivasaraghavan, 1994; Hines & Straus, 2007; Leonard, Bromet, Parkinson, Day & Ryan, 1985; O'Leary & Schumacher, 2003). A positive and consistent association was found for alcohol use and different types of IPV, including physical, psychological, and sexual abuse (Crane et al., 2016; Devries et al., 2013; Foran & O'Leary, 2008). However, when examining various types of alcohol use (e.g., alcohol abuse/dependence, episodic heavy drinking, alcohol quantity, and frequency), the results differed. Based on a meta-analysis of 285 studies, Cafferky et al. (2018) found that problematic alcohol use (e.g., abuse/dependence) is a stronger correlate than amount of alcohol consumption for physical IPV victimization, but not for perpetration. Crane et al. (2016) conducted a meta-analysis based on 22 studies to examine the association between acute alcohol consumption and male-to-female IPV and reported that alcohol amount did not show significant associations with IPV. Instead, problematic alcohol use was a stronger predictor of IPV, both for physical and sexual abuse. Overall, just consuming alcohol is not linked to IPV as much as being intoxicated as a result of episodic heavy drinking or alcohol abuse/dependence (Foran & O'Leary, 2008). This is consistent with the proposition of proximal effects model in that it may be necessary for alcohol to be consumed in a sufficient quantity to produce intoxication in order for the psychopharmacological effects on disinhibition to occur and increase the likelihood of IPV.

While the majority of earlier studies focused on cross-sectional associations, more recent work has examined the longitudinal effects of alcohol use on IPV, which allows for the examination of temporality. In a meta-analysis, Devries et al. (2013) summarized 14 longitudinal studies that examined physical and sexual IPV victimization and alcohol use among women and identified a bidirectional relationship. That is, a positive longitudinal link was found for alcohol use predicting later IPV, as well for IPV predicting later alcohol use. However, as Devries and colleagues pointed out, a causal relationship cannot be inferred, as the specific mechanism behind the relationship is unknown.

Overall, with respect to the large number of studies on the link between IPV and alcohol use, most studies focus on physical IPV and generally lack thoroughness on the alcohol measures (Shorey et al., 2018). Furthermore, although an increasing number of longitudinal studies have been conducted, proof of a causal relationship remains elusive. That said, Leonard (2005) suggested that, given the difficulty in testing a causal model coupled with the robustness of available data, we can confidently say that substance

COMPREHENSION ACTIVITY 3.1

ACTIVITY

To illustrate their prevalence and strong link, search "domestic violence" and "alcohol" in Google News. Select one story to summarize and critique. As an example, we did this in early 2022 and found this story: https://www.leaderlive.co.uk/news/19901654.ms-plea-domestic-abuse-can-follow-sporting-events-fuelled-alcohol/

SUMMARY

Concern over alcohol-fueled domestic violence secondary to the upcoming Six Nations Rugby Tournament. An organization is attempting to get men and boys to pledge to never commit, excuse, or remain silent about violence against women.

QUESTIONS TO CRITIQUE

1. Is alcohol intake related to partner violence? If so, how?
2. Is there strong and consistent evidence that domestic violence increases during major sporting events?
3. What is the evidence regarding pledges? Do they actually result in behavior change?

use is a strong contributor to (if not cause of) many instances of partner violence. Lastly, multiple meta-analyses (e.g., Crane et al., 2016; Foran & O'Leary, 2008) identified significant between-study variations when examining the associations, and suggest that moderators of relationships need to be examined.

IPV and Other Substance Use

Despite the extensive research on IPV and alcohol use, relatively fewer studies have examined the link between IPV and other substances. Existing research has identified an overall association between drug use/abuse and higher levels of IPV perpetration and victimization (Cafferky et al., 2018; Moore et al., 2008). Similar to alcohol use, various types of drug use also show different strengths of associations with IPV, such that the associations of drug use amount/frequency are smaller than that of drug problems or drug diagnoses (Moore et al., 2008). All abuse types, including physical abuse, psychological abuse, and sexual abuse, have been linked to increased drug use (Cafferky et al., 2018; Moore et al., 2008). In comparing among IPV types, the association with drugs is stronger for psychological IPV compared to sexual abuse, but differences did not emerge for physical abuse (Moore et al., 2008).

Among drug types, cocaine has consistently been found to associate with higher levels of IPV (Bennett et al., 1994; Gilbert et al., 2012; Grisso et al., 1999; Murphy et al., 2001; Parrott et al., 2003; Stuart et al., 2008). Mixed findings have been reported for marijuana, with some studies finding higher amounts may actually be inversely associated with IPV (Cherek et al., 1993; Myerscough & Taylor, 1985) while others finding that withdrawal increases IPV (Hoaken & Stewart, 2003; Moore & Stuart, 2005). For cigarette smoking, IPV victimization was found to heighten the risk of smoking (Crane et al., 2013). One longitudinal study also found that TDV (i.e., physical and sexual TDV combined) was associated with cigarette smoking one year later in a sample of older adolescents (Ackard et al., 2007). Synthesizing previous research, meta-analytic studies reported that the use of cocaine, marijuana, cigarettes, amphetamines, and opiates were all significantly associated with higher levels of IPV, whereas heroin, sedatives/anxiolytics, stimulants (other than cocaine), and hallucinogens did not show differences (Cafferky et al., 2018; Crane et al., 2013; Moore et al., 2008). Cafferky et al. (2018) also examined drug categories and found that both stimulant and nonstimulant drug use associated with physical IPV perpetration and victimization.

Research has also suggested a possible bi-directional relationship between IPV and drug use. In a longitudinal study of 241 women receiving emergency care, Gilbert et al. (2012) found that heroin use was associated with subsequent physical, sexual, and psychological abuse, while cocaine was associated with later physical and psychological abuse. Sexual IPV, on the other hand, was significantly associated with subsequent cocaine use.

A meta-analysis of 96 studies by Moore and colleagues (2008) found that cocaine had the strongest relationship to all three types of IPV. Marijuana showed a stronger association than opiates, but was no stronger than other drug types (Moore et al., 2008). Based on a meta-analysis of 285 studies, Cafferky et al. (2018) found that illicit drug abuse, relative to alcohol, was a stronger correlate of physical IPV victimization but not perpetration.

Overall, research is limited on the relationship between drug use and IPV, especially given the large number of drug types. Many studies do not distinguish between different types of drugs (e.g., Moore et al., 2018), and those that do distinguish suggest that different drug types may have varied relationships with IPV (Boles & Miotto, 2003; Stuart et al., 2008). More research—preferably longitudinal studies—is needed to identify these links. Similar to research on alcohol use, research on drug use is limited by focusing primarily on physical IPV and measurement variations (e.g., drug use amount vs. drug dependency).

Cyber Dating Abuse and Substance Use

Given the novelty of this behavior, little research has examined the association between CDA and substance use. Using a sample of 424 sixth graders who reported ever having a boyfriend/girlfriend, Peskin and colleagues (2017) did not find a link between CDA perpetration and any alcohol/drug use. Zweig et al. (2014) examined CDA victimization in a sample of 3,745 youth in three northeastern states and found that CDA victims reported more frequent alcohol, marijuana, any drug use, and serious drug use compared to their non-victim counterparts. However, when considered alongside other factors, including demographics, delinquency, mental health, and personality factors, the association diminished. A study of 1,187 adolescents from secondary schools in Belgium (Van Ouytsel et al., 2016) found that youth victimized by CDA more frequently engaged in heavy episodic drinking compared to those who did not report victimization, but not with marijuana and cigarette use. A recent longitudinal study (Lu et al., 2018) examined the cross-sectional and temporal associations between CDA victimization and a range of substance use (alcohol, cigarette, marijuana, and hard drugs) in a sample of 641 late adolescents in Texas. Cross-sectional associations were identified with all substances, with past year hard drug use as well as past month alcohol and marijuana use associated with CDA victimization one year later.

Findings on the link between CDA and substance use are mixed. The discrepancies are likely due to measure variation (e.g., frequency, any use), similar to research on IPV and alcohol use. Overall, there is a dearth of studies on this relationship and future research is needed—especially given the prevalence of CDA and its associations with traditional dating abuse (Temple et al., 2016).

Historical Context

IPV has maintained much scholarly, public, and policy attention since the 1970s, when it was first brought to attention by the battered women's movement with a strict focus on "wife abuse." Scholars including Strauss, Gelles, and Dobash are among the first to study IPV. Intimate partner violence has been studied in two major streams of work: the *family violence perspective* and the *feminist perspective* (Kurz, 1989). The family violence perspective refers to violence between husbands and wives as "spouse abuse," and views it as part of a pattern of violence occurring among all family members. This approach often relies on quantitative data through surveys and provides information on the prevalence and causality of IPV. The feminist perspective, on the other hand, places male–female relations at the center of analysis and views gender inequality as a key factor in the violence. Primarily utilizing qualitative data, this approach often relies on data from battered women, especially those who have come for support to law enforcement, hospitals, and shelters. While the feminist perspective focuses on battered women and argues that male dominance as "the" factor at the root of IPV, scholars of the family violence perspective suggest that violence is more dyadic in nature (Straus et al., 1980).

In 1995, Johnson suggested that the discrepancies between family violence and feminist perspectives were due to the fact that they were studying two distinct phenomena. Johnson identified two forms of IPV, *patriarchal terrorism*, which he later referred to as *intimate terrorism* (Johnson & Leone, 2005), and *common couple violence*, or *situational couple violence*. **Intimate terrorism** refers to the attempt to dominate one's partner and to exert general control over the relationship, using a wider range of power and control tactics, including violence (Johnson, 1995; Johnson & Leone, 2005). **Common couple violence**, on the other hand, involves specific arguments that escalate to violence but shows no relationship-wide pattern of controlling behaviors (Johnson & Leone, 2005). In their study using the National Violence Against Women Survey data, Johnson and Leone (2005) found that, compared to common couple violence, the violence in intimate terrorism was more frequent and severe, and less likely to desist. Furthermore, victims of intimate terrorism were more likely to be injured, exhibit more posttraumatic stress symptoms, miss work, and have left the abusive relationship.

Increasing attention has been given to the mutuality of partner violence—that is, whether the violence is unidirectional (e.g., male-to-female) or bidirectional (i.e., male-to-female and female-to-male). Studies over the last few decades have found that a vast majority of partner violence is characterized by mutual violence (Cascardi et al., 1992; Gray & Foshee, 1997; Langhinrichsen-Rohling et al., 1995; Temple et al., 2005). Indeed, in a review of 48 studies, Langhinrichsen-Rohling et al. (2012) concluded that bidirectional violence was common across all types of samples (including community and criminal justice samples).

Paralleling IPV research history, a large number of early studies on IPV and substance use focused on male-to-female IPV, particularly among batterers or marital treatment programs (e.g., Halford & Osgarby, 1993; Hutchison, 1999; Rosenbaum & O'Leary, 1981). Many previous studies interviewed battered women (or examined arrest records) and identified the proportion of times in which IPV occurred when an individual was under the influence of alcohol or drugs (Roberts, 1987). A number of other research compared batterers and community samples (e.g., Else et al., 1993; Julian & McKenry, 1993) or examined the association within community samples (e.g., Kaufman-Kantor & Straus, 1989). In recent years, an increasing number of studies have included female perpetration (e.g., Kelly & Halford, 2006; Shorey et al., 2012; Stuart et al., 2008).

Theoretical Perspectives

Several theoretical perspectives have been used to explain the associations between substance use and IPV (for reviews, see Foran & O'Leary, 2008; Moore et al., 2008). A group of theoretical perspectives posits a causal relationship between substance use and IPV, although the opposite relationship direction was also implied. General strain theory states that stressors such as physical abuse could lead to engagement in substance use as a coping mechanism to alleviate the emotions in response to stressors (Agnew, 2008). Lifestyle-routine activity theory (Gover, 2004; Mannon, 1997) suggests that deviant lifestyles, such as substance use, could put individuals at risk for becoming victims of abusive behaviors, as they are more often in situations in which capable guardians (e.g., parents or teachers for youth) or law enforcement who could provide protection are absent. Importantly, victims should never be blamed for their abuse; the fault always lies with the perpetrator.

Proximal effects model (Strauss et al., 2018) posits that substance use facilitates aggression, including IPV, directly through psychopharmacological effects. For example, alcohol intoxication depresses higher order executive functioning that aids in the inhibition of normative aggressive impulses, efficient social information processing, and decision-making, which could result in higher tendencies for aggression (Giancola et al., 2010). Drugs, on the other hand, may inhibit anxieties regarding perceived punishment from aggression, which results in a higher likelihood of aggressive behaviors. Drugs may also increase sensitivity to pain, which results in increased risk of reactive aggression (Pihl & Hoaken, 1997; Pihl & Peterson, 1995). Furthermore, Goldstein's (1995) tripartite framework suggests that aggression, including IPV, can occur in the context of procuring drugs (e.g., forcing a partner to obtain drugs) or to support a drug habit.

Also suggesting a causal relationship, the indirect effects model (Foran & O'Leary, 2008) postulates that substance use causes aggression that is mediated by other variables such as marital conflict and dissatisfaction. In other words, substance use increases conflicts in romantic relationships, which in turn increases the risk for IPV.

The spurious model, on the other hand, suggests that the link between substance use and IPV is not causal but due to other factors that correlate with both substance use and IPV, such as childhood IPV and substance abuse exposure, mental health issues, work-related stress, or antisocial personality (Jasinski et al., 1997; Osgood et al., 1988). Similarly, the general deviance theory (Harrison et al., 2001; Osgood et al., 1988) proposes that individuals involved in one type of deviant behavior are likely to be involved in other types of deviant behaviors, hence the correlation between substance use and IPV.

While all the theoretical frameworks described above focus on one possible way to explain the relationship between IPV and substance use, the biopsychosocial model (Cafferky et al., 2018; Moore & Stuart, 2005) describes the interplay between proximal and distal factors. Distal factors are the relatively stable and enduring individual characteristics that exist across a variety of conflictual situations, such as childhood abuse, family history of substance use, temperament, gender role expectations, norms, and peer influences. Proximal factors include substance influences, information processing, threat/provocation, impulsivity, emotional arousal, verbal behaviors, and setting of the encounter. Moore and Stuart (2005) suggest that distal factors influence violence indirectly through proximal factors.

Risk and Protective Factors

Various factors have been identified in examining the association between substance use and IPV. Age plays a potentially protective role. For example, in a study with adolescents, Reyes et al. (2011) found that the strong association between alcohol use and TDV perpetration weakened as adolescents aged.

Higher rates of substance use were also associated with IPV among sexual minorities. Wong et al. (2010) examined young men who have sex with men and found that physical IPV predicted recent illicit drug use. In a study of sexual minority women, Glass et al. (2008) found increases in physical violence were linked to having an alcohol-misusing partner or ex-partner.

Another factor to consider is pregnancy. Martin et al. (2003) studied 85 prenatal care patients and found that the link between IPV and substance use became stronger after pregnancy; that is, women who experienced each type of IPV (i.e., physical, psychological, and sexual) were more likely to use both alcohol and illicit drugs during pregnancy compared to pre-pregnancy. Among women substance users, experiencing physical and psychological IPV was linked to increased symptoms of substance disorders.

Among different racial groups, stronger associations have been found between drug use and IPV among African Americans, compared to Whites or Hispanics (Moore et al., 2008). Foshee et al. (2004) found that being Non-Hispanic White predicted chronic victimization from serious physical dating violence for males but not for females, suggesting that the racial difference on IPV and substance use associations may be further complicated by gender. Indeed, gender variations have been reported in the link between IPV and various types of substance use. Moore et al. (2011) collected data from 184 college students using electronic diary assessment methods and found that men were 7.03 times more likely to engage in psychological IPV on drinking days compared to non-drinking days, in comparison to an odds ratio of 1.60 for women. Cafferky et al. (2018) also concluded that alcohol use was a stronger correlate for males perpetrating physical IPV than for females. For victimization, mixed findings have been reported. Using longitudinal data from a sample of 725 young adults, Chen and White (2004) found that although problematic drinking significantly predicted physical IPV perpetration in both males and females, it was only associated with female physical IPV victimization. On the contrary, in a sample of 1,291 eighth and ninth graders, Foshee and colleagues (2004) found that drinking alcohol was associated with chronic serious physical

IPV victimization for males but not for females. In spite of significant association between CDA victimization and heavy episodic drinking for both males and females, male CDA victims were found to consume alcohol more frequently than non-victims, but no difference was found for females (Van Ouytsel et al., 2016).

Cocaine use has been positively linked to IPV victimization in females but not in males (Ackard et al., 2007; Moore et al., 2008). Ackard et al. (2007) found that TDV victimization was significantly associated with increased marijuana use in female adolescents, but not in males. Synthesizing research on alcohol and various types of drug use, Cafferky et al. (2018) concluded that overall substance use and alcohol use in particular are stronger correlates for male perpetration of physical IPV relative to females. Overall drug use, on the other hand, was a stronger correlate for female physical IPV victimization. However, no significant gender differences emerged for specific drug types (e.g., cocaine, heroin, amphetamines) and IPV perpetration or victimization.

The gender of who is being studied also appears important. An overall greater effect size of the associations between IPV and substance use have been identified for female reporters compared to male reporters (Cafferky et al., 2018; Moore et al., 2008). Moore and colleagues found that the effect sizes based on female reports of IPV were significantly greater than male reports, regardless of the gender of the substance user and IPV victim. That is, women generally report a stronger association than do men for all forms of aggression.

Prevention and Intervention

The established connection between IPV and substance use, particularly alcohol use, has resulted in interventions that target both behaviors. Indeed, treatment studies have found that reductions in drinking after alcoholism treatment were related to reductions in IPV (O'Farrell & Murphy, 1995), implying effectiveness of prevention programs targeting substance use in order to reduce IPV.

Guided by the Institute of Medicine's (1994) framework for classifying prevention programs, there are three types of prevention programs: selective, indicated, and universal. (For a detailed review, see Temple et al., 2009.) **Selective prevention programs** target a group of individuals at higher risk of certain risk behaviors, such as a violence prevention program for adolescents who misuse substances.

Indicated preventions, on the other hand, target high-risk individuals who have already exhibited the problem behavior (e.g., IPV, substance misuse). It differs from selective prevention programs in that it focuses on preventing the recurrence or the progression of the behavior. Stuart et al. (2009) summarized three types of **indicated prevention programs**: batterer programs (i.e., individuals arrested for domestic violence and court-referred to violence prevention programs), individual treatment for substance misuse, and behavioral couples therapy for substance use and IPV. Historically, batterer intervention programs have been found to show limited efficacy in preventing IPV (Babcock et al., 2004; Feder & Wilson, 2005), particularly among men arrested for IPV who misuse substances (DeMaris & Jackson, 1987; Hamberger & Hastings, 1990; Stuart et al., 2007). On the other hand, patients receiving individual treatment for substance misuse have shown to have reduced IPV perpetration and victimization. However, a connection between relapse to substance use and continued relationship aggression was documented (Stuart et al., 2009). Finally, behavioral couples therapy shows a consistent pattern of more abstinence from using alcohol and drugs, fewer substance use-related problems, more satisfied relationships, and lower risk of relationship separation for individuals who received behavioral couples therapy (Stuart et al., 2009). In light of these findings, behavioral couples therapy seems especially promising given the larger effect; however, this approach should only be considered if there is a history of low to moderate levels of IPV, if both partners independently agree to participate and do not express fear of negative consequences for doing so, and if both partners firmly commit to nonviolence. Regardless of approach, more attention must be given to relapse prevention.

Universal prevention programs are provided to an entire population (e.g., nation, adolescents, school, sixth-grade class). Generally speaking, these programs aim to prevent the onset of a problematic behavior. Several universal alcohol consumption prevention programs have shown to be effective in reducing violent behaviors, although the specific effects on IPV are unknown (Månsdotter et al., 2007; Simon et al., 2002; Sussman, 1996). One program that targets both IPV and substance use is *Fourth R* [Reading, w(R)iting, a(R)ithmetic, and Relationships], a healthy relationship school-based curriculum that focuses on the interrelated nature of risky behaviors (e.g., substance misuse, risky sexual behaviors, TDV). By targeting shared risk and protective factors and teaching healthy relationship skills, *Fourth R* has the potential to reduce a number of risky behaviors, including TDV. *Fourth R* has shown to be effective at increasing relationship skills and reducing problematic behaviors including physical DV (Crooks et al., 2008; Temple et al., 2021; Wolfe et al., 2009).

Conclusion

Mounting evidence illustrates the clear, bidirectional, and potentially causative link between substance use and partner violence. Thus, researchers, policy makers, and health professionals should not consider these critically important public health concerns in silos. Instead, we suggest the following:

- Prevention programs—whether universal, selected, or indicated—should target the shared risk and protective factors of multiple problem behaviors.
- Batterer intervention programs should address substance use disorders. Acquired skills in managing anger and healthy conflict resolution will be limited if the offender is using alcohol or drugs.
- Domestic violence shelters should provide access—preferably on site—to treatment for substance use.
- Substance use treatment programs should provide IPV prevention programming. They should also screen for and refer or provide necessary services for men and women in violent relationships.

COMPREHENSION ACTIVITY 3.2

ACTIVITY

Watch the following music video: https://www.youtube.com/watch?v=uelHwf8o7_U

DISCUSSION

1. Describe the relationship between substance use and violence both in the lyrics and in the video imagery.

Discussion Questions

1. Which theory(ies) that explain the relationship between IPV and substance use stand out to you and why? What are some ways to go about testing these theorized links?
2. Discuss the pros and cons of selected, indicated, and universal prevention programs for IPV and substance use. If you had all the money in the world, what type of prevention program would you choose and why? What if you had a limited amount of money?

Key Terms

Common couple violence: Also called "situational couple violence," involves specific arguments that escalate to violence but showing no relationship-wide pattern of controlling behaviors.

Cyber dating abuse: The control, harassment, stalking, and abuse of one's dating partner via technology and social media.

Dating violence: Physical, sexual, or psychological aggression by a current or former dating partner that can occur in heterosexual or same sex relationships. When teens are involved, referred to as teen dating violence or adolescent relationship abuse.

Indicated prevention programs: Programs targeting high-risk individuals who have already exhibited the behavior of interest in order to prevent its recurrence and stop its progression.

Intimate partner violence: Physical, sexual, or psychological aggression by a current or former partner or spouse that can occur in heterosexual or same-sex relationships.

Intimate terrorism: Initially referred to as "patriarchal terrorism" and known as "coercive controlling violence," intimate terrorism refers to the attempt to dominate one's partner and to exert general control over the relationship, domination that is manifested in the use of a wider range of power and control tactics, including violence.

Physical intimate partner violence: When one person hurts or tries to hurt a partner (or ex-partner) by hitting, kicking, or using any type of physical force.

Psychological intimate partner violence: Or emotional abuse. Acting in an offensive or degrading manner toward another, verbally or nonverbally, with the intent to harm another mentally or emotionally and to exert control over another person (e.g., social isolation, financial control).

Selective prevention programs: Programs directed toward subsets of individuals who may be at heightened risk for developing a problematic behavior.

Sexual intimate partner violence: Coercive behaviors to force a partner to take part in a sex act, sexual touching, or a non-physical sexual event (e.g., sexting) without consent.

Stalking: A pattern of repeated, unwanted attention and contact by a partner that causes fear or concern for the safety of oneself or someone close to the victim.

Universal prevention programs: Programs provided to an entire population of individuals (e.g., nation, adolescents, school, sixth-grade class) with the skills and information necessary to prevent the onset of a problematic behavior.

References

Ackard, D. M., Eisenberg, M. E., & Neumark-Sztainer, D. (2007). Long-term impact of adolescent dating violence on the behavioral and psychological health of male and female youth. *The Journal of Pediatrics, 151*(5), 476–481.

Agnew, R. (2008). General strain theory: Current status and directions for further research. In F. T. Cullen, J. P. Wright, & K. R. Blevins (Eds.), *Taking stock. The status of criminological theory* (vol. 15). Transaction Publishers.

Anderson, K. M., & Danis, F. S. (2007). Collegiate sororities and dating violence: An exploratory study of informal and formal helping strategies. *Violence Against Women, 13*(1), 87–100.

Archer, J. (2000). Sex differences in aggression between heterosexual partners: A meta-analytic review. *Psychological Bulletin, 126*(5), 651.

Babcock, J. C., Green, C. E., & Robie, C. (2004). Does batterers' treatment work? A meta-analytic review of domestic violence treatment. *Clinical Psychology Review, 23*(8), 1023–1053.

Bell, K. M., & Naugle, A. E. (2007). Effects of social desirability on students' self-reporting of partner abuse perpetration and victimization. *Violence and Victims, 22*(2), 243.

Bennett, L. W., Tolman, R. M., Rogalski, C. J., & Srinivasaraghavan, J. (1994). Domestic abuse by male alcohol and drug addicts. *Violence and Victims, 9*(4), 359.

Boles, S. M., & Miotto, K. (2003). Substance abuse and violence: A review of the literature. *Aggression and Violent Behavior, 8*(2), 155–174.

Cafferky, B. M., Mendez, M., Anderson, J. R., & Stith, S. M. (2018). Substance use and intimate partner violence: A meta-analytic review. *Psychology of Violence, 8*(1), 110.

Capaldi, D. M., Knoble, N. B., Shortt, J. W., & Kim, H. K. (2012). A systematic review of risk factors for intimate partner violence. *Partner Abuse, 3*(2), 231–280.

Carlson, B. E. (1987). Dating violence: A research review and comparison with spouse abuse. *Social Casework, 68*(1), 16–23.

Cascardi, M., Langhinrichsen, J., & Vivian, D. (1992). Marital aggression: Impact, injury, and health correlates for husbands and wives. *Archives of Internal Medicine, 152*(6), 1178–1184.

CDC. (2018). Intimate partner violence. https://www.cdc.gov/violenceprevention/intimatepartnerviolence/

CDC. (2021a). Violence prevention. https://www.cdc.gov/violenceprevention/intimatepartnerviolence/fastfact.html

CDC. (2021b). Preventing teen dating violence. https://www.cdc.gov/violenceprevention/intimatepartnerviolence/teendatingviolence/fastfact.html

Cherek, D. R., Roache, J. D., Egli, M., Davis, C., Spiga, R., & Cowan, K. (1993). Acute effects of marijuana smoking on aggressive, escape and point-maintained responding of male drug users. *Psychopharmacology, 111*(2), 163–168.

Choi, H. J., & Temple, J. R. (2016). Do gender and exposure to interparental violence moderate the stability of teen dating violence? Latent transition analysis. *Prevention Science, 17*(3), 367–376.

Crane, C. A., Godleski, S. A., Przybyla, S. M., Schlauch, R. C., & Testa, M. (2016). The proximal effects of acute alcohol consumption on male-to-female aggression: A meta-analytic review of the experimental literature. *Trauma, Violence, & Abuse, 17*(5), 520–531.

Crane, C. A., Hawes, S. W., & Weinberger, A. H. (2013). Intimate partner violence victimization and cigarette smoking: A meta-analytic review. *Trauma, Violence, & Abuse, 14*(4), 305–315.

Crooks, C. V., Wolfe, D. A., Hughes, R., Jaffe, P. G., & Chiodo, D. (2008). Development, evaluation and national implementation of a school-based program to reduce violence and related risk behaviours: Lessons from the Fourth R. *IPC Review, 2*(2), 109–135.

DeMaris, A., & Jackson, J. K. (1987). Batterers' reports of recidivism after counseling. *Social Casework, 68*(8), 458–465.

Devries, K. M., Child, J. C., Bacchus, L. J., Mak, J., Falder, G., Graham, K., ... & Heise, L. (2014). Intimate partner violence victimization and alcohol consumption in women: A systematic review and meta-analysis. *Addiction, 109*(3), 379–391.

Ehrensaft, M. K., Moffitt, T. E., & Caspi, A. (2004). Clinically abusive relationships in an unselected birth cohort: Men's and women's participation and developmental antecedents. *Journal of Abnormal Psychology, 113*(2), 258.

Else, L., Wonderlich, S. A., Beatty, W. W., Christie, D. W., & Staton, R. D. (1993). Personality characteristics of men who physically abuse women. *Psychiatric Services, 44*(1), 54–58.

Emery, S. T. (2017). Prevalence and correlates of the perpetration of cyber dating abuse among early adolescents. *Journal of Youth and Adolescence, 46*(2), 358–375.

Exner-Cortens, D., Eckenrode, J., & Rothman, E. (2013). Longitudinal associations between teen dating violence victimization and adverse health outcomes. *Pediatrics, 131*(1), 71.

Feder, L., & Wilson, D. B. (2005). A meta-analytic review of court-mandated batterer intervention programs: Can courts affect abusers' behavior? *Journal of Experimental Criminology, 1*(2), 239–262.

Foran, H. M., & O'Leary, K. D. (2008). Alcohol and intimate partner violence: A meta-analytic review. *Clinical Psychology Review, 28*(7), 1222–1234.

Foshee, V. A., Benefield, T. S., Ennett, S. T., Bauman, K. E., & Suchindran, C. (2004). Longitudinal predictors of serious physical and sexual dating violence victimization during adolescence. *Preventive Medicine, 39*(5), 1007–1016.

Garthe, R. C., Sullivan, T. N., & McDaniel, M. A. (2017). A meta-analytic review of peer risk factors and adolescent dating violence. *Psychology of Violence, 7*(1), 45.

Giancola, P. R., Josephs, R. A., Parrott, D. J., & Duke, A. A. (2010). Alcohol myopia revisited clarifying aggression and other acts of disinhibition through a distorted lens. *Perspectives on Psychological Science, 5*, 265–278.

Gilbert, L., El-Bassel, N., Chang, M., Wu, E., & Roy, L. (2012). Substance use and partner violence among urban women seeking emergency care. *Psychology of Addictive Behaviors, 26*(2), 226.

Glass, N., Perrin, N., Hanson, G., Bloom, T., Gardner, E., & Campbell, J. C. (2008). Risk for reassault in abusive female same-sex relationships. *American Journal of Public Health, 98*(6), 1021–1027.

Gover, A. R. (2004). Risky lifestyles and dating violence: A theoretical test of violent victimization. *Journal of Criminal Justice, 32*(2), 171–180.

Gray, H. M., & Foshee, V. (1997). Adolescent dating violence: Differences between one-sided and mutually violent profiles. *Journal of Interpersonal Violence, 12*, 126–141.

Grisso, J. A., Donald Hirschinger, N., Sammel, M., Brensinger, C., Santanna, J., ... Teeple, L. (1999). Violent injuries among women in an urban area. *The New England Journal of Medicine, 341*, 1899–1905.

Halford, W. K., & Osgarby, S. M. (1993). Alcohol abuse in clients presenting with marital problems. *Journal of Family Psychology, 6*(3), 245.

Hamberger, L. K., & Hastings, J. E. (1990). Recidivism following spouse abuse abatement counseling: Treatment program implications. *Violence and Victims, 5*(3), 157.

Harrison, L. D., Erickson, P. G., Adlaf, E., & Freeman, C. (2001). The drugs–violence nexus among American and Canadian youth. *Substance Use & Misuse, 36*(14), 2065–2086.

Herrera, V. M., Wiersma, J. D., & Cleveland, H. H. (2008). The influence of individual and partner characteristics on the perpetration of intimate partner violence in young adult relationships. *Journal of Youth and Adolescence, 37*(3), 284–296.

Hines, D. A., & Malley-Morrison, K. (2001). Psychological effects of partner abuse against men: A neglected research area. *Psychology of Men & Masculinity, 2*(2), 75.

Holt, M. K., Finkelhor, D., & Kantor, G. K. (2007). Multiple victimization experiences of urban elementary school students: Associations with psychosocial functioning and academic performance. *Child Abuse & Neglect, 31*(5), 503–515.

Hutchison, I. W. (1999). Alcohol, fear, and woman abuse. *Sex Roles, 40*, 893–920.

Jasinski, J. L., Asdigian, N. L., & Kantor, G. K. (1997). Ethnic adaptations to occupational strain: Work-related stress, drinking, and wife assault among Anglo and Hispanic husbands. *Journal of Interpersonal Violence, 12*(6), 814–831.

Johnson, M. P. (1995). Patriarchal terrorism and common couple violence: Two forms of violence against women. *Journal of Marriage and the Family, 57*(2), 283–294.

Johnson, M. P., & Leone, J. M. (2005). The differential effects of intimate terrorism and situational couple violence: Findings from the National Violence Against Women Survey. *Journal of Family Issues, 26*(3), 322–349.

Julian, T. W., & McKenry, P. C. (1993). Mediators of male violence toward female intimates. *Journal of Family Violence, 8*, 39–56.

Kaufman-Kantor, G., & Straus, M. A. (1989). Substance abuse as a precipitant of wife abuse victimizations. *The American Journal of Drug and Alcohol Abuse, 15*(2), 173–189.

Kelly, A. B., & Halford, W. K. (2006). Verbal and physical aggression in couples where the female partner is drinking heavily. *Journal of Family Violence, 21*(1), 11–17.

Kurz, W., & Fisher, D. J. (1989). *Fundamentals of solidification.* Trans Tech Publications.

Langhinrichsen-Rohling, J., Misra, T. A., Selwyn, C., & Rohling, M. L. (2012). Rates of bidirectional versus unidirectional intimate partner violence across samples, sexual orientations, and race/ethnicities: A comprehensive review. *Partner Abuse, 3*(2), 199–230.

Langhinrichsen-Rohling, J., Neidig, P., & Thorn, G. (1995). Violent marriages: Gender differences in levels of current violence and past abuse. *Journal of Family Violence, 10*, 159–176.

Leonard, K. E. (2005). Alcohol and intimate partner violence: When can we say that heavy drinking is a contributing cause of violence? *Addiction, 100*(4), 422–425.

Leonard, K. E., Bromet, E. J., Parkinson, D. K., Day, N. L., & Ryan, C. M. (1985). Patterns of alcohol use and physically aggressive behavior in men. *Journal of Studies on Alcohol, 46*(4), 279–282.

Lu, Y., Van Ouytsel, J., Walrave, M., Ponnet, K., & Temple, J. R. (2018). Cross-sectional and temporal associations between cyber dating abuse victimization and mental health and substance use outcomes. *Journal of Adolescence, 65*, 1–5.

Mannon, J. M. (1997). Domestic and intimate violence: An application of routine activities theory. *Aggression and Violent Behavior, 2*(1), 9–24.

Månsdotter, A. M., Rydberg, M. K., Wallin, E., Lindholm, L. A., & Andréasson, S. (2007). A cost–effectiveness analysis of alcohol prevention targeting licensed premises. *European Journal of Public Health, 17*(6), 618–623.

Martin, S. L., Beaumont, J. L., & Kupper, L. L. (2003). Substance use before and during pregnancy: Links to intimate partner violence. *The American Journal of Drug and Alcohol Abuse, 29*(3), 599–617.

Moore, T. M., Elkins, S. R., McNulty, J. K., Kivisto, A. J., & Handsel, V. A. (2011). Alcohol use and intimate partner violence perpetration among college students: Assessing the temporal association using electronic diary technology. *Psychology of Violence, 1*(4), 315.

Moore, T. M., & Stuart, G. L. (2005). A review of the literature on marijuana and interpersonal violence. *Aggression and Violent Behavior, 10*(2), 171–192.

Moore, T. M., Stuart, G. L., Meehan, J. C., Rhatigan, D., Hellmuth, J. C., & Keen, S. M. (2008). Drug abuse and aggression between intimate partners: A meta-analytic review. *Clinical Psychology Review, 28*, 247–274.

Myerscough, R., & Taylor, S. P. (1985). The effects of marijuana on human physical aggression. *Journal of Personality and Social Psychology, 49*(6), 1541.

Nahapetyan, L., Orpinas, P., Song, X., & Holland, K. (2014). Longitudinal association of suicidal ideation and physical dating violence among high school students. *Journal of Youth and Adolescence, 43*(4), 629–640.

O'Farrell, T. J., & Murphy, C. M. (1995). Marital violence before and after alcoholism treatment. *Journal of Consulting and Clinical Psychology, 63*(2), 256.

O'Leary, K. D., & Maiuro, R. D. (Eds.). (2001). *Psychological abuse in domestically violent relationships*. Springer.

O'Leary, K. D., & Schumacher, J. A. (2003). The association between alcohol use and intimate partner violence: Linear effect, threshold effect, or both? *Addictive Behaviors, 28*, 1575–1585.

Osgood, D. W., Johnston, L. D., O'Malley, P. M., & Backman, J. G. (1988). The generality of deviance in late adolescence and early adulthood. *American Sociological Reviews, 53*, 80–92.

Parker, E. M., Debnam, K., Pas, E. T., & Bradshaw, C. P. (2016). Exploring the link between alcohol and marijuana use and teen dating violence victimization among high school students: The influence of school context. *Health Education & Behavior, 43*(5), 528–536.

Parrott, D. J., Drobes, D. J., Saladin, M. E., Coffey, S. F., & Dansky, B. S. (2003). Perpetration of partner violence: Effects of cocaine and alcohol dependence and posttraumatic stress disorder. *Addictive Behaviors, 28*(9), 1587–1602.

Pihl, R. O., & Hoaken, P. N. S. (1997). Clinical correlates and predictors of violence in patients with substance use disorders. *Psychiatric Annals, 27*(11), 735–740.

Pihl, R. O., & Peterson, J. (1995). Drugs and aggression: Correlations, crime and human manipulative studies and some proposed mechanisms. *Journal of Psychiatry and Neuroscience, 20*(2), 141–149.

Reyes, H. L. M., Foshee, V. A., Bauer, D. J., & Ennett, S. T. (2012). Heavy alcohol use and dating violence perpetration during adolescence: Family, peer and neighborhood violence as moderators. *Prevention Science, 13*(4), 340–349.

Roberts, A. R. (1987). Psychosocial characteristics of batterers: A study of 234 men charged with domestic violence offenses. *Journal of Family Violence, 2*(1), 81–93.

Rosenbaum, A., & O'Leary, K. D. (1981). Marital violence: Characteristics of abusive couples. *Journal of Consulting and Clinical Psychology, 49*(1), 63.

Schluter, P. J., Abbott, M. W., & Bellringer, M. E. (2008). Problem gambling related to intimate partner violence: Findings from the Pacific Islands families study. *International Gambling Studies, 8*(1), 49–61.

Schumacher, J. A., Feldbau-Kohn, S., Smith Slep, A. M., & Heyman, R. E. (2001). Risk factors for male-to-female partner physical abuse. *Aggression and Violent Behavior, 6*, 281–352.

Sears, H. A., Byers, E. S., & Price, E. L. (2007). The co-occurrence of adolescent boys' and girls' use of psychologically, physically, and sexually abusive behaviours in their dating relationships. *Journal of Adolescence, 30*(3), 487–504.

Shorey, R. C., Cornelius, T. L., & Bell, K. M. (2008). A critical review of theoretical frameworks for dating violence: Comparing the dating and marital fields. *Aggression and Violent Behavior, 13*(3), 185–194.

Shorey, R. C., Fite, P. J., Choi, H., Cohen, J. R., Stuart, G. L., & Temple, J. R. (2015). Dating violence and substance use as longitudinal predictors of adolescents' risky sexual behavior. *Prevention Science, 16*(6), 853–861.

Shorey, R. C., Temple, J. R., Febres, J., Brasfield, H., Sherman, A. E., & Stuart, G. L. (2012). The consequences of perpetrating psychological aggression in dating relationships: A descriptive investigation. *Journal of Interpersonal Violence, 27*(15), 2980–2998.

Shortt, S. E. D. (2011). *Victorian lunacy: Richard M. Bucke and the practice of late nineteenth-century psychiatry.* Cambridge University Press.

Silverman, J., Raj, A., Mucci, L., & Hathaway, J. (2001). Dating violence against adolescent girls and associated substance use, unhealthy weight control, sexual risk behavior, pregnancy, and suicidality. *Journal of the American Medical Association, 286*, 572–579.

Simon, T. R., Sussman, S., Dahlberg, L. L., & Dent, C. W. (2002). Influence of a substance-abuse-prevention curriculum on violence-related behavior. *American Journal of Health Behavior, 26*(2), 103–110.

Smith, S. G., Chen, J., Basile, K. C., Gilbert, L. K., Merrick, M. T., Patel, N., Walling, M., & Jain, A. (2017). The National Intimate Partner and Sexual Violence Survey (NISVS): 2010-2012 state report. National Center for Injury Prevention and Control, Centers for Disease Control and Prevention. https://www.cdc.gov/violenceprevention/pdf/NISVS-StateReportBook.pdf

Smith, S. G., Zhang, X., Basile, K. C., Merrick, M. T., Wang, J., Kresnow, M., & Chen, J. (2018). The National Intimate Partner and Sexual Violence Survey: 2015 data brief—updated release. National Center for Injury Prevention and Control, Centers for Disease Control and Prevention. https://www.cdc.gov/violenceprevention/pdf/2015data-brief508.pdf.

Stith, S. M., Smith, D. B., Penn, C. E., Ward, D. B., & Tritt, D. (2004). Intimate partner physical abuse perpetration and victimization risk factors: A meta-analytic review. *Aggression and Violent Behavior, 10*(1), 65–98.

Stöckl, H., Devries, K., Rotstein, A., Abrahams, N., Campbell, J., Watts, C., & Moreno, C. G. (2013). The global prevalence of intimate partner homicide: A systematic review. *The Lancet, 382*(9895), 859–865.

Strauss, C. V., Johnson, E. E. H., Stuart, G. L., & Shorey, R. C. (2018). Substance use and adolescent dating violence: How strong is the link. In D. A. Wolfe & J. R. Temple (Eds.), *Adolescent dating violence: Theory, research, and prevention* (pp. 135–157). Academic Press.

Straus, M. A., Gelles, R. J., & Steinmetz, S. K. (1980). *Behind closed doors.* Sage.

Stuart, G. L., O'Farrell, T. J., & Temple, J. R. (2009). Review of the association between treatment for substance misuse and reductions in intimate partner violence. *Substance Use & Misuse, 44*(9),1298–1317.

Stuart, G. L., Temple, J., Moore, T. M., Follansbee, K., Bucossi, M., & Hellmuth, J. C. (2008). The role of drug use in a conceptual model of intimate partner violence in men and women arrested for domestic violence. *Psychology of Addictive Behaviors, 22*, 12–24.

Stuart, G. L., Temple, J. R., & Moore, T. M. (2007). Improving batterer intervention programs through theory-based research. *Journal of the American Medical Association, 298*(5), 560–562.

Sussman, S. (1996). Development of a school-based drug abuse prevention curriculum for high-risk youth. *Journal of Psychoactive Drugs, 28*, 169–182.

Temple, J. R., Baumler, E., Wood, L., Thiel, M., Peskin, M., & Torres, E. (in press). A dating violence prevention program for middle school youth: A cluster randomized trial. *Pediatrics*.

Temple, J. R., Choi, H. J., Brem, M., Wolford-Clevenger, C., Stuart, G. L., Peskin, M. F., & Elmquist, J. (2016). The temporal association between traditional and cyber dating abuse among adolescents. *Journal of Youth and Adolescence, 45*(2), 340–349.

Temple, J. R., Stuart, G. L., & O'Farrell, T. J. (2009). Prevention of intimate partner violence in substance-using populations. *Substance Use & Misuse, 44*(9–10), 1318–1328.

Temple, J. R., Weston, R., & Marshall, L. L. (2005). Physical and mental health outcomes of women in nonviolent, unilaterally violent, and mutually violent relationships. *Violence and Victims, 20*(3), 335.

Vagi, K. J., Olsen, E. O. M., Basile, K. C., & Vivolo-Kantor, A. M. (2015). Teen dating violence (physical and sexual) among U.S. high school students: Findings from the 2013 National Youth Risk Behavior Survey. *JAMA Pediatrics, 169*(5), 474–482.

Van Ouytsel, J., Ponnet, K., Walrave, M., & Temple, J. R. (2016). Adolescent cyber dating abuse victimization and its associations with substance use, and sexual behaviors. *Public Health, 135*, 147–151.

Wolfe, D. A., Crooks, C., Jaffe, P., Chiodo, D., Hughes, R., Ellis, W., … Donner, A. (2009). A school-based program to prevent adolescent dating violence: A cluster randomized trial. *Archives of Pediatrics & Adolescent Medicine, 163*(8), 692–699.

Wong, C. F., Weiss, G., Ayala, G., & Kipke, M. D. (2010). Harassment, discrimination, violence, and illicit drug use among young men who have sex with men. *AIDS Education and Prevention, 22*(4), 286–298.

Zweig, J. M., Dank, M., Yahner, J., & Lachman, P. (2013). The rate of cyber dating abuse among teens and how it relates to other forms of teen dating violence. *Journal of Youth and Adolescence, 42*, 1063–1077.

Zweig, J. M., Lachman, P., Yahner, J., & Dank, M. (2014). Correlates of cyber dating abuse among teens. *Journal of Youth and Adolescence, 43*(8), 1306–1321.

Spotlight on Special Issues

Substance Use, Intimate Partner Violence, and Service Provision for Queer Clients

Holly Hardin-Ramella, MA

Queer victim-survivors are often left out of conversations related to intimate partner violence, and when they are discussed, it is often an afterthought or the discussion is focused on only a specific group within the queer spectrum (Harden et al., 2020). While intimate partner violence consists of power and control dynamics that are present in all relationships, it is important to understand the unique barriers and needs of queer victim-survivors (Harden et al., 2020; Jean-Charles, 2014). However, before moving further into that conversation, it is important to understand that *queer* is an intentionally vague term meant to broadly categorize those who self-identify outside of heteronormative definitions of sexuality and gender. Said differently, contemporary definitions of queer may refer to anyone who identifies as lesbian, gay, transgender, queer or questioning, intersex, asexual, or other identities such as pangender or pansexual. Queer can be an identity and a community, meaning that someone may be trans, or may identify as gay, but may also situate themselves within the larger queer community (Thomas & Hsieh, 2020). For the purposes of this discussion, queer may be used to refer to individual identity or the broader community.

Findings have shown that intimate partner violence is as frequent in queer relationships as it is in heterosexual relationships (Allen et al., 2007). The systemic oppression and stigma faced by the queer community creates barriers to intervention or accessing services and resources that may address or provide aid to queer individuals experiencing intimate partner violence. Formal interventions such as therapy and mental health services may be inaccessible due to cost, and this is often compounded for the queer community. For instance, even if someone in the queer community is insured, or has the means to pay out of pocket for therapy or mental health care, finding quality mental health care that affirms their identity and experience can prove difficult. The queer community may struggle to find therapists who share their identity, they may experience misgendering, or may feel they have to educate their provider on their experiences and identities due to a lack of understanding, which can all be harmful and serve as a deterrent for seeking out these services (Green et al., 2020). Likewise, studies have shown that often safety resources, such as domestic violence shelters or women's resource centers, fail to provide inclusive, accessible, and relevant programming or aid for queer victim-survivors (Bornstein et al., 2006; Harden et al., 2020).

Substance use is often analyzed as an accelerant in intimate partner violence. Studies have shown that rates of substance use and misuse are higher among individuals in the queer community (McCabe et al., 2009; Medley et al., 2015). The relationship between queer identity and substance use is complex. Historically, spaces that were catered to and safe for queer individuals have been bars or events that revolve around alcohol and drug use (see, for example, Hunt et al., 2019). In more recent years, alternative spaces such as public libraries, coffee shops, and community centers have emerged as an alternative; however, accessibility to these spaces may be limited by location, hours of operation, or, as the COVID-19 pandemic has underscored, environmental or public health crises may shut down these safe and sober spaces queer individuals have used to build community or be affirmed in altogether (Blum, 2020). This can result in increased isolation, but also decreased accessibility to healthy coping mechanisms. There is a culmination of factors that create an environment that encourages potentially harmful self-soothing methods like substance use for queer individuals, particularly those seeking coping mechanisms in response to intimate partner violence. Making matters worse are other interrelated systemic barriers and discrimination against queer populations. For example, some states do not have legal protections against employment discrimination for queer populations, creating barriers related to job discrimination that can limit financial stability, and increase stress for queer people (Meyer, 2016). Discrimination in healthcare and substance use disorder treatment services can also create barriers for queer individuals in accessing necessary care to address substance use or violent victimization (Girouard et al., 2019).

Research has shown that when responding to intimate partner violence, questions that inquire about substance use are important in danger assessments when identifying lethality risks, but studies also elucidate the impact substance use may have on victim-survivors coping and healing. Victim-survivors are 70% more likely to drink alcohol heavily than those who have not experienced intimate partner violence (Soper, 2004). Given this, prevention and intervention are deeply connected, and also historically inaccessible and understudied for queer populations. Moving forward, agencies providing direct services to victim-survivors should create substance use support programs centering queer communities. Counseling and other healing services should be equipped to address the complex lived experiences of queer clients. Centering queer folks means ensuring that the program or service meets the specific needs of queer clients. In order to do this, agencies must have training to educate staff and volunteers on the unique barriers and complex needs of queer populations, and policies and procedures accompanying the training that will hold staff and volunteers accountable if they engage in harmful behavior with queer clients. Training must also empower staff and volunteers to understand oppression and the resilience of queer populations. While elevating and validating lived experiences of queer clients is absolutely essential to centering the needs of this population, queer clients should not be consulted as a resource for education, or asked to inform an agency or service on the barriers and oppression the larger queer community faces. Asking queer clients to do so places an undue burden on an individual to speak for an entire community and ultimately centers the needs of the service provider over the client. Other steps, such as hiring queer staff, and not just for queer outreach positions, receiving technical assistance from national agencies such as FORGE (n.d.) or the NYC Anti-Violence Project (2020), or partnering with other organizations locally to train staff on working with queer communities, may all improve access and services for queer victim-survivors of violence who may also need substance use disorder intervention or treatment.

These suggestions, which focus specifically on creating policies, procedures, and training based on the lived experiences of the queer community, may initially seem at odds with the limited resources available for all victim-survivors of intimate partner violence and/or those with substance use disorders. However, intersectional feminist scholars suggest that those who are most marginalized have the most complete picture of systemic barriers and oppression, and that centering those vantage points in the making of policies and procedures and developing training will create better and more comprehensive programming for all populations affected by intimate partner violence, substance use disorders, or the combination of both (Ackerly and True, 2010; Hesse-Biber, 2013). These suggestions, combined with the somewhat limited body of research on the experiences of the queer community and queer individuals as they pertain to intimate partner violence and substance use, creates an urgent call for researchers in these substantive areas to shift their focus from heteronormative populations to experiences of those with marginalized identity characteristics.

References

Ackerly, B., & True, J. (2010). *Doing feminist research in political and social science.* Palgrave Macmillan.

Allen, M., Branco, P. L. V., Burnett, D., Hernandez, A., & List-Warrilow, J. (2007). *Lesbian, gay, bisexual and trans (LGBT) communities and domestic violence: Information and resources.* The National Resource Center on Domestic Violence.

Bornstein, D. R., Fawcett, J., Sullivan, M., Senturia, K. D., & Shiu-Thornton, S. (2006). Understanding the experiences of lesbian, bisexual and trans survivors of domestic violence. *Journal of Homosexuality, 51*(1), 159–181. https://doi.org/10.1300/J082v51n01_08

Green, A. E., Price-Feeney, M., & Dorison, S. (2020). *Breaking barriers to quality mental health care for LGBTQ youth.* The Trevor Project.

Harden, J., McAllister, P., Spencer, C. M., & Stith, S. M. (2022). The dark side of the rainbow: Queer women's experiences of intimate partner violence. *Trauma, Violence, & Abuse, 23*(1), 301–313. https://doi.org/10.1177/1524838020933869

Hesse-Biber, S. N. (Ed.). (2013). *Feminist research practice: A primer* (2nd ed.). Sage Publications.

Hunt, G., Antin, T., Sanders, E., & Sisneros, M. (2019). Queer youth, intoxication and queer drinking spaces. *Journal of Youth Studies, 22*(3), 380–400. https://doi.org/10.1080/13676261.2018.1508826

FORGE Empowering. Healing. Connecting. (n.d.). Retrieved October 29, 2020, from https://forge-forward.org/

Jean-Charles, R. M. (2014). Toward a victim-survivor narrative: Rape and form in Yvonne Vera's *Under the Tongue* and Calixthe Beyala's *Tu t'Appelleras Tanga. Research in African Literatures, 45*(1), 39–62.

McCabe, S. E., Hughes, T. L., Bostwick, W. B., West, B. T., & Boyd, C. J. (2009). Sexual orientation, substance use behaviors and substance dependence in the United States. *Addiction, 104*(8), 1333–1345. https://doi.org/10.1111/j.1360-0443.2009.02596.x

Medley, G., Lipari, R., Bose, J., Cribb, D., Kroutil, L., & McHenry, G. (2016). Sexual orientation and estimates of adult substance use and mental health: Results from the 2015 National Survey on Drug Use and Health. NSDUH Data Review. https://www.samhsa.gov/data/sites/default/files/NSDUH-SexualOrientation-2015/NSDUH-SexualOrientation-2015/NSDUH-SexualOrientation-2015.htm

Meyer, I. H. (2016). The elusive promise of LGBT equality. *American Journal of Public Health, 106*(8), 1356–1358. https://doi.org/10.2105/AJPH.2016.303221

NYC Anti-Violence Project. (2020). Retrieved October 29, 2020, from https://avp.org/

Soper, R. G., MD. (2014, October 6). Intimate partner violence and co-occurring substance abuse/addiction. American Society of Addiction Medicine. Retrieved October 29, 2020, from https://www.asam.org/Quality-Science/publications/magazine/read/article/2014/10/06/intimate-partner-violence-and-co-occurring-substance-abuse-addiction

Thomas, S. S., & Hsieh, C. (2020, September 21). What does it really mean to be queer? *Cosmopolitan.* https://www.cosmopolitan.com/sex-love/a25243218/queer-meaning-definition/

CHAPTER FOUR

Substance Use and Child Maltreatment

Samantha M. Brown, PhD, and Jennifer L. Bellamy, PhD

Introduction

Child maltreatment is a heterogeneous phenomenon, spanning emotional, physical, and **sexual abuse** and **neglect**. Accordingly, different states and localities, professions, and cultural groups hold divergent views regarding how types of child maltreatment are defined or what constitutes child abuse and neglect. Despite differences in definitions of maltreatment and perceptions of parenting behaviors, more broadly, there is a consensus regarding acceptable and unacceptable acts of omission or commission in the care of children. Specifically, **child abuse** is generally characterized by acts of commission, whereas **child neglect** is characterized by acts of omission by a parent or caregiver (English et al., 2005). The **Child Abuse Prevention and Treatment Act** (CAPTA; P.L. 93–247), as amended by the CAPTA Reauthorization Act of 2010 (P.L. 111–320), defines child abuse and neglect, at a minimum, as follows:

> *Any recent act or failure to act on the part of a parent or caretaker which results in death, serious physical or emotional harm, sexual abuse or exploitation; or an act or failure to act, which presents an imminent risk of serious harm.*

In the United States, **child protective services** is the government agency responsible for ensuring the safety, permanency, and well-being of children exposed to abuse and neglect (i.e., the child welfare system; Child Welfare Information Gateway, 2013). Although federal law provides a foundation for defining child abuse and neglect, each state has its specific definition (U.S. DHHS, ACF, ACYF, Children's Bureau, 2021). A brief description of the types of child maltreatment is provided in Table 4.1.

TABLE 4.1 Types of Child Maltreatment

Maltreatment Type	Description
Physical abuse	Violent handling, choking, burning, hitting, or shaking
Emotional abuse	Threats of harm, rejection, humiliation, isolation, unreasonable restriction of behaviors
Sexual abuse	Sexual exposure, sexual touching, rape, sexual exploitation, encouraging prostitution
Neglect	Lack of supervision, failure to meet basic needs (food, clothing, shelter, education, medical care), inadequate nurturing or affection

In some states, risk factors, such as parental alcohol and other drug use, may substantiate child maltreatment in one or more of these domains. **Substantiation** means that the child welfare authority has determined that a caregiver is responsible for child abuse and/or neglect. For example, reports of child neglect may be made if a child is alcohol- or drug-exposed at birth, or lives in a home where the manufacturing or distribution of drugs is present (Petersen et al., 2014). According to the American Public Health Association, **substance misuse** is defined as the inappropriate use of alcohol or other drugs (American Public Health Association, 2021). In the context of child maltreatment, substance use is typically problematic when it affects a parent's ability to function effectively in a caregiving role; or when a child is physically exposed to harmful substances (Children's Bureau, 2014). In a broader context, **substance use disorder** is defined as the recurrent use of alcohol and/or drugs that causes clinically significant impairment, including health problems, disability, and failure to meet major responsibilities at work, school, or home (SAMHSA, 2019).

Variability in these definitions across states makes it difficult to clearly define and describe the incidence and prevalence of child maltreatment. **Incidence** is the rate of new occurrences of child maltreatment, and **prevalence** is the number of occurrences of child maltreatment at any given time. For example, without a consistent definition across states, under- or over-reporting the true incidence of child abuse and neglect is likely to occur. Some states have more specific definitions of different types of maltreatment that list specific behaviors or indicators. In contrast, other states are much broader with their definitions and leave a lot of room for interpretation by professionals.

Similarly, inconsistent definitions make it difficult to understand the overall prevalence of child abuse and neglect in the United States. Without consistent definitions, comparisons cannot be made across geographic regions to determine how child maltreatment differentially affects specific areas. When only some states identify parental substance use as a type of maltreatment, the magnitude of the co-occurrence of parental substance use and child maltreatment is unclear, thereby affecting the ability to develop appropriate programmatic and policy responses to address these issues. This challenge is further complicated as child maltreatment is likely underreported. Therefore, even less is known about the co-occurrence of child maltreatment and substance use among families that do not come to the attention of child protective services. This chapter will explore the intersection of substance use and child maltreatment by describing the scope of the problem, historical context, theoretical perspectives, risk and protective factors, and prevention and intervention.

Scope of the Problem

Because many cases of child abuse and neglect are not reported, multiple children may be the subject of a single report, and definitions vary significantly by jurisdiction, it is tough to produce an accurate estimate of the incidence of child maltreatment. In 2019, estimates of the extent of child maltreatment in the United States ranged from 656,000 (substantiated cases of child abuse and/or neglect) to 4,378,000 (Child Protective Services investigations; U.S. DHHS, ACF, ACYF, Children's Bureau, 2021). Some studies that compare self-reported child maltreatment and official reports propose that maltreatment may be even more widespread than these numbers suggest (Negriff et al., 2017).

The prevalence of child maltreatment also varies by type. Neglect is the most common type of maltreatment, affecting approximately 75% of children investigated for child maltreatment, followed by **physical abuse** (17.5%) and sexual abuse (9.3%; U.S. DHHS, ACF, ACYF, Children's Bureau, 2021). Approximately 15% of children are victims of two or more maltreatment types (U.S. DHHS, ACF, ACYF, Children's Bureau, 2021). Moreover, **child fatalities**, or deaths of children resulting from child abuse and neglect, are at a rate of 2.5 for every 100,000 children in the United States, with boys having a higher child fatality rate than girls (U.S. DHHS, ACF, ACYF, Children's Bureau, 2021). Utilizing national samples, other researchers have found that over one year, 5.6% of children experienced **emotional abuse**, 4.7% experienced neglect, 4.0% experienced physical abuse, and 0.1% experienced sexual abuse by a caregiver (Finkelhor et al., 2014). The same study found that the lifetime prevalence of maltreatment was 11.6% for neglect, 10.3% for emotional abuse, 8.9% for physical abuse, and 0.7% for sexual abuse (Finkelhor et al., 2014). Most forms of child maltreatment are perpetrated by a parent, except sexual abuse, where in 20% of cases, the parent is the perpetrator, 21% another adult relative, and 21% an unrelated adult (Hodgdon et al., 2018).

Parental substance use also places children at increased risk for child maltreatment and can affect up to 80% of all child welfare cases (National Center on Addiction and Substance Abuse at Columbia University, 2005; Seay, 2015; Traube, 2012; Young, et al., 2007). However, wide variations exist in the reported prevalence rates of co-occurring parental substance use and child maltreatment. Indeed, many Statewide Automated Child Welfare Information Systems (SACWIS) do not require states to collect information on the percentage of families impacted by parental substance use (Seay, 2015; Young et al., 2007), and prevalence rates of parental substance use may vary based on how substance use is defined as well as the type of maltreatment and child welfare involvement (Seay, 2015). In addition, the burgeoning research on adverse childhood experiences (ACEs) suggests that child maltreatment frequently co-occurs with other household problems, such as parental substance use (Felitti et al., 1996). In addition, the overlap between child maltreatment and substance use varies by maltreatment type. For example, parental substance use is more often linked to instances of neglect than abuse (Steenrod & Mirick, 2017). Regardless of the type of child maltreatment, estimates of substance use vary widely by the type of involvement with child protective services. For example, among families receiving in-home services (when families receive services, but children remain in their homes), estimates of substance use range from 26% to 68%, whereas for families with children placed in foster care, estimates range from 5.2% to 79% (Seay, 2015).

Historical Context

Child maltreatment and substance use have long been identified as serious social problems, although recognition of and attention to their relationship to one another is relatively more recent. Substance use increasingly became a modern social problem mainly due to the progress of scientific technologies and the development of substances for medical-related purposes. Moreover, given the medical benefits of some substances, funding for alcohol and drug use research has substantially increased since the 1960s (Committee on Opportunities in Drug Abuse Research, Division of Neuroscience and Behavioral Health, Institute of Medicine, 1996). Advancements in the understanding of addiction and discoveries in successful medical treatments contributed to changing attitudes toward substance use. Over the past couple of decades, substance use has also become recognized as a form of child maltreatment. Family involvement with child protective services became mandated in some jurisdictions when parental substance use is a presenting problem (Child Welfare Information Gateway, 2014).

The broad conceptualization of child maltreatment has a more complicated history. The identification of certain parental behaviors as contradictory to community norms, which resulted in religious groups intervening with families, dates back to colonial times (Morgan, 1966). However, our current understanding of child maltreatment as a social problem in the United States originated in the 19th century (Giovannoni, 1989) and coincides with many advances toward our current modern, post-industrial society. Child maltreatment has been linked to economic advancements such as industrialization, urban growth, and child labor. The first legislative action involving the abuse of children indicated that parents may not engage in unacceptable behavior nor endanger their children or allow others to do so. Children were often removed to orphanages or foster care in such cases where abuse might have been identified (Giovannoni, 1989).

In New York City, the Society to Prevent Cruelty to Children (SPCC) was established in 1874 due to the lack of a designated agency responsible for intervening with maltreated children. The development of the SPCC—more commonly known as a division of the American Humane Association—demonstrated a shift from focusing solely on abandoned children to intervening with the entire family unit (Levine & Levine, 2012). Moreover, the organization played a significant role in adopting legislation that included assault and battery against children in criminal law.

Several changes to understanding child maltreatment occurred in the 1950s through the 1960s. For example, the American Humane Association influenced how child maltreatment was defined and intervened with by delineating types of maltreatment as acts of commission (abuse) and acts of omission (neglect). Several medical definitions of child abuse and neglect came following this, known as **battered child syndrome** (Kempe et al., 1962). The work of Kempe and his colleagues prompted the passage of laws in all 50 states requiring medical professionals to report on suspected child abuse and neglect (Foster, 1976). This, in turn, revived a national conversation about child maltreatment as a serious social problem and encouraged community organizations to improve the management and treatment of child abuse and neglect (Giovannoni, 1989).

A new wave of research and legislation involved the passage of the Child Abuse Prevention and Treatment Act (CAPTA; P.L. 93–247). CAPTA has been amended several times since its original enactment in 1974, but continues to provide the present-day federal definition of child abuse and neglect. One notable amendment of CAPTA includes the requirement of states to implement policies and procedures regarding parental substance use. Since CAPTA, several organizations have also been developed to increase awareness of the etiology and consequences of child maltreatment. These include the National Clearinghouse on Child Abuse and Neglect, National Resource Center on Family Violence, and National Adoption Information Clearinghouse (Child Welfare Information Gateway, n.d.).

Legal and Policy Responses

To address the research and practice concerns related to parental substance use and child maltreatment, legal and social policy has been constructed at the state and federal levels in the United States. Because state definitions of child abuse and neglect vary, some states have expanded their civil definitions of maltreatment to include "a caregiver's use of a controlled substance that impairs the ability to adequately care for a child and/or exposure of a child to illegal drug activity" (Child Welfare Information Gateway, 2014, p. 5). Some states also include children's exposure to illegal drug activity in their criminal statutes (Child Welfare Information Gateway, 2019).

Federal policy also requires states to address the negative impact of parental substance use and child maltreatment. For states to receive funding from CAPTA, they must have policies and procedures in place regarding the reporting and care of substance-exposed newborns. For example, medical professionals must report pregnant mothers to child protective services when affected by substance use. In some states, prenatal drug exposure is immediately classified as child abuse and involves child welfare involvement and mandated admission to substance use treatment (Child Welfare Information Gateway, 2014). Consequently, mixed evidence exists regarding the effectiveness of CAPTA in preventing child maltreatment and whether these mandated reporting laws make children safer.

The **Family Violence Prevention and Services Act** (FVPSA) also provides a federal funding stream to support emergency shelter and supportive services for victims of intimate partner violence and their children. Although FVPSA does not focus solely on child abuse and neglect (Fernandes-Alcantara, 2017), it is part of the amendments to CAPTA as a response to the knowledge that intimate partner violence and child maltreatment are not isolated problems. Specifically, FVPSA allows states to provide high-quality prevention services to reduce child maltreatment and better address the unique needs of vulnerable populations. The primary goals of FVPSA include better data collection on programming for vulnerable populations, improved training for professionals responding to adults and children exposed to violence, and strengthened coordination among service providers working with families exposed to abuse, neglect, and intimate partner violence.

As previously noted, substance-misusing parents involved with the child welfare system may experience multiple expectations regarding addiction and parenting treatment. Some policies, such as the **Adoption and Safe Families Act** (ASFA), may create an added burden on families mandated to attend substance use treatment during their involvement with child welfare. ASFA encourages expedited reunification and case closures among families with young children, and families are required to show reasonable progress toward service plan goals. The goal of this policy was to prevent children languishing, year after year, in foster care without a permanent home. One way to measure this success is by demonstrating competent parenting and abstinence (Marsh & Smith, 2011). However, the deadlines associated with the requirements of ASFA are inconsistent with research supporting substance use treatment. Namely, the length of time substance use treatment may be required to attain lasting positive outcomes is far longer than the current time limits imposed by the child welfare system (Conners et al., 2006). The disconnect between service goals and moving cases too quickly to reunification may, in turn, create obstacles for treatment success and lead to long-term negative consequences, such as high re-entry rates into the child welfare system (Kimberlin et al., 2009; Terling, 1999).

Theoretical Perspectives

A unifying conceptual model that undergirds both parental substance use and child maltreatment has not fully been developed in the field (Neger & Prinz, 2015). However, several theoretical perspectives aim to better understand the etiology of child maltreatment in isolation, and some of these perspectives have also been applied in the context of parental substance use. To explain the interrelationships between these co-occurring issues, Neger and Prinz (2015) broadly propose that the pathways linking parental substance use and child maltreatment involve deficits in parent emotional regulation, knowledge of parenting, and child development; increases in psychosocial stressors and drug-seeking behavior; and decreases in pleasures associated with parenting. Given that this conceptual framework is in its infancy, and a single, comprehensive approach to understanding child maltreatment remains absent from the literature, a brief description of several salient theoretical perspectives used to draw inferences about maltreatment occurrence and its consequences are described below.

Attachment Theory

The formation of attachment relationships may explain both the behavior of maltreated children and maltreating parents (Crittenden & Ainsworth, 1989). According to Bowlby (1969), establishing a safe and secure attachment between a child and their parent is essential during the first year of life. Across infancy, children develop internal working models of caregivers' availability, supportiveness, and reliability (Bretherton, 1992). **Internal working models** are mental representations of the self and others. These models influence the direction of children's developmental trajectories, including how children regulate their physiological and behavioral responses both in the presence and absence of their parents (Cassidy, 1994). When secure attachments are established, young children learn to expect a safe, stable, and supportive environment and confidently explore novel situations and quickly recover from potentially stressful experiences (Bretherton, 1992; Gunnar & Hostinar, 2015). Secure attachments contribute to the promotion of adaptive biological and behavioral responses in terms of understanding one's self-image and future relationships. In contrast, insecure or disorganized attachments lead to negative representations of the self and expectations regarding the availability and trustworthiness of others (Bowlby, 1969).

Children exposed to maltreatment are particularly at risk for developing anxious, insecure, or disorganized attachments (Cicchetti et al., 2006). These children often experience conflicts in the attachment relationship. Their parent is supposed to be their source of security, and yet they experience parenting behaviors that are stressful, frightening, and inconsistent. The most apparent evidence of impairments in internal working models is from research investigating the Strange Situation procedure, in which abused children are found to be anxiously attached to their mothers (Ainsworth et al., 1978). The original Strange Situation procedure consisted of eight episodes and involved several simulations of stressful experiences that aim to uncover patterns of parent-child attachment. In brief, a child is first introduced to a strange environment, such as a new playroom, and then to a stranger while their parent is present. These interactions are then compared to the child's response to their parent leaving them alone in the room with the stranger, the parent returning and the stranger leaving, the parent leaving while the child is left alone, the stranger returning, and finally, the parent returning to the room (Ainsworth & Wittig, 1969).

Distorted internal working models of the self and others may also exist in parents who maltreat their children (Crittenden & Ainsworth, 1989). Insensitive and unresponsive parenting behaviors may result from parents' attachment histories or various risk factors that impair parenting. For example, parents who are abusive toward their children may have internal working models associated with conflict, control, and rejection (Crittenden & Ainsworth, 1989). They may, in turn, respond to their children with more harsh and negative behaviors. Conversely, parents who are neglectful toward their children may have internal working models tied to the concept of helplessness (Crittenden & Ainsworth, 1989). Often this parent will avoid their parenting responsibilities and rely on others to care for their children. The quality of the parent-child relationship may also be influenced by risk factors that exacerbate maladaptive parenting, such as parental substance use. Parental substance use has been linked to insecure and disorganized attachment in early infancy (Barnard & McKeganey, 2004; Pajulo et al., 2006).

Biological Theory

Another approach to understanding child maltreatment is through biological perspectives. As with **attachment theory**, **biological theories** support the intergenerational transmission of abusive parenting behaviors as a pathway through which parents' own childhood experiences may shape the childrearing practices they use with their children. Primarily tested within animal models, it has been hypothesized that an increased risk for abusive behavior toward one's offspring is partly due to brain-based differences derived from one's own early childhood experiences. For example, baby rhesus monkeys exposed to variable maternal parenting styles, such as rejection and abuse, produced lower serotonin levels than baby rhesus monkeys with low or no exposure to maternal rejection and abuse (Maestripieri et al., 2006). Low levels of the hormone serotonin—a chemical that transmits impulses in the brain—are linked to mood disorders and aggression in both humans and monkeys. In work conducted by Maestripieri and colleagues (2006), baby rhesus monkeys with low serotonin levels went on to become abusive mothers themselves, suggesting that exposure to abuse can negatively affect brain development. Therefore, a biological basis for the intergenerational transmission of maltreatment may exist and have important implications for maltreatment in humans. More recent research suggests other biological pathways and markers that might help explain the cycle of maltreatment from one generation to the next.

There is also evidence to support a biological basis for substance use. Some individuals may be particularly vulnerable to substance use due to the development of specific brain regions responsible for behavioral control. Indeed, adolescents and young adults—populations in which these brain areas are still maturing—are more likely to have high addiction rates than older adults (Wagner & Anthony, 2002). Biological theories, such as the self-medication hypothesis (Khantzian, 1985) or the incentive salience model (Berridge, 2007), are reward-based approaches used to explain substance use. In brief, these approaches suggest that individuals may use substances as a method to alleviate negative affect and symptomology, and the motivation to use substances is associated with specific brain regions, such as those responsible for the dopamine or stress systems (Koob & Volkow, 2010). Given the proposal of various biological theories, several brain pathways have been identified that may underlie susceptibility to problematic substance use (Luscher & Malenka, 2011).

Ecological Theory

Ecological theories aim to provide the most comprehensive explanation of child abuse and neglect by incorporating multiple pathways that transact across various ecological levels (Belsky, 1993; Cicchetti & Rizley, 1981). Given the recognition that several factors are associated with child maltreatment and its outcomes, the ecological-transactional theory of child maltreatment was developed to provide an inclusive perspective for linking differing etiological factors to conceptualize maltreatment occurrence (Cicchetti et al., 2000). This theory bridges an ecological model of child maltreatment in which maltreatment occurrence is a result of forces within the individual (ontogenic development), family (microsystem), community (exosystem), and culture (macrosystem; Belsky, 1980) with a transactional model where environmental, family, and child characteristics mutually influence each other (Cicchetti & Rizley, 1981).

Factors that transact across these various ecological levels are classified into two broad categories: (1) potentiating factors, which increase the probability of maltreatment, and (2) compensatory factors, which decrease or mitigate the risk of maltreatment (Cicchetti & Rizley, 1981). Enduring potentiating factors (e.g., psychopathology, chronic stress) may increase the risk of maltreatment exposure, whereas enduring compensatory or protective factors (e.g., social support, secure employment) are aspects of a family's environment that reduce the risk of maltreatment. Therefore, child maltreatment is more likely to occur only when potentiating factors override compensatory factors (Cicchetti et al., 2000).

The ecological-transactional theory suggests that potentiating and compensatory factors occur within each level of the child and family's ecology, and the factors that are present within a given level can influence consequences in the nearby areas of one's environment (Cicchetti et al., 2000). Factors that transact across ecological levels to contribute to maltreatment occurrence range from abuse-eliciting characteristics and the developmental stage of children, to biological and psychological disturbance in parents, dysfunctional family interaction patterns, social pressures, and cultural beliefs and attitudes. A brief example of possible potentiating and compensatory factors from Cicchetti and colleagues' (2000) ecological-transactional theory of child maltreatment is presented in Table 4.2. Although factors emphasized across ecological levels can also influence the likelihood of parental substance use, parental substance use as a risk factor of child maltreatment is highlighted at the microsystem level.

While factors presented at each ecological level may serve as antecedents to, and consequences of, child maltreatment, the distance at which a child encounters multiple vulnerabilities and safeguards may differentially

TABLE 4.2 Transacting Factors Associated with Child Maltreatment and Child Development

Ecological Level	Description	Potentiating Factors	Compensatory Factors
Macrosystem	Cultural values and beliefs that may be abuse-promoting	Acceptance of a violent culture and parenting practices	Rejection of a violent culture and parenting practices
Exosystem	Formal and informal social structures that impact the child's and family's immediate environment	Neighborhood violence; employment unavailability	Supportive social networks; adequate community resources
Microsystem	Family environment and immediate context in which child maltreatment may take place	Parental substance use; parent's own developmental history; negative parent-child interactions	Sensitive caregiving; positive parental coping strategies
Ontogenic development (child)	Factors within the child that affect adaptation	Anxious, insecure, or disorganized attachment to parent associated with poor child self-concept and unhealthy internal working models	Positive self-concept; adaptive physiological and emotional regulation

impact the risk of maltreatment and children's developmental outcomes. Cicchetti and colleagues (2000) propose that factors associated with a child's more proximal ecologies are the most influential contributors to child development. However, the accumulation of risk factors across distal and proximal ecological levels and the collection of protective factors within these levels also play a role.

Feminist Theory

Feminist theory aims to understand gender inequality and has been applied within the context of substance use and child maltreatment. One underpinning of this theory is that women play a more passive role in substance use culture, whereas men are active participants (Ettorre, 1989). Feminist theory has also linked substance use and child maltreatment with other household risk factors, such as intimate partner violence. It is well-established that intimate partner violence often co-occurs with substance use and child maltreatment, and feminist theory suggests that the expression of male dominance and social control in families is associated with masculinist substance using and increases the risk of child abuse and neglect (Ettorre, 1989; Stark & Flitcraft, 1988). Through the feminist lens, it is postulated that men are often the perpetrators of severe maltreatment compared to women; thus, gender identity and male authority better explain maltreatment occurrence in families (Stark & Flitcraft, 1988). Indeed, some family systems involve rigid gender identities and inequities between a man and woman. Family systems characterized by such rigid gender roles may, in turn, place women in a dilemma of helplessness; they may be deprived of their responsibility to care for their children or use the parenting role to exert control over their children (Stark & Flitcraft, 1988).

Consequently, when child protective services intervene in abuse and neglect cases, mothers are often assigned the responsibility of the abuse and withheld resources to care for their children appropriately. This, in turn, overburdens mothers as more frequently being named the perpetrators of child maltreatment and has deleterious consequences for children. Feminist theorists indicate that the best way to prevent child maltreatment is to empower women and treat them as adequate caregivers of their children (Stark & Flitcraft, 1988).

Risk and Protective Factors

Although substance use is one of the most salient risk factors implicated in child abuse and neglect, a combination of overlapping individual, familial, community, and societal risk factors often undergird both parental substance use and child maltreatment. Regarding child characteristics, younger children are often more susceptible to these co-occurring issues, as well as children with developmental disabilities or medical needs. For example, among children 6 months to 4 years old, and 5 to 6 years old, maternal misuse of substances increases the odds of neglect by 2.85 and 4.16 times, respectively (Clément et al., 2016). Children exposed to alcohol and/or other drugs in utero are more likely to experience major medical problems (Huestis & Choo, 2002), growth deficits (Bada et al., 2002), congenital anomalies (Little et al., 2004), and behavior problems (Linares et al., 2006). Children with chronic illnesses or disabilities experience child maltreatment at three times the rate of children that do not have chronic illnesses or disabilities (Sullivan & Knutson, 2000).

Parental characteristics are also associated with co-occurring substance use and child maltreatment. Although the terms parent, mother, and father are used interchangeably throughout this section, it should be noted that most research on parenting is based on studies with mothers. Differences between mothers and fathers are highlighted when available. The parental characteristics associated with co-occurring substance use and child maltreatment include low levels of education (Cox et al., 2003), depressive symptoms (Dubowitz et al., 2011; Swendsen et al., 2010), and young age (Zhou et al., 2006). In addition, low parental warmth and use of physical discipline (Slack et al., 2004) and deficits in social information processing (Berlin et al., 2011) are associated with child maltreatment. Mothers with high perceived parental stress are 1.39 times more likely to self-report neglectful behaviors toward their children. In contrast, fathers are more likely to engage in child maltreatment if they experience stress related to outside factors, particularly perceiving themselves as impoverished or experiencing work-related stress (Clément et al., 2016). Notably, stress serves as a shared precipitant to both substance use and child maltreatment, suggesting that stress may operate as a mechanistic link between these problems. Compared to non-substance users, substance-using parents experience higher cumulative stressors that are shown to negatively impact parenting, which in turn places these families at an increased risk for child welfare involvement (Curenton et al., 2009; Nair et al., 2003). Parental stress and substance use have been linked to a lower tolerance for child misbehavior and unreasonable expectations regarding child development and behavior, authoritarian parenting attitudes, and increased rigidity and intrusiveness in caregiving behaviors (Burns et al., 1991; Cicchetti & Olsen, 1990; Donohue et al., 2006; Hien & Honeyman, 2000; Rodriguez, 2010). Conversely, protective factors, such as parental knowledge of child development and sensitive and responsive caregiving behaviors, have been linked to a lower incidence of child abuse and neglect (McMillin et al., 2016; Thomas & Zimmer-Gembeck, 2011).

At the family level, factors such as poverty status (Slack et al., 2004), social isolation (Berlin et al., 2011), violence (Carbone-Lopez et al., 2006; Cox et al., 2003), and family conflict (Stith et al., 2009; Zhou et al., 2006) have been shown to increase risk of substance use and/or child maltreatment. Although most families with low income do not maltreat their children, and maltreatment occurs at every income level, poverty has been linked to all types of child maltreatment, even among cases not reported to child protective services (Sedlak & Broadhurst, 1996; Slack et al., 2004). Substance use is similarly often associated with other problems, including intimate partner violence (Carbone-Lopez et al., 2006), which in turn is linked to maladaptive family functioning and increased risk of maltreatment (Cox et al., 2003). Children in homes characterized by intimate partner violence are twice as likely as children not exposed to intimate partner violence to be reported to child protective services (Casanueva et al., 2009). Children in families with diverse family structures, such as single parents, same-sex parents, and multi-generational families with grandparents serving as primary caregivers, may experience unique stressors and differentially experience exposure to maltreatment and parental substance use (Dolbin-Macnab & O'Connell, 2021; Steenrod & Mirick, 2017; Wu et al., 2015). For example, single parenthood and a larger number of children in the home are associated with maltreatment (Dubowitz et al., 2011; Merrit, 2009; Sedlak et al., 2010); and grandparents may experience physical, social, and mental health challenges in assuming caregiving responsibilities for children (Lent & Otto, 2018).

Broader community and societal factors are also linked to parental substance use and child abuse and neglect. Families living in impoverished and disadvantaged communities, as well as those who are less engaged with community services, may be at increased risk of substance use and maltreatment (Boardman et al., 2001; Merritt, 2009; Klein, 2011; Sidebotham et al., 2002), whereas those with access to social support and higher levels of community involvement are at decreased risk (Kim & Maguire-Jack, 2015; MacLeod & Nelson, 2000). Cultural beliefs centered on physical and verbal punishment also play a role in parenting styles, particularly among fathers. Cultural factors and beliefs are associated with more punitive parenting behaviors among fathers in some cultures (Ferrari, 2002); and fathers are overrepresented in cases that include some of the most physically damaging and even lethal forms of maltreatment (Sinal et al., 2000; Stiffman et al., 2002). Other gender inequities and expectations can also affect both mothers' and fathers' behaviors, as well as the expectations placed on them for caring for and protecting children. For example, although fathers are less often the perpetrators of maltreatment, mothers are more often held legally accountable for failing to protect their children from an abusive partner. Cultural and social norms are also predictive of substance use. This is demonstrated by the changing cultural attitudes about acceptable drug use, such as with marijuana and opioids. In states where marijuana has been legalized, individuals report increases in the approval of marijuana use and decreases in perceived harm of regular use (Kosterman et al., 2016). However, there are also negative consequences associated with changing cultural influences. The opioid epidemic is one such example, whereby norms shifted regarding increases in prescribing opioids, contributing to more opioid overdoses (Centers for Disease Control and Prevention, 2018).

Vignette: Mr. and Mrs. Reed, Part 1

Mr. and Mrs. Reed, 33 years old, were brought to the attention of child protective services when their 5-year-old son, Jacob, had several consecutive days of unexcused absences from school. Mr. Reed identifies himself as White and Mrs. Reed identifies herself as Latina. At the time of the initial investigation, Mr. and Mrs. Reed were living with Mrs. Reed's mother, and Jacob was the only child in the home. The child protective services caseworker assigned to the case observed bruising on Mrs. Reed's arms and suspected possible intimate partner violence between the couple. Mr. and Mrs. Reed stated that they had difficulties getting Jacob to school due to a lack of transportation. Jacob's grandmother reported that Mr. and Mrs. Reed had recently been using alcohol and prescription opioids, and observed them sleeping throughout the day. Jacob's grandmother also expressed that, due to chronic pain, she was unable to transport Jacob to school. Mr. and Mrs. Reed confirmed recent alcohol and other drug use and informed the caseworker that it was challenging to remain sober in their current living environment as other family members would frequently host parties in the home. The caseworker learned that Mr. and Mrs. Reed had several strengths, including stable employment, sensitive caregiving behaviors, engagement in community activities, and connection to Mrs. Reed's family culture. However, Jacob was temporarily placed with a foster caregiver after Mr. and Mrs. Smith entered intensive alcohol and drug counseling.

Sociodemographic Factors

The intersection between parental substance use and child maltreatment and the impact on families varies across diverse sociodemographic characteristics. Parents are named as perpetrators in most maltreatment cases (77.5%), followed by a relative (6.5%), multiple or other relationships (3.8%), and unmarried partner of parent (3.4%; U.S. DHHS, ACF, ACYF, Children's Bureau, 2021). Most perpetrators are female (53.0%; U.S. DHHS, ACF, ACYF, Children's Bureau, 2021). Indeed, mothers are likely more often named perpetrators because they provide most of the direct caregiving to children in the United States. Administrative data suggest that most perpetrators of abuse and neglect are White (48.9%), followed by Black (21.1%) or Latinx (19.7%; U.S. DHHS, ACF, ACYF, Children's Bureau, 2021). Notably, approximately 11% and 28% of perpetrators of child maltreatment misuse alcohol and other drugs, respectively. Young women with low education, in particular, report the greatest substance use (Centers for Disease Control and Prevention, 2021); this includes approximately 5% to 8% of pregnant women (U.S. DHHS, SAMHSA, 2013).

Although findings are mixed, parental substance use and child maltreatment exposure rates differ according to the victimized child's race and ethnicity. American Indian or Alaska Native children have the highest rate of exposure to maltreatment, followed by children identified as Black, multiple races, Pacific Islander, White, Latinx, and Asian (U.S. DHHS, ACF, ACYF, Children's Bureau, 2021). Racial and ethnic differences also exist with regard to specific characteristics of child maltreatment, including the timing, type, severity, and chronicity. For example, although similar rates of neglect have been found among White and Black families, higher rates of physically abusive behaviors have been found in Black families (Maguire-Jack et al., 2018). Yet, these data are often limited in that racial and ethnic minority children are systematically overrepresented in child protective services, largely due to racism and/or other forms of oppression at multiple levels, including high rates of surveillance, which may lead to an overestimation or over reporting of the actual occurrence of child maltreatment among these families (Dettlaff & Boyd, 2020; Lanier et al., 2014).

Low socioeconomic status (SES) can confound racial and ethnic differences in the prevalence of parental substance use and child maltreatment exposure. Indeed, poverty is among the most significant predictors of both substance use and child maltreatment, and poverty differentially affects racial and ethnic minoritized families (Connell-Carrick, 2003; DiLauro, 2004; Sedlak et al., 2010; Testa & Smith, 2009). Among Black and Latina mothers, low SES is significantly associated with child abuse potential (Espinosa et al., 2017). Compared to White children, Black children are more likely to live in poverty and have higher official report rates for maltreatment, especially neglect (Drake & Rank, 2009; U.S. DHHS, National Center on Child Abuse and Neglect, 2010). Consequently, the variation in maltreatment occurrence and parental substance use across race and ethnicity and SES may be due, in part, to the larger community context with which these families live. For example, White children characterized by low SES do not generally live in poor communities; conversely, Black children characterized by low SES generally live in poor communities and experience more significant systemic inequities than their White counterparts (Drake & Rank, 2009; Jonson-Reid et al., 2013). As such, disparities in community-level SES factors may uniquely affect rates of maltreatment by race and ethnicity.

Differences in exposure to parental substance use and child maltreatment are also associated with the child's age. Children under the age of 1 year are at the highest risk (U.S. DHHS, ACF, ACYF, Children's Bureau, 2021). These very young children are more often cared for at home, making their maltreatment less likely to be observed by others, and they are unable to report their maltreatment or seek help, further reducing the likelihood of detection and intervention. For many young children, substance exposure begins prenatally (Young et al., 2009), with documented prenatal substance use exposure rates as high as 30% in some populations (Chasnoff, 2010). For example, research has found that substance use exposure was highest among Black infants (4.1%) and the lowest among Latinx infants (1.0%; Putnam-Hornstein et al., 2016). White and Latinx infants were predominantly exposed to parental amphetamine and cannabis use, whereas Black infants were exposed to parental use of cannabis and cocaine (Putnam-Hornstein et al., 2016).

Given that some children of parents with substance use may use alcohol and other drugs, differences are also seen across sociodemographic characteristics in later adolescent and young adult substance use. Although children who experience maltreatment, generally, are at high risk for substance use disorders, the intergenerational effects of parental substance use on the substance use outcomes of children may further exacerbate this risk (Dunn et al., 2002). Indeed, younger victims of abuse and neglect are more likely to start using substances at a younger age than their non-victimized peers (Kilpatrick et al., 2000). Furthermore, White adolescents are more likely to become heavier drinkers and substance-dependent than adolescents of other races and ethnicities (Kilpatrick et al., 2000; Lee et al., 2012). Other studies have mixed findings regarding the increased risk of substance use by child and adolescent sex. One study found that exposure to child maltreatment and parental substance use predicts later substance use problems among females (Stein et al., 2002). In contrast, another study found that males exposed to abuse and parental substance use were at greater risk of alcohol and marijuana use relative to females (Kilpatrick et al., 2000).

Consequences of Child Maltreatment and Parental Substance Use

The co-occurrence of parental substance use and child maltreatment is linked to a range of long-term consequences for children. Substance use and problematic parenting are associated in many ways and increase the risk of poor health, attention problems, and aggression in children (Osborne & Berger, 2009). These children are also more likely to experience anxiety, depression, and posttraumatic stress disorder (PTSD) than their non-exposed counterparts (Conners et al., 2004; Osborne & Berger, 2009; Turney & Wildeman, 2016). Compared to the general population, a disproportionate number of adults (25.2% compared to 4.5%) with a history of child maltreatment meet the criteria for PTSD (Pecora et al., 2005). Furthermore, children with a substance-misusing parent are at an increased risk of engaging in future substance use themselves (Appleyard et al., 2011; Dunn et al., 2002; Zlotnick et al., 2004). Similarly, approximately 30% of abused and neglected children will continue the intergenerational cycle of maltreatment (Children's Bureau, 2013).

Several consequences are associated with parental substance use and child maltreatment within the context of child welfare involvement. Due to the severity of problems experienced, children with co-occurring exposure to maltreatment and substance use are more likely to be placed in foster care and remain in placement longer when compared to maltreated children from non-substance-using families (U.S. DHHS, National Clearinghouse on Child Abuse and Neglect, 2003). In addition, these children are more likely to have multiple placement changes, remain in the child welfare system longer, and have a parent whose rights are terminated (Harris-McKoy et al., 2014; U.S. DHHS, National Clearinghouse on Child Abuse and Neglect, 2003).

Societal costs are also associated with both substance use and child maltreatment. It is estimated that $28 billion is spent annually on child maltreatment services, with approximately $1.7 billion per year linked to support services, including substance use services (DeVooght et al., 2014). Substance use treatment alone costs the United States over $400 billion annually (Uhl & Grow, 2004). The economic burden, coupled with the deleterious outcomes of child maltreatment and substance use, is substantial, and indicates the importance of effective prevention, intervention, and treatment programming for this vulnerable population.

Vignette: Mr. and Mrs. Reed, Part 2

Visitation with Jacob had been consistent until two months into the open child protective services case, when Mr. and Mrs. Reed did not show up for a scheduled visit. They admitted that they had relapsed with alcohol and did not want Jacob to see them intoxicated. The caseworker contacted Mr. and Mrs. Reed's alcohol and drug counselor and found that they regularly attended their weekly therapy sessions and were progressing with their treatment plan. However, after the missed visit, Jacob began wetting the bed, and the foster caregiver reported that it had been challenging to get him up for school because he seemed overly tired. Jacob worked with a play therapist and continued with supervised visitation with Mr. and Mrs. Reed.

Prevention and Intervention

Several evidence-supported interventions have been developed and implemented to prevent child maltreatment and its harmful and costly consequences. Programs aimed to address child maltreatment are often designed to reduce risk factors and enhance protective factors by nurturing parenting attitudes and skills, reducing parental stress, and building supportive social networks (Centers for Disease Control and Prevention, 2021). Although preventing and treating child abuse and neglect requires a comprehensive approach that reaches all levels of a child's ecology, including individual, family, community, and societal levels, much work in the field fails to utilize this perspective to guide child maltreatment programming. Many programs to prevent or reduce child maltreatment are found to have small or inconsistent findings regarding their effectiveness (Euser et al., 2015).

Among the effective approaches to prevent child maltreatment to date, home visiting has evidenced positive changes in parenting outcomes, the home environment, and children's development (Chen & Chan, 2016; Howard & Brooks-Gunn, 2009). For example, **Nurse Family Partnership** is often identified as one of the most effective home visiting programs to prevent child abuse and neglect among low-income, first-time mothers (Nurse-Family Partnership, n.d.). Women whom a nurse visits during pregnancy and after birth demonstrate reductions in child maltreatment, number of pregnancies, use of welfare services, and criminal behavior compared to women not visited by nurses, with effects lasting up to 15 years after participating in the program (Olds et al., 1997). Nurse-visited mothers also report less impairment in the parenting role due to drug and alcohol use (Olds et al., 2010).

Another effective home-based program is **SafeCare**, which teaches parents how to best interact with their children, respond appropriately to children's behaviors, recognize hazards in the home environment, and identify health-related concerns. Effectiveness studies demonstrate that families' participation in *SafeCare* significantly improves their health, safety, and parenting (Gershater-Molko et al., 2003). In addition, positive changes in mothers' parenting, depression, and stress are associated with positive changes in children's behavior among families participating in the program (Carta et al., 2013). Notably, *SafeCare* has been widely used in rural communities and with families across diverse racial and ethnic backgrounds (Chaffin et al., 2012).

Absent from most prevention and intervention programs is a dual focus on parental substance use and child maltreatment. Given the high prevalence of these co-occurring issues, this presents a significant need to prevent and treat child abuse and neglect. Although it is well-known that child abuse and neglect is a multifaceted problem, many programs that target parental substance use and child maltreatment are implemented in isolation; consequently, parenting interventions that have been adapted or developed specifically for families at risk of maltreatment tend to focus on targeting singular factors. Interventions, such as **parent-child interaction therapy** (Herschell & McNeil, 2007) or the **Triple P—Positive Parenting Program** (Sanders, 1999), have been refined to reduce maltreatment by targeting harsh parenting practices. These interventions are effective because they move beyond parent support groups to provide parent training, and sessions are implemented within a moderate duration (e.g., ~12 sessions; Euser et al., 2015). Although these programs demonstrate fewer maltreatment occurrences, they do not necessarily address other factors that place parents at risk for maltreatment, including parental substance use.

In light of the pervasiveness of parental substance use and child maltreatment, a growing body of research is examining the extent to which programs address these co-occurring concerns. A review of the few dual treatment programs available demonstrated that these programs generally have a positive effect on reducing parental substance use and improvement of parenting- and maltreatment-related outcomes (Neger & Prinz, 2015). Several studies showed programs having a positive impact through various mechanisms, including emotional regulation, psychosocial functioning, parenting knowledge, and preoccupation with substances (Neger & Prinz, 2015). A summary of combined substance use and parenting interventions and their outcomes published in the past 15 years are presented in Table 4.3.

TABLE 4.3 Parenting and Parental Substance Use Programs

Program	Authors	Parental Substance Use Outcomes	Parenting and Maltreatment-Related Outcomes
Attachment and Biobehavioral Catch-up	Berlin et al., 2014	Abstinence throughout participation in program	Increases in sensitive parenting behaviors
Engaging Mom's Program	Dakof et al., 2010	Decreases in alcohol and drug use	Improvements in child welfare permanency outcomes; decreases in child abuse potential
Family Behavior Therapy	Donohue et al., 2014	Decreases in hard drug use	Decreases in child abuse potential
Mindfulness-Informed Intervention for Child Welfare-Involved Families	Brown et al., 2021	Decreases in substance misuse	Decreases in parenting stress and parental rigidity
Mothers and Toddlers Program	Suchman et al., 2010	Decreases in drug use	Increases in supportive parenting behaviors
Multisystemic Therapy—Building Stronger Families	Schaeffer et al., 2013	Decreases in alcohol and drug use	Decreases in psychological aggression toward youth and substantiated incidents of maltreatment
Parenting Skills & Behavioral Couples Therapy	Lam et al., 2009	Increases in the percentage of days abstinent	Decreases in open cases with child protective services
Parents Under Pressure	Dawe & Harnett, 2007	Decreases in methadone dose	Decreases in child abuse potential and parental rigidity

Despite needed improvements in the methodological rigor of programs aimed to address parental substance use and parenting, in general, some programs may be critical in the prevention and treatment of child maltreatment and parental substance use. Only four of the dual programs noted above precisely assess the outcomes of families involved with child welfare. These included the **Mindfulness-Informed Intervention for Child Welfare-Involved Families**, **Parenting Skills and Behavioral Couples Therapy** (PSBCT), **Engaging Moms Program** (EMP), and **Multisystemic Therapy—Building Stronger Families** (MST-BSF) programs, which were implemented with families involved in drug court and child protective services. Mindfulness techniques have particularly gained growing support in both the addictions and parenting fields, and the mindfulness-informed intervention presented here demonstrated reductions in both rigid parenting practices and substance use (Brown et al., 2021). When interventions target co-occurring risk factors, such as parental substance use and poor parenting, larger effects are found for preventing and reducing child maltreatment (van der Put et al., 2018). However, only the PSBCT, EMP, and MST-BSF programs assessed child welfare–specific outcomes, such as open child protective services cases (Lam et al., 2009), permanency outcomes (Dakof et al., 2010), and substantiated incidents of child maltreatment (Schaeffer et al., 2013). Given the scarcity of programs with the dual focus to address parental substance use and parenting for families involved with child welfare, this highlights the need for prevention and intervention development in this area and better measurement to assess the certainty with which these programs truly reduce the risk of child abuse and neglect among families with parental substance use.

However, several barriers exist that might interfere with the ability to successfully implement programs in child welfare that target both parental substance use and child maltreatment. First, child welfare-involved parents with substance use are less likely to comply with treatment recommendations or are more likely to leave treatment early (Traube, 2012). In addition, a lack of coordination between other mandated services, substance use treatment, and parent training may place an undue burden on families, making it difficult for them to meet the multiple demands associated with child welfare involvement. Furthermore, child welfare policy also interferes with treatment success among these parents. Child welfare agencies are often required to establish safe, stable, and permanent homes for children in an expedited time frame—generally within one year—yet successful parenting and substance use treatment often involves more time to devote to recovery.

Although program barriers exist, the most promising child maltreatment prevention and intervention programs are multifaceted and target parental substance use and parenting. However, few programs that address myriad ecological factors have been rigorously designed and tested, nor have they been implemented within the child welfare system. Useful programs should therefore include carefully developed theoretical underpinnings along with empirically sound research, such as the use of comparison or control groups, to accurately assess program effectiveness within the context of child protection outcomes.

Vignette: Mr. and Mrs. Reed, Part 3

Based on Mr. and Mrs. Reed's progress in alcohol and drug counseling, demonstration of supportive parenting and consistency during visitation with Jacob, and engagement with Jacob's school, the caseworker recommended and the court agreed that Jacob be reunified with them. Jacob also showed improvements in his wellness and excelled during his transition home. In addition, Mr. and Mrs. Reed had obtained transitional housing where they could live independently as a family and continue to thrive with supportive services and an environment that is more supportive of sobriety. They expressed their intent to abstain from alcohol and prescription opioids and commitment to Jacob's safety and well-being.

Conclusion

Despite differences in definitions of child abuse and neglect, there is a general consensus that an act or failure to act in the caregiving role, and that which presents an imminent risk of serious harm to a child, constitutes child maltreatment. While there is no single risk factor identified as contributing to child maltreatment, ecological and transactional models have evolved to better understand the causes and consequences of child abuse and neglect. Notably, one prominent risk factor associated with child maltreatment is parental substance use. Parental substance use has become increasingly recognized as a form of child maltreatment, and exposure to co-occurring child maltreatment and parental substance use has deleterious effects on children's lives. Up to three quarters of cases brought to the attention of child protective services involve parental substance use. Maltreated children of parents with substance use often remain in child protective services longer and experience poorer developmental, physical, and mental health outcomes. The etiology and consequences associated with child maltreatment and parental substance use highlight the need for targeted programs and policies that address these co-occurring issues. Few programs exist that address parental substance use and child maltreatment simultaneously, but outcomes of the extant dual treatment programs are positive with respect to reducing parental substance use and improving parenting. In addition, policies that aim to integrate the demands of the child welfare system with an understanding of successful treatment of parental substance use may better address the unique needs of this population.

Discussion Questions

1. What are the challenges to accurately identifying maltreatment and/or intervening in alleged cases of maltreatment?
2. What factors relate to the occurrence of both child maltreatment and substance use?
3. How do issues of bias and discrimination relate to the occurrence, identification, and treatment of co-occurring substance use and child maltreatment?
4. In the case of the Reed family, what other types of prevention and intervention approaches could the caseworker have introduced to lead to positive outcomes?

Key Terms

Adoption and Safe Families Act: A law that aims to address child safety, permanency, and well-being by focusing on expedited family reunification and case closures as well as the termination of parental rights.

Attachment and Biobehavioral Catch-up: An intervention designed to help caregivers provide nurturing care and positive interactions with their children.

Attachment Theory: A theory concerning the relationships between people, particularly among young children and their primary caregiver.

Battered Child Syndrome: A term that was previously used to describe a medical condition in children who have received serious injuries as a result of physical abuse.

Biological Theory: A perspective that suggests that our thoughts, feelings, and behaviors are a consequence of our genetics and physiology.

Child Abuse: Acts of commission toward a child by a parent or caregiver.

Child Abuse Prevention and Treatment Act: A law that provides financial assistance for demonstration programs for the prevention, identification, and treatment of child abuse and neglect.

Child Fatalities: Death of children as a result of abuse or neglect.

Child Maltreatment: Any recent act or failure to act on the part of a parent or caretaker which results in death, serious physical or emotional harm, sexual abuse or exploitation; or an act or failure to act, which presents an imminent risk of serious harm.

Child Neglect: Acts of omission toward a child by a parent or caregiver.

Child Protective Services: The government agency responsible for ensuring the safety, permanency, and well-being of children exposed to abuse and neglect; also known as the child welfare system.

Ecological Theory: A theory suggesting that the different environments or systems that individuals encounter across their lifespan can influence human behavior and development.

Emotional Abuse: Threats of harm, rejection, humiliation, isolation, or unreasonable restriction of behaviors toward a child.

Engaging Moms Program: A family-based intervention designed to assist mothers in regaining or retaining their parental rights by facilitating substance abuse treatment entry during participation in court-ordered programming.

Family Behavioral Therapy: A behavioral intervention that aims to address co-occurring concerns within families, such as substance use, child maltreatment, and family conflict.

Family Violence Prevention and Services Act: A law that provides financial assistance to support emergency shelter and related assistance for victims of domestic violence and their children.

Feminist Theory: A theory concerning gender inequality and women's experiences.

Incidence: The rate of new occurrences of child maltreatment.

Internal Working Model: A mental representation of the self and of others, which can influence a child's developmental trajectory.

Mindfulness-Informed Intervention for Child Welfare-Involved Families: An integrated intervention that incorporates mindfulness, cognitive-behavioral, and positive psychology strategies to improve family functioning and well-being.

Mothers and Toddlers Program: An attachment-based program designed to address parenting in mothers with substance use.

Multisystemic Therapy—Building Stronger Families: An intensive family and community-based intervention designed to reduce parental substance use, prevent child maltreatment, and improve family health and well-being.

Neglect: Lack of supervision; failure to meet basic needs, such as food, clothing, shelter, education, and medical care; or inadequate affection or nurturing of a child.

Nurse Family Partnership: A nurse home visitation program for mostly low-income, first-time mothers.

Parent-Child Interaction Therapy: A dyadic behavioral intervention for children and their parents.

Parenting Skills and Behavioral Couples Therapy: An integrative intervention that combines parent skills training and behavioral couples therapy to address parenting behavior and relationship functioning.

Parents Under Pressure Program: A home-based intervention that combines psychological principles related to parenting and child behavior within a case management model, designed to address family functioning.

Physical Abuse: Violent handling, choking, burning, hitting, or shaking of a child.

Prevalence: The number of occurrences of child maltreatment.

SafeCare: An evidence-based parent training program for the prevention of child maltreatment.

Sexual Abuse: Sexual exposure, sexual touching, rape, or sexual exploitation of a child.

Substance Misuse: The inappropriate use of alcohol or other drugs.

Substance Use Disorder: The recurrent use of alcohol and/or drugs that causes clinically significant impairment, including health problems, disability, and failure to meet major responsibilities at work, school, or home.

Substantiation: Child welfare authority determines that a caregiver is responsible for child abuse and/or neglect.

Triple P—Positive Parenting Program: A parenting and family support program designed to prevent and treat children's behavioral and emotional problems.

References

Ainsworth, M. S., Blehar, M. C., Waters, E., & Wall, S. (1978). *Patterns of attachment: A psychological study of the strange situation.* Lawrence Erlbaum.

Ainsworth, M. S., & Wittig, B. A. (1969). *Attachment and exploratory behavior of one-year-olds in a strange situation: Determinants of infant behavior.* Methuen.

American Public Health Association. (2021). *Substance misuse.* https://www.apha.org/topics-and-issues/substance-misuse

Appleyard, K., Berlin, L. J., Rosanbalm, K. D., & Dodge, K. A. (2011). Preventing early child maltreatment: Implications from a longitudinal study of maternal abuse history, substance use problems, and offspring victimization. *Prevention Science, 12,* 139–149. https://doi.org/10.1007/s11121-010-0193-2

Bada, H. S., Das, A., Bauer, C. R, Seetha, S., Lester, B., Wright, L. L., … Maza, P. L. (2002). Gestational cocaine exposure and intrauterine growth: Maternal lifestyle study. *Obstetrics & Gynecology, 5,* 916–924. https://doi.org/10.1016/S0029-7844(02)02199-3

Barnard, M., & McKeganey, N. (2004). The impact of parental problem drug use on children: What is the problem and what can be done to help? *Addiction, 99*(5), 552–559. https://doi.org/10.1111/j.1360-0443.2003.00665.x

Belsky, J. (1980). Child maltreatment: An ecological integration. *American Psychologist, 35,* 320–335.

Belsky, J. (1993). Etiology of child maltreatment: A developmental-ecological analysis. *Psychological Bulletin, 114*(3), 413–434. https://doi.org/10.1037/0033-2909.114.3.413

Berlin, L. J., Appleyard, K., & Dodge, K. A. (2011). Intergenerational continuity in child maltreatment: Mediating mechanisms and implications for prevention. *Child Development, 82*(1), 162–176. https://doi.org/10.1111/j.1467-8624.2010.01547.x

Berlin, L. J., Shanahan, M., & Carmody, K. A. (2014). Promoting supportive parenting in new mothers with substance-use problems: A pilot randomized trial of residential treatment plus an attachment-based parenting program. *Infant Mental Health Journal, 35*(1), 81–85. https://doi.org/10.1002/imhj.21427

Berridge, K. C. (2007). The debate over dopamine's role in reward: The case for incentive salience. *Psychopharmacology, 191,* 391–431. https://doi.org/10.1007/s00213-006-0578-x

Boardman, J. D., Finch, B. K., Ellison, C. G., Williams, D. R., & Jackson, J. S. (2001). Neighborhood disadvantage, stress, and drug use among adults. *Journal of Health and Social Behavior, 42,* 151–165.

Bowlby, J. (1969). *Attachment and loss.* Basic Books.

Bretherton, I. (1992). The origins of attachment theory: John Bowlby and Mary Ainsworth. *Developmental Psychology, 28*(5), 759–775.

Brown, S. M., Bender, K. A., Bellamy, J. L., Garland, E. L., Dmitrieva, J., & Jenson, J. M. (2021). A pilot randomized trial of a mindfulness-informed intervention for child welfare-involved families. *Mindfulness, 12,* 420–435. https://doi.org/10.1007/s12671-018-1001-5

Burns, K., Chethik, L., Burns, W. J., & Clark, R. (1991). Dyadic disturbances in cocaine-abusing mothers and their infants. *Journal of Clinical Psychology, 47*(2), 316–319.

Carbone-Lopez, K., Kruttschnitt, C., & MacMillan, R. (2006). Patterns of intimate partner violence and their associations with physical health, psychological distress, and substance use. *Public Health Reports, 121,* 382–392. https://doi.org/10.1177/003335490612100406

Carta, J. J., Lefever, J. B., Bigelow, K., Borkowski, J., & Warren, S. F. (2013). Randomized trial of a cellular phone-enhanced home visitation parenting intervention. *Pediatrics, 132* (Supplement 2), S167–S173.

Casanueva, C., Martin, S. L., & Runyan, D. K. (2009). Repeated reports for child maltreatment among intimate partner violence victims: Findings from the National Survey of Child and Adolescent Well-being. *Child Abuse & Neglect, 33,* 84–93. https://doi.org/10.1016/j.chiabu.2007.04.017

Cassidy, J. (1994). Emotion regulation within attachment relationships. *Monographs of the Society for Research in Child Development, 59*(2–3), 228–283.

Centers for Disease Control and Prevention. (2018). *Prescription opioid data.* https://www.cdc.gov/drugoverdose/data/prescribing.html

Centers for Disease Control and Prevention (2021). *Violence prevention: Risk and protective factors.* https://www.cdc.gov/violenceprevention/childabuseandneglect/riskprotectivefactors.html

Chaffin, M., Bard, D., Bigfoot, D. S., & Maher, E. J. (2012). Is a structured, manualized, evidence-based treatment protocol culturally competent and equivalently effective among American Indian parents in child welfare? *Child Maltreatment, 7*(3), 277–285.

Chasnoff, I. (2010). *The mystery of risk: Drugs, alcohol, pregnancy, and the vulnerable child.* NTI Upstream.

Chen, M., & Chan, K. L. (2016). Effects of parenting programs on child maltreatment prevention: A meta-analysis. *Trauma, Violence, & Abuse, 17,* 88–104. https://doi.org/10.1177/1524838014566718

Children's Bureau. (2013). *Long-term consequences of child abuse and neglect.* https://www.childwelfare.gov/pubs/factsheets/long_term_consequences.pdf

Children's Bureau. (2014). *Parental substance use and the child welfare system.* https://www.childwelfare.gov/pubPDFs/parentalsubstanceuse.pdf

Child Welfare Information Gateway. (n.d.). *Historical timeline of Child Welfare Information Gateway.* https://www.childwelfare.gov/aboutus/cwig-timeline/

Child Welfare Information Gateway. (2013). *How the child welfare system works.* U.S. Department of Health and Human Services, Children's Bureau. https://www.childwelfare.gov/pubPDFs/cpswork.pdf

Child Welfare Information Gateway. (2014). *Parental substance use and the child welfare system.* U.S. Department of Health and Human Services, Children's Bureau. http://centerforchildwelfare.org/kb/subabuse/ParentSubAbuseAndCW.pdf

Child Welfare Information Gateway. (2019). *Parental substance use as child abuse.* U.S. Department of Health and Human Services, Children's Bureau. https://www.childwelfare.gov/pubPDFs/parentalsubstanceuse.pdf

Cicchetti, D., & Olsen, K. (1990). The developmental psychopathology of child maltreatment. In M. Lewis and S. Miller (Eds.), *Handbook of developmental psychopathology* (pp. 261–279). Plenum Press.

Cicchetti, D., & Rizley, R. (1981). Developmental perspectives on the etiology, intergenerational transmission, and sequelae of child maltreatment. *New Directions for Child Development, 11,* 31–55. https://doi.org/10.1002/cd.23219811104

Cicchetti, D., Rogosch, F. A., & Toth, S. L. (2006). Fostering secure attachment in infants in maltreating families through preventive interventions. *Developmental Psychopathology, 18*(3), 623–649.

Cicchetti, D., Toth, S. L., & Maughan, A. (2000). An ecological-transactional model of child maltreatment. In A. J. Sameroff, M. Lewis, & S. M. Miller (Eds.), *Handbook of developmental psychopathology* (2nd ed., pp. 689–722). Springer.

Clément, M. E., Bérubé, A., & Chamberland, C. (2016). Prevalence and risk factors of child neglect in the general population. *Public Health, 138,* 86–92. https://doi.org/10.1016/j.puhe.2016.03.018

Committee on Opportunities in Drug Abuse Research, Division of Neuroscience and Behavioral Health, Institute of Medicine. (1996). *Pathways of addiction: Opportunities in drug abuse research.* National Academy Press.

Connell-Carrick, K. A. (2003). A critical review of the empirical literature: Identifying correlates of child neglect. *Child and Adolescent Social Work Journal, 20,* 389–425.

Conners, N. A., Bradley, R. H., Whiteside-Mansell, L. W., Liu, J. Y., Roberts, T. J., Burgdorf, K., ... Herrell, J. M. (2004). Children of mothers with serious substance abuse problems: An accumulation of risks. *American Journal of Drug & Alcohol Abuse, 29*(4), 743–758. https://doi.org/10.1081/ADA-120029867

Conners, N. A., Grant, A., Crone, C. C., & Whiteside-Mansell, L. (2006). Substance abuse treatment for mothers: Treatment outcomes and the impact of length of stay. *Journal of Substance Abuse Treatment, 31*(4), 447–456. https://doi.org/10.1016/j.jsat.2006.06.001

Cox, C. E., Kotch, J. B., & Everson, M. D. (2003). A longitudinal study of modifying influences in the relationship between domestic violence and child maltreatment. *Journal of Family Violence, 18,* 5–17.

Crittenden, P. M., & Ainsworth, M. D. S. (1989). Child maltreatment and attachment theory. In D. Cicchetti and V. Carlson (Eds.), *Child maltreatment: Theory and research on the causes and consequences of child abuse and neglect* (pp. 432–463). Cambridge University Press.

Curenton, S. M., McWey, L. M., & Bolen, M. G. (2009). Distinguishing maltreating versus nonmaltreating at-risk families: Implications for foster care and early childhood education interventions. *Families in Society, 90*(2), 176–182. https://doi.org/10.1037/t02445-000

Dakof, G. A., Cohen, J. B., Henderson, C. E., Duarte, E., Boustani, M., Blackburn, A., ... Hawes, S. (2010). A randomized pilot study of the engaging moms program for family drug court. *Journal of Substance Abuse Treatment, 38*(3), 263–274. https://doi.org/10.1016/j.jsat.2010.01.002

Dawe, S., & Harnett, P. (2007). Reducing potential for child abuse among methadone-maintained parents: Results from a randomized controlled trial. *Journal of Substance Abuse Treatment, 32,* 381–390. https://doi.org/10.1016/j.jsat.2006.10.003

Dettlaff, A. J., & Boyd, R. (2020). Racial disproportionality and disparities in the child welfare system: Why do they exist, and what can be done to address them? *Annals of the American Academy of Political and Social Science, 692*(1), 253–274. https://doi.org/10.1177/0002716220980329

DeVooght, K., Fletcher, M., & Cooper, H. (2014). *Federal, state, and local spending to address child abuse and neglect in SFY 2012.* Child Trends, The Annie E. Casey Foundation, and Casey Family Programs.

DiLauro, M. D. (2004). Psychosocial factors associated with types of maltreatment. *Child Welfare, 83,* 69–99.

Dolbin-Macnab, M. L., & O'Connell, L. M. (2021). Grandfamilies and the opioid epidemic: A systemic perspective and future priorities. *Clinical Child and Family Psychology Review, 24,* 207–223. https://doi.org/10.1007/s10567-021-00343-7

Donohue, B., Azrin, N. H., Bradshaw, K., Van Hasselt, V. B., Cross, C. L., Urgelles, J., … Allen, D. N. (2014). A controlled evaluation of family behavior therapy in concurrent child neglect and drug abuse. *Journal of Consulting and Clinical Psychology, 82*(4), 706–720. https://doi.org/10.1037/a0036920

Donohue, B., Romero, V., & Hill, H. H. (2006). Treatment of co-occurring child maltreatment and substance abuse. *Aggression and Violent Behavior, 11*(6), 626–640. https://doi.org/10.1016/j.avb.2005.08.007

Drake, B., & Rank, M. (2009). The racial divide among American children in poverty: Reassessing the importance of neighborhood. *Children and Youth Services Review, 31,* 1264–1271. https://doi.org/10.1016/j.childyouth.2009.05.012

Dubowitz, H., Kim, J., Black, M. M., Weisbart, C., Semiatin, J., & Magder, L. S. (2011). Identifying children at high risk for a child maltreatment report. *Child Abuse & Neglect, 35,* 96–104. https://doi.org/10.1016/j.chiabu.2010.09.003

Dunn, M. G., Tarter, R. E., Mezzich, A. C., Vanyukov, M., Kirisci, L., & Kirillova, G. (2002). Origins and consequences of child neglect in substance abuse families. *Clinical Psychology Review, 22*(7), 1063–1090. https://doi.org/10.1016/S0272-7358(02)00132-0

English, D. J., Bangdiwala, S. I., & Runyan, D. K. (2005). The dimensions of maltreatment: Introduction. *Child Abuse & Neglect, 29,* 441–460. https://doi.org/10.1016/j.chiabu.2003.09.023

Espinosa, A., Ruglass, L. M., Dambreville, N., Shevorykin, A., Nicholson, R., & Sykes, K. M. (2017). Correlates of child abuse potential among African American and Latina mothers: A developmental-ecological perspective. *Child Abuse & Neglect, 70,* 222–230. https://doi.org/10.1016/j.chiabu.2017.06.003

Ettorre, B. (1989). Women and substance use/abuse: Towards a feminist perspective or how to make dust fly. *Women's Studies International Forum, 12*(6), 593–602.

Euser, S., Alink, L. R. A., Stoltenborgh, M., Bakermans-Kranenburg, M. J., & van IJzendoom, M. H. (2015). A gloomy picture: A meta-analysis of randomized controlled trials reveals disappointing effectiveness of programs aiming at preventing child maltreatment. *Public Health, 15,* 1068. https://doi.org/10.1186/s12889-015-2387-9

Felitti, V. J., Anda, R. F., Nordenberg, D., Williamson, D. F., Spitz, A. M., Edwards, V., … Marks, J. S. (1998). Relationship of childhood abuse and household dysfunction to many of the leading causes of death in adults. The Adverse Childhood Experiences (ACE) study. *American Journal of Preventive Medicine, 14*(4), 245–258. https://doi.org/10.1016/s0749-3797(98)00017-8

Fernandes-Alcantara, A. L. (2017). *Family violence prevention and services act (FVPSA): Background and funding.* https://fas.org/sgp/crs/misc/R42838.pdf

Ferrari, A. M. (2002). The impact of culture upon child rearing practices and definitions of maltreatment. *Child Abuse & Neglect, 26*(8), 793–813. https://doi.org/10.1016/S0145-2134(02)00345-9

Finkelhor, D., Vanderminden, J., Turner, H., Hamby, S. & Shattuck, A. (2014). Child maltreatment rates assessed in a national household survey of caregivers and youth. *Child Abuse & Neglect, 38*(9), 1421–1435. https://doi.org/10.1016/j.chiabu.2014.05.005

Foster, H. (1976). Violence toward children: Medicolegal aspects. *The Bulletin of the American Academy of Psychiatry and the Law, 4*(4), 336–40.

Gershater-Molko, R. M., Lutzker, J. R., & Wesch, D. (2003). Project SafeCare: Improving health, safety, and parenting skills in families reported for, and at-risk for child maltreatment. *Journal of Family Violence, 18*(6), 377–386. https://doi.org/10.1023/A:1026219920902

Giovannoni, J. (1989). Definitional issues in child maltreatment. In D. Cicchetti & V. Carlson (Eds.), *Child maltreatment: Theory and research on the causes and consequences of child abuse and neglect* (pp. 3–37). Cambridge University Press.

Gunnar, M. R., & Hostinar, C. E. (2015). The social buffering of the hypothalamic-pituitary-adrenocortical axis in humans: Developmental and experiential determinants. *Social Neuroscience, 10*(5), 479–488. https://doi.org/10.1080/17470919.2015.1070747

Harris-McKoy, D., Meyer, A. S., McWey, L. M., & Henderson, T. L. (2014). Substance use, policy, and foster care. *Journal of Family Issues, 35*(10), 1298–1321. https://doi.org/10.1177/0192513X13481439

Herschell, A. D., & McNeil, C. B. (2007). Parent-child interaction therapy with physically abusive families. In J. M. Briesmeister & C. E. Schaefer (Eds.), *Handbook of parent training: helping parents prevent and solve problem behaviors* (3rd ed., pp. 234–265). Wiley.

Hien, D., & Honeyman, T. (2000). A closer look at the drug abuse-maternal aggression link. *Journal of Interpersonal Violence, 15*(5), 503–522. https://doi.org/10.1177/088626000015005004

Hodgdon, H. B., Spinazzola, J., Briggs, E. C., Liang, L., Steinberg, A. M., & Layne, C. M. (2018). Maltreatment type, exposure characteristics, and mental health outcomes among clinic referred trauma-exposed youth. *Child Abuse & Neglect, 82*, 12–22. https://doi.org/10.1016/j.chiabu.2018.05.021

Howard, K. S., & Brooks-Gunn, J. (2009). The role of home-visiting programs in preventing child abuse and neglect. *Future Child, 19*(2), 119–146.

Huestis, M. A., & Choo, R. E. (2002). Drug abuse's smallest victims: In utero drug exposure. *Forensic Science International, 128*, 20–30. https://doi.org/10.1016/S0379-0738(02)00160-3

Jonson-Reid, M., Drake, B., & Zhou, P. (2013). Neglect subtypes, race, and poverty: Individual, family, and service characteristics. *Child Maltreatment, 18*, 30–41. https://doi.org/10.1177/1077559512462452

Kempe, C. H., Silverman, F., Steele, B. F., Droegenmueller, W., & Silver, H. K. (1962). The battered-child syndrome. *Journal of the American Academy of Child Psychiatry, 2*(1), 210–211. https://doi.org/10.1001/jama.1962.03050270019004

Khantzian, E. J. (1985). The self-medication hypothesis of addictive disorders: Focus on heroin and cocaine dependence. *American Journal of Psychiatry, 142*(11), 1259–1264. https://doi.org/10.1176/ajp.142.11.1259

Kilpatrick, D. G., Acierno, R., Saunders, B., Resnick, H. S., Best, C. L., & Schnurr, P. O. (2000). Risk factors for adolescent substance abuse and dependence data from a national sample. *Journal of Consulting and Clinical Psychology, 68*, 19–30.

Kim, B., & Maguire-Jack, K. (2015). Community interaction and child maltreatment. *Child Abuse & Neglect, 41*, 146–157. https://doi.org/10.1016/j.chiabu.2013.07.020

Kimberlin, S. E., Anthony, E. K., & Austin, M. J. (2009). Re-entering foster care: Trends, evidence, and implications. *Children and Youth Services Review, 31*, 471–481. https://doi.org/10.1016/j.childyouth.2008.10.003

Klein, S. (2011). The availability of neighborhood early care and education resources and the maltreatment of young children. *Child Maltreatment, 16*(4), 300–311. https://doi.org/10.1177/1077559511428801

Koob, G. F., & Volkow, N. D. (2010). Neurocircuitry of addiction. *Neuropsychopharmacology, 35,* 217–238. https://doi.org/10.1038/npp.2009.110

Kosterman, R., Bailey, J. A., Guttmannova, K., Jones, T. M., Eisenberg, N., Hill, K. G., & Hawkins, J. D. (2016). Marijuana legalization and parents' attitudes, use, and parenting in Washington state. *Journal of Adolescent Health, 59*(4), 450–456. https://doi.org/10.1016/j.jadohealth.2016.07.004

Lam, W. K. K., Fals-Stewart, W., & Kelley, M. L. (2009). Parent training with behavioral couples therapy for fathers' alcohol abuse: Effects on substance use, parental relationship, parenting, and CPS involvement. *Child Maltreatment, 14*(3), 243–254. https://doi.org/10.1177/1077559509334091

Lanier, P., Maguire-Jack, K., Walsh, T., Drake, B., & Hubel, G. (2014). Race and ethnic differences in early childhood maltreatment in the United States. *Journal of Developmental and Behavioral Pediatrics, 35*(7), 419–426. https://doi.org/10.1097/DBP.0000000000000083

Lee, C., Cronley, C., White, H. R., Mun, E., Stouthamer-Loeber, M., & Loeber, R. (2012). Racial differences in the consequences of childhood maltreatment for adolescent and young adult depression, heavy drinking, and violence. *Journal of Adolescent Health, 50,* 443–449. https://doi.org/10.1016/j.jadohealth.2011.09.014

Lent, J. P., & Otto, A. (2018). Grandparents, grandchildren, and caregiving: The impacts of America's substance use crisis. *Generations, 42*(3), 15–22.

Levine, M., & Levine, A. G. (2012). Coming full circle: A social context for Henry Kempe's work. *American Journal of Orthopsychiatry, 82*(2), 167–173. https://doi.org/10.1111/j.1939-0025.2012.01155.x

Linares, T. J., Singer, L. T., Kirchner, H. L., Short, E. L., Min, M. O., Hussey, P., … Minnes, S. (2006). Mental health outcomes of cocaine-exposed children at 6 years of age. *Journal of Pediatric Psychology, 31,* 85–97. https://doi.org/10.1093/jpepsy/jsj020

Little, J., Cardy, A., & Munger, R. G. (2004). Tobacco smoking and oral clefts: A meta-analysis. *Bulletin of the World Health Organization, 82*(3), 213–218.

Luscher, C., & Malenka, R. C. (2011). Drug-evoked synaptic plasticity in addiction: From molecular changes to circuit remodeling. *Neuron, 69,* 650–663. https://doi.org/10.1016/j.neuron.2011.01.017

MacLeod, J., & Nelson, G. (2000). Programs for the promotion of family wellness and the prevention of child maltreatment: A meta-analytic review. *Child Abuse & Neglect, 24*(9), 1127–1146. https://doi.org/10.1016/S0145-2134(00)00178-2

Maestripieri, D., Higley, J. D., Lindell, S. G., Newman, T. K., McCormack, K. M., & Sanchez, M. M. (2006). Early maternal rejection affects the development of monoaminergic systems and adult abusive parenting in rhesus macaques. *Behavioral Neuroscience, 120*(5), 1017–1024. https://doi.org/10.1037/0735-7044.120.5.1017

Maguire-Jack, K., Cao, Y., & Yoon, S. (2018). Racial disparities in child maltreatment: The role of social service availability. *Children and Youth Services Review, 86,* 49–55. https://doi.org/10.1016/j.childyouth.2018.01.014

Marsh, J. C., & Smith, B. D. (2011). Integrated substance abuse and child welfare services for women: A progress review. *Child and Youth Services Review, 33*(3), 466–472. https://doi.org/10.1016/j.childyouth.2010.06.017

McMillin, S. E., Bultas, M. W., Zander, T., Wilmott, J., Underwood, S., Broom, M. A., … Zand, D. H. (2016). The role of maternal knowledge of child development in predicting risk for child maltreatment. *Clinical Pediatrics, 55*(4), 374–376. https://doi.org/10.1177/0009922815586054

Merritt, D. H. (2009). Child abuse potential: Correlates with child maltreatment rates and structural measures of neighborhoods. *Children and Youth Services Review, 31,* 927–934. https://doi.org/10.1016/j.childyouth.2009.04.009

Morgan, E. S. (1966). *The puritan family.* Harper & Row.

Nair, P., Schuler, M. E., Black, M. M., Kettinger, L., & Harrington, D. (2003). Cumulative environmental risk in substance abusing women: Early intervention, parenting stress, child abuse potential and child development. *Child Abuse & Neglect, 27*(9), 993–995.

National Center on Addiction and Substance Abuse at Columbia University. (2005). *Family matters: Substance abuse and the American family.* https://www.ojp.gov/ncjrs/virtual-library/abstracts/family-matters-substance-abuse-and-american-family

Neger, E. N., & Prinz, R. J. (2015). Interventions to address parenting and parental substance abuse: Conceptual and methodological considerations. *Clinical Psychology Review, 39,* 71–82. https://doi.org/10.1016/j.cpr.2015.04.004

Negriff, S., Schneiderman, J. U., & Trickett, P. K. (2017). Concordance between self-reported childhood maltreatment versus case record reviews for child welfare-affiliated adolescents: Prevalence rates and associations with outcomes. *Child Maltreatment, 22*(1), 34–44. https://doi.org/10.1177/1077559516674596

Nurse-Family Partnership. (n.d.). Nurse-family partnership is often cited as the intervention for preventing child abuse and neglect. https://www.nursefamilypartnership.org/about/proven-results/prevent-child-abuse-neglect/

Olds, D. L., Eckenrode, J., Henderson, C. R. Jr., Kitzman, H., Powers, J., Cole, R., ... Luckey, D. (1997). Long-term effects of home visitation on maternal life course and child abuse and neglect. Fifteen-year follow-up of a randomized trial. *Journal of the American Medical Association, 278,* 637–643.

Olds, D. L., Kitzman, H. J., Cole, R. E., Hanks, C. A., Arcoleo, K. J., Anson, E. A., ... Stevenson, A. J. (2010). Enduring effects of prenatal and infancy home visiting by nurses on maternal life course and government spending. *Archives of Pediatric and Adolescent Medicine, 164*(5), 419–424. https://doi.org/10.1001/archpediatrics.2010.49

Osborne, C., & Berger, L. M. (2009). Parental substance abuse and child well-being: A consideration of parents' gender and coresidence. *Journal of Family Issues, 30*(3), 341–370. https://doi.org/10.1177/0192513X08326225

Pajulo, M., Suchman, N., Kalland, M., & Mayes, L. C. (2006). Enhancing the effectiveness of residential treatment for substance abusing pregnant and parenting women: Focus on maternal reflective functioning and mother-child relationship. *Infant Mental Health Journal, 27*(5), 448–465. https://doi.org/10.1002/imhj.20100

Pecora, P. J., Kessler, R. C., Williams, J., O'Brien, J., Downs, A. C., English, D., ... Holmes, K. E. (2005). *Improving family foster care: Findings from the Northwest Foster Care Alumni study.* Casey Family Programs.

Petersen, A., Joseph, J., & Feit, M. (2014). *New directions in child abuse and neglect research.* The National Academic Press.

Putnam-Hornstein, E., Prindle, J. J., & Leventhal, J. M. (2016). Prenatal substance exposure and reporting of child maltreatment by race and ethnicity. *Pediatrics, 138,* 1–10. https://doi.org/10.1542/peds.2016-1273

Rodriguez, C. M. (2010). Personal contextual characteristics and cognitions: Predicting child abuse potential and disciplinary style. *Journal of Interpersonal Violence, 25*(2), 315–335. https://doi.org/10.1177/0886260509334391

[SAMHSA] Substance Abuse and Mental Health Services Administration. (2019). *Mental health and substance use disorders.* https://www.samhsa.gov/find-help/disorders

Sanders, M. R. (1999). Triple P-Positive Parenting Program: Towards an empirically validated multilevel parenting and family support strategy for the prevention of behavior and emotional problems in children. *Clinical Child and Family Psychology Review, 2,* 71–90. https://doi.org/10.1023/A:1021843613840

Schaeffer, C. M., Swenson, C. C., Tuerk, E. H., & Henggeler, S. W. (2013). Comprehensive treatment for co-occurring child maltreatment and parental substance abuse: Outcomes from a 24-month pilot study of the MST-building stronger families program. *Child Abuse & Neglect, 37,* 596–607. https://doi.org/10.1016/j.chiabu.2013.04.004

Seay, K. (2015). How many families in child welfare services are affected by parental substance use disorders? A common question that remains unanswered. *Child Welfare, 94*(4), 19–51.

Sedlak, A., & Broadhurst, D. (1996). *The third national incidence study on child abuse and neglect (NIS-3)*. U.S. Department of Health and Human Services.

Sedlak, A., Mettenburg, J., Basena, M., Petta, I., McPherson, K., Greene, A., … Li, S. (2010). *Fourth national incidence study of child abuse and neglect (NIS-4): Report to Congress.* U.S. Department of Health and Human Services, Administration for Children, Youth, and Families.

Sidebotham, P. D., Heron, J., Golding, J., & ALSPAC Study Team. (2002). Child maltreatment in the 'children of the nineties': Deprivation, class, and social networks in a UK sample. *Child Abuse & Neglect, 26,* 1243–1259. https://doi.org/10.1016/S0145-2134(02)00415-5

Sinal, S. H., Petree, A. R., Herman-Giddens, M., Rogers, M. K., Enand, C., & Durant, R. H. (2000). Is race or ethnicity a predictive factor in shaken baby syndrome? *Child Abuse & Neglect, 24*(9), 1241–1246. https://doi.org/10.1016/S0145-2134(00)00177-0

Slack, K. S., Holl, J. L., McDaniel, M., & Yoo, J. (2004). Understanding the risks of child neglect: An exploration of poverty and parenting characteristics. *Child Maltreatment, 9*(4), 395–408. https://doi.org/10.1177/1077559504269193

Stark, E., & Flitcraft, A. H. (1988). Women and children at risk: A feminist perspective on child abuse. *International Journal of Health Services, 18,* 97–118. https://doi.org/10.2190/3K8F-KDWD-QYXK-2AX5

Steenrod, S., & Mirick, R. (2017). Substance use disorders and referral to treatment in substantiated cases of child maltreatment. *Child & Family Social Work, 22*(3), 1141–1150. doi:10.1111/cfs.12331

Stein, J. A., Leslie, M. B., & Nyamathi, A. (2002). Relative contributions of parent substance use and childhood maltreatment to chronic homelessness, depression, and substance abuse problems among homeless women: Mediating roles of self-esteem and abuse in adulthood. *Child Abuse & Neglect, 26,* 1011–1027. https://doi.org/10.1016/S0145-2134(02)00382-4

Stiffman, M., Schnitzer, P., Adam, P., Kruse, R., & Ewigman, B. (2002). Household composition and risk of fatal child maltreatment. *Pediatrics, 109*(4), 615–621.

Stith, S. M., Liu, T., Davies, L. C., Boykin, E. L., Alder, M. C., Harris, J. M., … Dees, J. E. M. E. G. (2009). Risk factors in child maltreatment: A meta-analytic review of the literature. *Aggression and Violent Behavior, 14*(1), 13–29. https://doi.org/10.1016/j.avb.2006.03.006

Suchman, N. E., DeCoste, C., Castiglioni, N., McMahon, T. J., Rounsaville, B., & Mayes, L. (2010). The mothers and toddlers program, an attachment-based parenting intervention for substance using women: Post-treatment results from a randomized clinical pilot. *Attachment and Human Development, 12*(5), 483–504. https://doi.org/10.1080/14616734.2010.501983

Sullivan, P. M., & Knutson, J. F. (2000). Maltreatment and disabilities: A population-based epidemiological study. *Child Abuse & Neglect, 24*(10), 1257–1273. https://doi.org/10.1016/S0145-2134(00)00190-3

Swendsen, J., Conway, K. P., Degenhardt, L., Glantz, M., Jin, R., Marikangas, K. R., … Kessler, R. C. (2010). Mental disorders as risk factors for substance use, abuse, and dependence: Results from the 10-year follow-up of the National Comorbidity Survey. *Addiction, 105*(6), 1117–1128. https://doi.org/10.1111/j.1360-0443.2010.02902.x

Terling, T. (1999). The efficacy of family reunification practices: Reentry rates and correlates of reentry for abused and neglected children reunited with their families. *Child Abuse & Neglect, 23*(12), 1359–1370. https://doi.org/10.1016/S0145-2134(99)00103-9

Testa, M. F., & Smith, B. (2009). Prevention and drug treatment. *The Future of Children, 19*(2), 147–167.

Thomas, R., & Zimmer-Gembeck, M. J. (2011). Accumulating evidence for parent-child interaction therapy in the prevention of child maltreatment. *Child Development, 82*(1), 177–192. https://doi.org/10.1111/j.1467-8624.2010.01548.x

Traube, D. (2012). The missing link to child safety, permanency, and well-being: Addressing substance misuse in child welfare. *Social Work Research, 36*(2), 83–87.

Turney, K., & Wildeman, C. (2016). Mental and physical health of children in foster care. *Pediatrics, 138*(5), E20161118-e20161118.

Uhl, G. R., & Grow, R. W. (2004). The burden of complex genetics in brain disorders. *Archives of General Psychiatry, 61*(3), 223–229. https://doi.org/10.1001/archpsyc.61.3.223

U.S. Department of Health & Human Services, Administration for Children and Families, Administration on Children, Youth, and Families, Children's Bureau. (2021). *Child maltreatment 2019.* https://www.acf.hhs.gov/cb/research-data-technology/statistics-research/child-maltreatment

U.S. Department of Health and Human Services, National Clearinghouse on Child Abuse and Neglect. (2003). *Substance abuse and child maltreatment.* http://nccanch.acf.hhs.gov

U.S. Department of Health and Human Services, National Center on Child Abuse and Neglect. (2010). *Child maltreatment 2008: Reports from the states to the national child abuse and neglect data system.* U.S. Government Printing Office.

U.S. Department of Health and Human Services, Substance Abuse and Mental Health Services Administration. (2013). *The NSDUH report, data spotlight: 6.8 million adults had both mental illness and substance use disorder in 2011.* https://www.samhsa.gov/data/sites/default/files/spot111-adults-mental-illness-substance-use-disorder/spot111-adults-mental-illness-substance-use-disorder.pdf

van der Put, C. E., Assink, M., Gubbels, J., Boekhout van Solinge, N. (2018). Identifying effective components of child maltreatment interventions: A meta-analysis. *Clinical Child and Family Psychology Review, 21*(2), 171–202. https://doi.org/10.1007/s10567-017-0250-5

Wagner, F., & Anthony, F. (2002). From first drug use to drug dependence: Developmental periods of risk for dependence upon marijuana, cocaine, and alcohol. *Neuropsychopharmacology, 26*, 479–488. https://doi.org/10.1016/S0893-133X(01)00367-0

Wu, E., El-Bassel, N., McVinney, D. L., Hess, L., Fopeano, M. V., Hwang, H. G., … Mansergh, G. (2015). The association between substance use and intimate partner violence within black male same-sex relationships. *Journal of Interpersonal Violence, 30*(5), 762–781. https://doi.org/10.1177/0886260514536277

Young, N. K., Boles, S. M., & Otero, C. (2007). Parental substance use disorders and child maltreatment: Overlap, gaps, and opportunities. *Child Maltreatment, 12*(2), 137–149. https://doi.org/10.1177/1077559507300322

Young, N. K., Gardner, S., Otero, C., Dennis, K., Chang, R., Earle, K., & Amatetti, S. (2009). *Substance-exposed infants: State responses to the problem.* Substance Abuse and Mental Health Services Administration. https://ncsacw.samhsa.gov/files/Substance-Exposed-Infants.pdf

Zhou, Y., Hallisey, E. J., & Freymann, G. R. (2006). Identifying perinatal risk factors for infant maltreatment: An ecological approach. *International Journal of Health Geographics, 4*, 53–64. https://doi.org/10.1186/1476-072X-5-53

Zlotnick, C., Tam, T., & Robertson, M. J. (2004). Adverse childhood events, substance abuse, and measures of affiliation. *Addictive Behaviors, 29*, 1177–1181. https://doi.org/10.1016/j.addbeh.2004.01.005

Spotlight on Special Issues

The Opioid Epidemic and Child Protective Services

Margaret I. Campe, PhD

The link between substance use disorders (SUDs) and child maltreatment has been well-documented. (See, for example, Cunningham & Finlay, 2013; Ghertner et al., 2018; Smith et al., 2007.) The opioid epidemic in particular has placed an elevated burden on child protective service (CPS) agencies. Likewise, these burdens extend to health care systems as well as myriad social service agencies that respond to the direct and latent effects of opioid use disorder (OUD) and support CPS efforts for reunification once a child has been removed from the home (Connell et al., 2007).

In response to a growing number of parents with OUD, as well as maternal opioid use resulting in large numbers of infants being born with neonatal abstinence syndrome (NAS), CPS agencies have had to adapt their interventions. As cited by Brown and colleagues in the previous chapter, there have been several programs aimed at dually treating SUD and addressing child maltreatment that have shown signs of efficacy. For example, the Sobriety Treatment and Recovery Teams (START) program was developed to coordinate efforts between CPS agencies and SUD treatment providers, while also pairing parents in the START program with mentors who are in long-term recovery (Huebner et al., 2012). Additionally, there has been a relatively large amount of research done to elucidate the immediate effects, such as extreme irritability, tremors, seizures, poor feeding, trouble sleeping, among others, of NAS on infants (March of Dimes, 2019). The opioid epidemic has rapidly increased the number of children being born with NAS, with the Centers for Disease Control reporting a rise from 1.5 per 1,000 to 6.5 per 1,000 births between 1999 and 2014 (Haight et al., 2018).

Although there are ongoing efforts to increase access to treatment options for parents and pregnant women, including medication for OUD, little is known about the long-term effects of maternal OUD on children. Part of the difficulty in determining long-term effects of NAS are the high rates of potentially confounding variables, as well as the lack of longitudinal studies beyond the first few years of life. Maternal OUD is often comorbid with other SUDs, and other socio-environmental factors that place children and infants at risk for developmental, both cognitive and physical, delays or other pathological disorders (Logan et al., 2013). Despite the difficult nature of determining long-term outcomes for children exposed to maternal OUD, the importance of doing so is becoming increasingly critical. Infants born with NAS are getting older and entering into systems such as K–12 public education, and may need specialized accommodations or access to additional or different resources such as specialized counseling and therapy.

While increased numbers of infants are being born with NAS due to maternal OUD, children who did not have in utero exposure to opioids or other drugs, but who have had a parent or caregiver with OUD, may also face extensive barriers. Child protective service agencies may be made aware of parental OUD through any number of different channels and children may be removed from the home. However, if reunification is not achieved quickly, often older children in foster care get bounced around from placement to placement, and sibling groups are separated into different placements, which may induce additional trauma or compound the effects of prior traumatic experiences (National Conference of State Legislatures, 2020). Without a consistent, stable, and caring home or living environment, continuity of health and mental health care or other resources may be difficult to achieve for these children. Moreover, if a child is not living in a consistent location, resources such as individual education plans in school may be more difficult to get into place. Children in these situations may end up aging out of the foster care system without having been provided the knowledge or ability about how or where to access vital resources as an adult (Massinga & Pecora, 2004).

The opioid epidemic is increasing the strain put on CPS agencies and other health, mental health, social, and community resources. However, Winstanley and Stover (2019) point out that only approximately 2% of federally funded research on SUD is focused on children and families. Research that focuses on reducing opioid overdose deaths and curbing OUD among adults is important and is a foundational step in reducing the negative effects of OUD on children and families. There are a lot of promising programs and largescale, federally funded projects, such as the National Institutes of Health HEALing Communities Initiatives, taking a multi-pronged approach to reducing opioid overdoses and combatting OUD. But even as research and interventions advance, children and families continue to be negatively impacted by SUD and OUD.

More research on the effects of maternal and parental OUD on children long-term is needed to implement successful and holistic interventions to mitigate negative long-term outcomes for children exposed to parental or maternal OUD.

References

Connell, C. M., Bergeron, N., Katz, K. H., Saunders, L., & Tebes, J. K. (2007). Re-referral to child protective services: The influence of child, family, and case characteristics on risk status. *Child Abuse & Neglect, 31*(5), 573–588. https://doi.org/10.1016/j.chiabu.2006.12.004

Cunningham, S., & Finlay, K. (2013). Parental substance use and foster care: Evidence from two methamphetamine supply shocks. *Economic Inquiry, 51*(1), 764–782.

Ghertner, R., Waters, A., Radel, L., & Crouse, G. (2018). The role of substance use in child welfare caseloads. *Children and Youth Services Review, 90*(C), 83–93.

Haight, S. C., Ko, J. Y., Tong, V. T., Bohm, M. K., & Callaghan, W. M. (2018). Opioid use disorder documented at delivery hospitalization—United States, 1999–2014. *MMWR. Morbidity and Mortality Weekly Report, 67*(31), 845–849. https://doi.org/10.15585/mmwr.mm6731a1

Huebner, R. A., Willauer, T., & Posze, L. (2012). The impact of Sobriety Treatment and Recovery Teams (START) on family outcomes. *Families in Society, 93*(3), 196–203. https://doi.org/10.1606/1044-3894.4223

Logan, B. A., Brown, M. S., & Hayes, M. J. (2013). Neonatal abstinence syndrome: Treatment and pediatric outcomes. *Clinical Obstetrics and Gynecology, 56*(1), 186–192. https://doi.org/10.1097/GRF.0b013e31827feea4

March of Dimes. *Neonatal abstinence syndrome (NAS).* (2019). https://www.marchofdimes.org/complications/neonatal-abstinence-syndrome-(nas).aspx

Massinga, R., & Pecora, P. J. (2004). Providing better opportunities for older children in the child welfare system. *The Future of Children, 14*(1), 151–175. https://doi.org/10.2307/1602759

National Conference of State Legislatures. (2020). *Child welfare.* https://www.ncsl.org/research/human-services/child-welfare.aspx

Winstanley, E. L., & Stover, A. N. (2019). The impact of the opioid epidemic on children and adolescents. *Clinical Therapeutics, 41*(9), 1655–1662. https://doi.org/10.1016/j.clinthera.2019.06.003

CHAPTER FIVE

Substance Use and Elder Abuse

Georgia J. Anetzberger, PhD, ACSW

Introduction

Elder abuse may be the most recent component of family violence to receive broad recognition and formal response. However, with the aging of the Baby Boomers and hence our overall population, it is likely to dominate family violence in societal prevalence and costs for years to come. In the context of elder abuse, substance abuse is seen as a major correlate, particularly as a characteristic of the **perpetrator** but sometimes of the **victim** as well.

This chapter explores elder abuse and its connections to substance abuse across several topics. The Introduction defines key terms. Scope of the Problem considers elder abuse prevalence and reporting. Historical Context examines the long history associating elder abuse with substance abuse, both with respect to self-**neglect** and elder mistreatment. Theoretical Perspectives identifies the major theoretical approaches to understanding elder abuse that link substance abuse as a problem correlate. The topic of Risk and Protective Factors considers research connecting substance abuse to elder abuse, mostly as a characteristic of the perpetrator but sometimes as a characteristic of the victim. Problem Effects looks at elder abuse signs (including screening tools to facilitate detection) as well as the consequences and costs of abuse, particularly for victims. The chapter ends with the exploration of Prevention and Intervention, focused on the latter (since the development of preventive measures remains in its infancy), including related major federal public policy and key service systems.

Many topics include a case study, which sometimes is woven into the text to illustrate or illuminate points and always is employed to emphasize the variation and dynamics of lived situations of elder abuse. All case studies are real in that they represent situations the author has encountered as a practitioner, administrator, or researcher doing elder abuse work. Names and other specifics were altered to preserve anonymity and for confidentiality. However, the essence of each situation remains, especially in attempting to describe the meaning of elder abuse for involved parties. In addition, the role of substance abuse is highlighted throughout. The unfortunate reality is that all too often substance abuse has a presence in elder abuse situations, across forms and demographics.

Vignette: Joe and Carmen

Joe and Carmen, age 84 and 78 respectively, both with multiple chronic conditions, brought their niece, Maria, from Europe to live with them in their suburban home and help with daily tasks. After two years Maria took a job, coming home drunk every pay day, often evoking tirades of angry cursing and name-calling at the couple if they made requests of her or criticized her behavior, finally beating up her uncle so badly that he was hospitalized. After this incident Joe sought a restraining order to remove Maria from the home. Later he removed the order and Maria returned, as did her anger and abuse.

Joe and Carmen are victims of elder abuse perpetrated by their niece Maria, who tends to inflict harm when drunk on alcohol. The vignette represents one of several ways in which elder abuse and substance abuse are related. Here the victims do not abuse alcohol, but the perpetrator does, although seemingly limited to binging on specific occasions. The relationship between victims and perpetrator is complicated. They are kin and co-residents, and Maria is **caregiver** for the older couple. Finally, the mistreatment represents polyvictimization or multiple forms, in this instance both **emotional abuse** and **physical abuse**.

Elder Abuse

To best understand the vignette, and others introduced later in this chapter, it is important to define key terms, beginning with **elder abuse**. Although there is no universally accepted definition of this concept, there is growing agreement about its essential features. Increasingly, elder abuse has come to serve as an umbrella term that always includes elder mistreatment and often includes self-neglect and fraud as well (Anetzberger, 2012).

The Centers for Disease Control and Prevention (2019) defines elder mistreatment as "an intentional act or failure to act, by a caregiver or another person in a relationship involving an expectation of trust that causes or creates a risk of harm to an older adult." This definition is similar to those offered by the National Research Council (2003) and World Health Organization (WHO; 2019). The National Center on Elder Abuse (NCEA; 2019a) indicates that elder mistreatment can assume six different forms: physical abuse, emotional abuse, **sexual abuse**, **exploitation**, neglect, and **abandonment**. Various other sources add, collapse, or rename forms. For example, WHO (2002) adds serious loss of dignity and respect; some state adult protective service (APS) laws collapse abandonment into neglect; and among the terms synonymous with emotional abuse are psychological abuse, verbal abuse, and mental anguish (Wallace & Crabb, 2017).

Self-neglect (which usually includes self-abuse) is characterized by NCEA (2019b) as "behavior of an elderly person that threatens his/her own health or safety." The National Adult Protective Services Association (NAPSA; 2019) defines self-neglect as when older adults "fail to meet their own essential physical, psychological, or social needs, which threatens their health, safety, and well-being." Unlike NAPSA, NCEA excludes self-neglect situations in which the older adult is mentally capable and voluntarily elects to engage in unsafe or unhealthy acts. However, by statutory provision, generally APS must accept reports of these situations, but is unable to intervene after investigation unless the older adult agrees. Various other sources add qualifications to these definitions, for instance, limiting self-neglect to persistent acts or repeated service refusals (Pavlou & Lachs, 2008). Finally, sometimes subtypes are identified for self-neglect (Burnett et al., 2014), with hoarding situations or the environmental subtype typically given special attention in the self-neglect literature and by the mass media, as evidenced through such newspaper headlines as "800 dogs seized at home in Arizona."

Fraud, as an aspect of elder abuse, has received increased attention in recent years, with the aging Baby Boomers and their considerable collective assets seen as vulnerable to unscrupulous persons seeking access to them through undue influence and illegal acts for profit and personal gain. Daily news underscores concern about fraud, illustrated by "Scam costs woman $6,000" and "Elderly relatives target of **scams**." Fraud is differentiated from financial exploitation by the perpetrator's relationship to the victim, with the former committed by strangers and the latter by persons in positions of trust. Still, research suggests that even in instances of fraud the perpetrator may use friendship and romance to manipulate and control victims (DeLiema, 2018). Fraud is often defined as "the deliberate intent to deceive with promises of goods, services, or other financial benefits that in fact do not exist or that were never intended to be provided" (Titus et al., 1995, p. 54). Associated scams can be wide ranging, from sweepstakes scams to grandparent scams (U.S. Senate Special Committee on Aging, 2018).

Older Adult

What is considered an "older adult" within the context of elder abuse (or substance abuse for that matter) can be as elusive as obtaining agreement on how to define elder abuse itself. Variation exists across research and public policy. For instance, the only nationally representative U.S. studies on elder abuse prevalence differ on age onset, with the earlier one using 57 (Laumann et al., 2008) and the later one using 60 (Acierno et al., 2010). However, typically the onset age employed in defining elder abuse is either 60 years (mirrored after the Older Americans Act, enacted in 1965 as the first federal initiative aimed at providing comprehensive services for older adults) or 65 years (mirrored after the Social Security Act, established in 1935, which provides old age insurance, with this the original eligibility age for full retirement benefits).

There are occasions when considered age onset is younger, usually either 50 or 55 years. Most commonly this occurs in reference to "domestic violence in later life," recognized as a subtype of domestic violence (or intimate partner violence) by the Wisconsin Coalition Against Domestic Violence beginning in the 1990s. Its subsidy, the National Clearinghouse on Abuse in Later Life (NCALL), defines domestic violence in later life as "the willful abuse, neglect, abandonment, or financial exploitation of an older adult who is age 50+ by someone in an ongoing, trust-based relationship (i.e., spouse, partner, family member, or caregiver)" (NCALL, 2019).

Although most state APS or elder abuse reporting laws make **vulnerability**, such as disability or impairment, the determinative for program eligibility, in a handful of states age (alone or in combination with vulnerability) determines eligibility. For example, Ohio's APS law identifies age onset as 60 years and then adds that the older adult must be someone who is either "handicapped by the infirmities of aging or who has a physical or mental impairment which prevents the person from providing for the person's own care or protection" (Ohio Revised Code 5101.60(B)).

Substance Abuse

Healthy People 2020 names substance abuse as a major public health concern, defining it as "a set of related conditions associated with the consumption of mind- and behavior-altering substances that have negative behavioral and health outcomes (U.S. Office of Disease Prevention and Health Promotion, 2019). In the fifth edition of the *Diagnostic and Statistical Manual of Mental Disorders* (American Psychiatric Association, 2013) the term "substance abuse" is replaced by "substance use disorder," meaning "a medical condition wherein one or more substances result in clinically significant impairment or distress." The *Manual* also recognizes ten separate classes of substances or drugs.

The Substance Abuse and Mental Health Services Administration (SAMHSA; 2019) identifies the following as the most common substance use disorders in the United States: alcohol, tobacco, cannabis, stimulant, hallucinogen, and opioid. According to the National Survey on Drug Use and Health (SAMHSA, 2017), during 2016, 20.1 million Americans age 12 or over had a substance use disorder, 15.1 million due to alcohol misuse and 7.4 million due to illicit drugs. Among the latter group, marijuana and prescription pain relievers were most frequently misused. Opioid misuse affected nearly 12 million persons that year.

Kuerbis et al. (2014) identify four categories of substance abuse found among older adults: alcohol, tobacco, illicit drugs, and prescribed and over-the-counter medications. Cohen and Eisdorfer (2017) consider alcohol and medication misuse and abuse of greatest concern because of their relatively high prevalence and potentially serious consequences for older adults, citing an abuse range of 2%–20% for alcohol and 50%–75% for vulnerability to dangerous drug-drug interactions. In contrast, less than 2% of older adults are reported as recent users of illicit drugs, with marijuana most common.

Scope of the Problem

Vignette: Margaret

Margaret, age 65, is watching the door, waiting for her daughter to come. She needs help and believes that Susan will provide it, if only she would show up, which she never does. Susan died years ago, but Margaret, brain damaged from decades of alcohol abuse, does not remember. Margaret is alone, ill, and incontinent, living in squalor and waste in a small, cramped trailer, located on the edge of this rural, sparsely populated county.

Prevalence and Incidence

Elder abuse is not a rare occurrence, whether it represents elder mistreatment, like Joe and Carmen's situation, self-neglect like Margaret's, or even fraud, as seen in the daily media feed. Among older adults, elder abuse is as common as Alzheimer's disease or injuries from falls that result in emergency department visits. However, it receives far less attention from policy makers, particularly those at the federal level, or support from funders, including those that might finance research, public awareness activities, or problem interventions. According to the U.S. Government Accountability Office (2011), methods to understand and respond to elder abuse are fragmented and under-resourced. Elder abuse fares especially poorly in comparison to intimate partner violence and child abuse. It is estimated that federal spending on elder abuse is 54 times less than that on violence against women and 588 times less than that on child abuse (Dong, 2017), aspects of family violence of similar or lesser scope.

The prevalence of elder mistreatment varies among nations worldwide. A systematic review and meta-analysis of the related literature suggests a pooled global frequency of 15.7%, with the problem more common in Asia and Europe than in the Americas (Yon et al., 2019). Recent U.S. large-scale studies provide elder mistreatment rates from 7.6% to 11% for community-dwellers (Laumann et al., 2008; Acierno et al., 2010; Lachs & Berman, 2011). The most common forms of elder mistreatment vary somewhat by nation and study. However, generally, both globally and in the United States, emotional abuse and financial exploitation are more common than neglect, physical abuse, or sexual abuse.

Less is known about the scope of self-neglect, largely due to fewer studies and a lack of uniformity in definitions and methods. From available research, the collective assessment suggests that self-neglect incidence is low, between 0.5 and 7 older adults per 1,000 annually (Dyer & Reyes-Ortiz, 2017).

In contrast to self-neglect, the perceived prevalence of elder fraud is high and growing (Ritter, 2017). For example, the AARP National Fraud Victim Study concluded that, although adults aged 60 and older represent just 15% of the U.S. population, they account for 30% of investment fraud victims (Pak & Shadel, 2011). In addition, the Federal Trade Commission's national study on prevalence of elder fraud found that 7.3% of adults aged 65 to 74, and 6.5% of those aged 75 and older, report past-year fraud (Anderson, 2012). Moreover, looking specifically at traditional retirement states, a large-scale study of older adults in Florida and Arizona discovered that nearly 6 in 10 respondents had experienced attempted fraud during the past year, with about 14% actually victimized (Holtfreter et al., 2014). Finally, a recent systematic review and meta-analysis of elder fraud and scams in the United States resulted in a pooled one-year prevalence rate of 5.4%, suggesting that about 1 in 18 cognitively intact, **community-dwelling** older adults are victims of fraud and scams each year (Burnes et al., 2017).

Reporting

Self-neglect, like Margaret's, may be the most frequently reported aspect of elder abuse to APS nationwide (Aurelien et al., 2018a), but far fewer situations get referred for investigation than actually occur. More discouraging, given its prevalence, is how little elder mistreatment, like Joe's and Carmen's, receives attention by authorities across service systems charged with investigation and intervention. However, perhaps most alarming, situations of financial exploitation and fraud rarely get referred to those who might assist. Studies and reports that reflect this hidden nature of elder abuse follow. After more than 40 years, elder abuse still struggles to gain public attention and national agenda prominence and remains decades behind child abuse and intimate partner violence in empirical study and knowledge-building (NCEA, 2019c).

Various service systems are required to receive and respond to reports of elder abuse involving older adults living in the community. Among the most important are APS and law enforcement. Yet, research spanning more than three decades attests to how little reporting actually happens.

An early elder mistreatment investigation conducted in the metropolitan Boston area concluded that only 1 in 14 situations comes to public attention, despite mandatory reporting laws (Pillemer & Finkelhor, 1988). A decade later, the first National Elder Abuse Incidence Study found that for every reported incident of elder abuse, five go unreported (NCEA & Westat, Inc., 1998). More recently, the New York State Elder Abuse Prevalence Study discovered that among all forms of elder mistreatment only 1 in 24 incidents were reported, just 1 in 44 specifically for financial exploitation, and for neglect only 1 in 57 (Lachs & Berman, 2011).

Over the years many reasons have been given for elder abuse non-reporting by professionals. They include questions about confidentiality, uncertainty about whether or when to report, lack of knowledge about the problem or systems that can help, deficient use of screening tools, lack of confidence in the agency charged with handling the report, fear of being sued, or unwillingness to become legally involved (Almogue et al., 2010; Hess, 2011; Miller, 2017). Likewise, there exist many barriers to elder abuse reporting by victims. Among them are unawareness that they are being exploited, a sense of self-reliance for problem-solving without outside help, social isolation, fear that the elder abuse may get worse after reporting or result in their institutional placement, desire to protect family members from trouble by the police, and language and cultural barriers (Daly et al., 2012; Jackson & Hafemeister, 2014; Ziminski Pickering & Rempusheski, 2014).

Principal reporting sources to APS have shown some variation over time. In 2017 reports that resulted in investigations were most likely to come from helping professionals (44.9%), especially those in social services and health care. The next most common reporters were family members (11.5%) and law enforcement, legal, or judicial professionals (7%). Just 6.1% represented self-reports (Aurelien et al., 2018b). This represents a change from a survey of APS reporting compiled more than a decade before (National Committee for the Prevention of Elder Abuse & National Adult Protective Services Association, 2005). At that time, reporters were less likely to be members of the helping professions (16.7%) and more likely to be family members (17%). The percentages of reporters from the law enforcement, legal, and judicial professions and from the victim themselves varied little between 2004 and 2017.

Like other aspects of elder abuse, fraud is underreported, as the following sample of studies reveals. Research on attempted investor fraud showed that only 17% of potential victims reported the attempt to authorities (Innovative Research Group, 2007). Indeed, the previously cited AARP National Fraud Victim Study found that older fraud victims were significantly less likely to report the occurrence to authorities than younger adult victims (Pak & Shadel, 2011). However, other research suggests that older adults are more willing to report fraud when it is seen as a consumer issue than when it is viewed as a crime (Beals et al., 2017). Still, sometimes fraud reporting may need to rely on persons other than the victims. A recent study commissioned by Allianz Life Insurance Company of North America revealed that one fourth of caregivers of older adults who had experienced fraud either had discovered the problem themselves or from someone other than the fraud victim (Beckman, 2016).

Historical Context

The perceived association between elder abuse and substance abuse has a long history. It began more than a half century ago and shows variation between self-neglect and elder mistreatment. That said, widespread professional and public recognition of elder abuse as a social problem, public health concern, and crime, affecting significant numbers of older adults, worthy of empirical investigation and the attention of policy makers, is more recent, perhaps only in the last two or three decades. This section will examine the beginnings of elder abuse recognition and, with it, substance abuse as a potential correlate. More recent recognition, research, and interventions will be addressed in later sections.

Self-Neglect

The first aspect of elder abuse to be acknowledged as a social concern was self-neglect (and fraud, to the extent that it may occur in the wake of self-neglect). Beginning in the 1950s, discussions were held in large urban communities, like Chicago and Cleveland, about the growing numbers of older adults, often mentally incapacitated, who were residing alone outside of institutions without nearby family support. Local leaders across professional disciplines believed that such persons could neglect themselves (or be subjected to exploitation) without appropriate intervention (Cole, 1962). Protective care (eventually called APS) evolved from this concern, developed through demonstration projects beginning in the late 1960s and expanded nationwide during the mid-1970s from impetus and funding out of Title XX of the Social Security Act (Burr, 1982).

Early studies of self-neglect (called by various names, including Diogenes syndrome and senile or social breakdown syndrome) often came from physicians. MacMillan and Shaw (1966) were among the earliest to note an association between self-neglect and substance abuse. After examining 72 self-neglectors, they concluded that "isolation, a certain type of personality, bereavement, and alcoholism were found to be important [explanatory] factors" (p. 1037). Later reports echo this discovery. For example, Snowdon (1987) surveyed community health centers, identifying 83 subjects living in unclean conditions, with 40% who were or had been heavy drinkers. Still other researchers found self-neglectors more likely to abuse substances than either the general population or victims of elder mistreatment. For instance, Longres (1995) combined quantitative data from the Wisconsin Elder Abuse Reporting System with in-depth interviews using a purposive sample of elder abuse investigators and found that alcohol or drug abuse was three times more common among older adult self-neglecters than victims of elder mistreatment.

Elder Mistreatment

In contrast to self-neglect, the earliest acknowledgements of elder mistreatment took the form of brief mentions in publications by scholars noting overlooked kinds of victimization. The first, by Butler (1975, p. 156), describes two situations that he labels a "battered old person syndrome," wherein older adults are beaten by an adult child. Substance abuse is not identified as characteristic of the victim or perpetrator in either situation. The second acknowledgement, two years later, embeds the "battered elderly parent" within a larger context of the cycle of violence within families. Here three cases are described, one specifically identifying the abusing son as alcoholic (Steinmetz, 1977, pp. xxi–xxii). It is from these earliest acknowledgements that recognition of elder mistreatment grew as an issue for older adults, and, with it, attention to substance abuse as a key risk factor for its occurrence.

The earliest actual studies of elder mistreatment were presented at gerontology conferences held in 1978. Rathbone-McCuan (1978) discussed eleven such cases at the International Congress of Gerontology, eight illustrating abuse and three illustrating neglect. Among the abuse cases, half identify the family member who inflicts harm as doing so when drinking. Lau and Kosberg (1978) presented their research at the Annual Scientific Meeting of the Gerontological Society of America. Using one year's case records ($N = 404$) from an agency serving older adults and chronically ill clients living in the community, 9.6% of older adult clients were found to have been abused, usually physically (74%) or psychologically (51%). The investigations divided the perpetrators into normal and non-normal caregivers, identifying mental, developmental, or substance abuse disorders as characteristic of the latter group.

From these beginnings, interest grew among elder mistreatment researchers in substance abuse as a topic worth investigating, with particular interest in alcohol abuse. Early research on perpetrators found those with alcohol or drug problems less able to cope with stress and more tolerant of abuse infliction (Pillemer, 1985; Anetzberger, 1987). Surveys of senior service providers found alcoholism listed among the primary perceived correlates to elder abuse occurrence (Douglass et al., 1980; O'Malley et al., 1979). Finally, early elder abuse comparison group studies bolstered thinking that alcohol abuse by perpetrators helped explain the occurrence of elder mistreatment. For instance, Wolf et al. (1986) found that among a sample of 59 abused and 49 non-abused older adults, one third of the abusive and none of the non-abusive caregivers had a drinking problem. Greenberg et al. (1990) similarly discovered that among 204 substantiated elder abuse cases with an adult child as the perpetrator, 44% of the sons and 14% of the daughters had alcohol or drug problems. Lastly, Anetzberger et al. (1994) compared 23 adult children who inflicted physical abuse on their elder parents with 39 adult children who cared for their elder parents but had no history of abusing them. The investigators found that the abusing offspring were more likely to drink alcohol frequently and heavily and to have been identified as having a drinking problem.

Theoretical Perspectives

Only a year after presenting exploratory research on elder abuse, one of its investigators, Kosberg (1979), delivered a paper on theoretical issues, underscoring the importance of theory in any follow-up study and identifying family violence approaches as starting points for considered use. The intervening 40-plus years have seen little progress in elder abuse theory development and testing, and rare movement outside of established family violence theory. Rebukes of the field for being atheoretical are many, among organizations ranging from the National Research Council (2003) to the National Institute of Justice (2014), and among individual commentators ranging from Kapp (1995) to Jackson (2018).

Some "truths" exist in describing the current status of elder abuse theory. First, there is no universally accepted theoretical approach, and it is unlikely that any single one will suffice for this problem of broad definition and great complexity, with many forms and multiple contexts. Second, many theoretical approaches have been proposed, but most were borrowed from the literature of other abused populations, where the dynamics may differ. Third, the popularity of various approaches has waxed and waned over time, but generally interpersonal ones have seemed to dominate (Burnight & Mosqueda, 2011) and ecological ones appear to be gaining momentum (Roberto & Teaster, 2017). Fourth, no theoretical approach to elder abuse has been rigorously tested, although select theories have received some support through empirical investigation (Jackson & Hafemeister, 2013).

Among the many theoretical approaches applied to elder abuse, the following may have application in understanding those situations in which either the perpetrator (elder mistreatment) or victim (primarily self-neglect) has substance abuse as a problem:

- Psychopathology theory: Problems in psychosocial functioning, like substance abuse, can promote or provoke elder abuse.
- Vulnerability theory: Impairment and incapacity, which may result from substance abuse, can render an older adult at risk of self-neglect or abuse by others.
- Structural theory: Circumstances, such as excessive stress upon a caregiver who then uses substances to cope or escape, can contribute to an older adult's vulnerability to abuse.
- General adaptation theory: Elder abuse can result from traits of the perpetrator and victim (including substance abuse), characteristics of the physical and social environments, and transactions between them.

Risk and Protective Factors

Because problem causes are unknown, the field of elder abuse turns to risk factors for guidance in problem detection, assessment, and prevention

(Anetzberger, 2013). Risk factors are commonly accepted conditions that have been found through research to be closely linked to elder abuse occurrence. Their usefulness in detection is to alert those in contact with older adults that prevailing circumstances may contribute to elder abuse and, therefore, to be on the lookout for examples or signs of the problem. For assessment, risk factors become areas of inquiry and examination in order to know what interventions may be needed. Perhaps most important, however, is the role of risk factors in problem prevention, where they offer a framework in determining strategies for impeding the likelihood of elder abuse occurrence or reoccurrence.

Anetzberger (2000) offers an explanatory model for elder abuse. In it the problem is seen primarily as a function of perpetrator characteristics, and secondarily, victim characteristics. Context is important as well, both that which brings perpetrator and victim together (such as caregiving or cohabitation of adult offspring and their older adult parents) and that which triggers elder abuse occurrence (such as criticisms from the older adult or that person's combative behavior as a result of dementia). Within the model, substance abuse is a potential consideration throughout. It can be a perpetrator characteristic, decreasing that person's ability to function effectively, injuring personal relations and jeopardizing employment or caregiving, perhaps resulting in financial or other dependence. It can be a victim characteristic, creating vulnerabilities that can affect health and undermine living conditions, reduce capacity to assess danger, or foster provocative behavior. Substance abuse also can affect context, as when it becomes the reason an adult son is now unemployed and needing to reside with his elderly mother and when, as seen in the case study with Maria, someone loses their inhibitions and becomes physically abusive following binge drinking.

As noted earlier in this chapter, there is a long-recognized association between elder abuse and substance abuse, with the bulk of it surrounding substance abuse as a risk factor for the perpetrator of elder mistreatment and for victims of self-neglect. The paragraphs which follow highlight research illustrative of these associations. However, in reading them, it is important to keep in mind that evidence on elder abuse risk factors is "still not very well established" (Chen & Dong, 2017, p. 93), "wide ranging" (Moyer, 2013, p. 48), and relatively weak on "risk factors of victims and perpetrators that includes contextual factors (e.g., … substance abuse)" (Stahl, 2015, p. 3).

Despite these research limitations, perpetrator substance abuse has emerged as the dominant predictor of elder mistreatment, empirically overshadowing such other studied perpetrator characteristics as physical and mental health problems, housing and financial dependency, and stress and burden from caregiving. It is consistently recognized in literature reviews on elder abuse risk factors (e.g., Erlingsson et al., 2003; Roberto, 2016), which reflects the sizable body of research linking perpetrator substance abuse and elder mistreatment (e.g., Amstadter et al., 2010; Brownell et al., 1999; Labrum & Solomon, 2018; O'Keeffe et al., 2007; Perez-Carceles et al., 2009; Rennison & Rand, 2003). Research by Conrad et al. (2016) well illustrates the strong correlation between perpetrator substance abuse and elder mistreatment. Using data from 948 cases, with 323 alleged perpetrators, they found 26.9% of them to have substance abuse problems. Substance abuse was associated with financial exploitation, physical abuse, and emotional abuse, but not with neglect. Further, substance-abusing perpetrators tended to be male, commit multiple abuse forms, and not provide care to their older adult victims. From her review of such studies, Jackson (2016) estimates that between 20% and 50% of elder mistreatment perpetrators are substance abusers. Moreover, she notes that substance abuse has been shown to be a perpetrator risk factor across elder mistreatment forms (Jackson, 2018).

Although considerably less than for perpetrators, the elder abuse literature suggests a correlation between victim substance abuse and elder mistreatment (Erlingsson et al., 2003; Johannesen, & LoGiudice, 2013). For instance, Friedman et al. (2011) undertook a case-control study on severe physical abuse, discovering that abuse victims were more likely than controls to report substance abuse. Additionally, in comparing alcohol use in a large sample of elder mistreatment victims and non-victims from seven European cities, Tredal et al. (2013) found that psychologically abused victims were more likely to use alcohol. The same did not apply to physical or sexual abuse victims, however, contrary to Friedman et al.'s results above.

Still, the elder abuse literature associates older adult substance abuse more with self-neglect than elder mistreatment. Substance abuse, particularly alcoholism, is listed among the key risk factors for self-neglect (e.g., Day & Leahy-Warren, 2008; O'Brien et al., 1999; Snowden et al., 2007). Indeed, several studies have uncovered a link between older adult self-neglect and substance abuse (e.g., Dong et al., 2010; Dyer et al., 2007; Payne & Gainey, 2005). In explaining the connection, Blondell (1999) discusses how substance abuse can result in neglect of basic safety and psychosocial needs. In addition, Ramsey-Klawsnik (2006) explains the ill-effect of substance abuse on judgment and decision-making, management of home and finances, and ability to fulfill personal and social responsibilities, all of which can lead to a situation of self-neglect. (See Table 5.1 for examples from research of elder abuse, substance abuse, and intersectionalities.)

TABLE 5.1 Elder Abuse, Substance Abuse, and Intersectionality: Examples from Research

- Findings from the National Elder Mistreatment Study indicated that emotional abuse committed by persons with substance abuse and/or mental health conditions tends to be associated with victims of the female gender (Labrum & Solomon, 2018).
- Internationally, female gender is an important risk factor for alcohol-related elder abuse, especially in certain regions, like Africa (World Health Organization, 2006).
- In a case control study of severe physical elder abuse, compared with non-abused cases, abused victims tended to be female and to have a neurological disorder and/or to abuse drugs or alcohol (Friedman et al., 2011).
- Conrad et al. (2016), studying the role of substance abuse in elder mistreatment, found that alleged perpetrators with substance abuse problems who committed multiple forms of abuse were more likely to be of the male gender.
- Labrum (2017) discovered an association between elder abuse perpetrators with behavioral health problems, including substance abuse, and co-residence with the victim.
- In a national examination of the association of state-reported domestic elder abuse with regional levels of substance abuse, Jogerst et al. (2011) found that high investigation rates were correlated with lower median household income, lower proportion of high school graduation, and higher population of Hispanics.

Vignette: Paul and Dave

Paul, aged 72 years and widowed, lives in a downtown condominium that he owns. When he suffers a stroke and needs care, he asks his only child, Dave, to move in. Dave, with a long history of schizophrenia and drug abuse, has had difficulty keeping jobs. Because he needs housing and financial support, he accepts his father's offer. The long-term conflict between father and son quickly returns, with Paul finding Dave ineffective and Dave finding Paul controlling. Dave proves incapable of providing care to the man he credits with causing his problems, saying, "He enjoyed the agony of his son being mentally weak." Although the yelling and beatings began months before, the authorities were called in when Dave took Paul and "bounced him up and down the stairs."

Problem Effects

Signs

The effects of elder abuse can be described across three dimensions: signs, consequences, and costs. Our knowledge about them decreases as we descend the list. Filling the gaps received recognition in the Elder Justice Roadmap, a strategic plan developed "by the field, for the field" of elder abuse, with 122 recommendations across the four domains of research, policy, education, and direct services (Connolly et al., 2014, p. 2).

The Roadmap was funded by the U.S. Department of Justice, with support from the U.S. Department of Health and Human Services. A two-year undertaking, it involved 750 subject matter experts and stakeholders from around the country and included in its methodology concept mapping of identified priorities, facilitated discussions on key topics, and interviews with influential leaders on ways to promote an agenda on elder justice. In the aftermath of Roadmap development, a steering committee was formed to further its dissemination as well as to encourage and track recommendation implementation.

Among the Roadmap's 122 recommendations, only two address elder abuse effects. First-wave priority is given to measuring the economic costs of the problem, and high priority is given to identifying forensic markers for detection purposes. Besides these, the Roadmap makes scant mention of existing gaps in understanding elder abuse effects, and no real emphasis on addressing them. Actually, there has been considerable interest and sometimes much activity around each effect dimension, but none has achieved an acceptable standard. This means that Paul's situation may go undetected due to lack of knowledge about elder abuse signs or availability of screening tools consistently able to detect the problem. It also means that the consequences of elder abuse infliction and costs to society remain incompletely understood, with advocacy to effect related policy change challenging at best.

Signs also are called symptoms, indicators, and markers. They are the result of elder abuse occurrence, manifestations of its infliction. For example, signs of physical abuse might involve bruises or broken bones, and signs of neglect might be dehydration and physical weakness. However, there can be ambiguity about the origin of particular signs, since those just identified for physical abuse could result from a simple fall, and those given for neglect from acute illness (Anetzberger, 2001).

Research on forensic markers is limited. Studies differentiating accidental bruising from bruising caused by elder abuse represent a welcome exception (Mosqueda et al., 2005; Wiglesworth et al., 2009). Daly (2017) lists possible signs (which she calls defining characteristics) by elder mistreatment form.

Signs listed have emerged from research. They then can be organized onto screening tools (often along with examples and risk factors) to assist in elder abuse detection. For example, defining characteristics for emotional abuse range from agitation and alcohol abuse to suicidal ideation and being withdrawn. Among the screening tools Daly identifies to enable emotional abuse detection is the Psychological Elder Abuse Scale (Wang et al., 2007), with 32 possible indicators.

Daly includes 18 screening tools to illustrate those available for detecting elder abuse. Among them, just one third include items on substance abuse. More of these target the perpetrator (e.g., Does anyone in your family drink a lot?) than the victim (e.g., has alcohol/medication problem), but occasionally the same item targets both perpetrator and victim (e.g., Are there problems with use of alcohol or drugs or medications?).

There are a large number and variety of elder abuse screening tools, and notable momentum to evaluate their effectiveness. Existing tools are wide-ranging in type (checklists to guidelines), length (a handful of items to dozens of them), comprehensiveness (single elder mistreatment form to multiple forms), applicable setting (community service to health care), and other features. Their importance rests with fostering elder abuse recognition, which then can enable situation referral to agencies that can offer intervention. In addition, screening tools can serve to heighten problem awareness and insure a systematic process of observation and documentation.

Many elder abuse screening tools have been tested. They include the Elder Assessment Instrument (Fulmer & O'Malley, 1987), Hwalek-Sengstock Elder Abuse Screening Test (Neale et al., 1991), Vulnerability to Abuse Screening Scale (Schofield et al., 2002), Elder Abuse Suspicion Index (Yaffe et al., 2008), Self-Neglect Severity Scale (Kelly et al., 2008), and Older Adult Financial Exploitation Measure (Conrad et al., 2010). Despite this progress, recently the U.S. Preventive Services Task Force (2018) failed again to recommend universal screening for elder abuse, stating that "current evidence is insufficient to assess the balance of benefits and harms of screening" (p. 3). Still, the American Medical Association and a few other health care professional organizations recommend screening for all geriatric patients. After conducting a systematic review of research on elder abuse screening tools published between 1995 and 2015, identifying 33 in the process, Schofield (2017) concluded that future study should result in a brief general measure for widespread use, more robust evaluation of developed instruments, and determination of the overall effectiveness of elder abuse screening. Clearly, these are worthy aims for the next phase of tool development and testing.

Consequences

The consequences of elder abuse specific to situations involving substance abuse are unknown. In part this reflects insufficient research on elder abuse consequences overall. However, it also evidences a lack of interest, and perhaps empirical challenge, to date in exploring the effects of any individual risk factor.

For the purposes of this chapter, consequences represent the harmful outcomes of elder abuse on victims. The literature does not address its impact on perpetrators, whether in terms of emotional distress, criminal sanction, or anything else. However, after reviewing research about elder abuse consequences on victims, Podnieks and Thomas (2017) were able to classify them into studies showing higher mortality, severe physical or emotional suffering (e.g., malnutrition, dehydration, depression, anxiety), and more hospitalization and institutionalization.

With respect to higher mortality, several largescale prospective studies reveal elder mistreatment and self-neglect victims die sooner than non-victims. For example, an early investigation into the mortality of elder abuse conducted by Lachs et al. (1998) compared 2,812 community-dwelling older adults with a subset seen by APS, following them for 9 years. The researchers learned that victims of elder mistreatment were three times and victims of self-neglect nearly two times more likely than non-victims to die within that period. More recently, Dong et al. (2009) looked at the mortality rates for older adults in the Chicago Aging Project over a 7-year period. They discovered that those reported to social service agencies for self-neglect were nearly six times more likely than non-self-neglecters to die within one year. For elder mistreatment, they found that those with confirmed abuse were two times and those with suspected abuse nearly 1.5 times more likely than non-abused older adults to die during that period.

Several studies suggest the toll that elder mistreatment has on victim health and well-being. Collectively they reveal that victims suffer poor emotional health (e.g., more likely evidence of post-traumatic stress disorder or irritability) and poorer physical health (e.g., chronic pain, heart problems). For instance, using a cross-sectional design, Begle et al. (2011) examined the relationship between elder mistreatment and negative emotional symptoms among 902 older adults, discovering emotional, but not physical, abuse significantly correlated with higher levels of emotional symptoms. Additionally, using data from the National Elder Mistreatment Study, Cisler et al. (2012) found that each form of abuse increased the likelihood of self-reported emotional symptoms.

Finally, elder abuse can result in greater victim use of health services and residential care. In various such studies, Dong et al. (e.g., Dong & Simon, 2013a, 2013b), using the Chicago Aging Project sample of community-dwelling older adults, found elder abuse victims more likely to use the emergency department, be hospitalized, and receive a hospice referral than were non–elder abuse victims.

Costs

As mentioned earlier in this section, less research has examined costs than the other dimensions of elder abuse effects. Therefore, it is little wonder that this dimension received first-wave priority in the Elder Justice Roadmap.

Most of what is known about costs relates to victim losses from financial exploitation and fraud. There are two exceptions worth noting. Franzini and Dyer (2008) compared 131 cases of elder self-neglect with 131 controls, discovering that the self-neglecters had lower health care costs prior to hospitalization and equivalent during hospitalization in spite of dementia diagnosis. Teaster (2011) examined three cases representing different kinds of elder abuse, calculating all costs associated with interventions. The predominately physical abuse case (with neglect substantiated as well) incurred $120,213.40 in medical care costs, including $44,643.40 for a nursing home stay. The self-neglect case received $1,485 in social services. Finally, the predominantly financial exploitation case (with physical abuse and neglect substantiated, too) cost $81,304 in legal and related services (like psychological consultation), adjusted to $281,304 when financial losses to the victim were included.

The research on financial exploitation and fraud suggests that the losses can be staggering to elder abuse victims. Three types of studies are illustrative. The first type attempts to calculate losses for a single state, extrapolating from available case data. More specifically, Gunther (2010) estimated that in 2010 Utah older residents lost $339 million or an average of $85,253 per victim, with 57% stolen by family members. Griffin et al. (2017) estimated that Maine older adult residents lost between $174.7 million and $451.5 million between 2010 and 2016.

The second type of study looks at limited client groups to determine losses. Jackson and Hafemeister (2010) interviewed 71 APS caseworkers in Virginia and either the financially exploited older adult client or another person that the client knew well, but not the perpetrator. Study findings indicate that the losses from financial exploitation totaled $4.6 million, averaging $87,967 per client, with 86% unable to recover any lost funds or assets. DeLiema (2015) examined 62 cases of financial exploitation or fraud seen by the Los Angeles County Elder Abuse Forensic Center, uncovering victim losses totaling $19 million and 15 properties.

Lastly, the most publicized studies came up with national estimates. The earlier and better known is the MetLife Mature Market Institute (2011) Study of Elder Financial Abuse. Using a mixed methods approach that focused on literature review and articles gathered from the NCEA Newsfeed, it estimated that $2.9 billion was lost in 2010 from financial exploitation experienced by over one million older adult victims. Surveying family caregivers of older adults, True Link Financial (2015) estimated that older Americans lose $36.48 billion annually to financial abuse, specifically $16.99 billion to business or charity pressure tactics, $12.76 billion to criminal activity, and $6.67 billion to deceit or theft by trusted others, such as family members or paid helpers. (See Table 5.2 for highlights of data presented under the topics of scope of the problem and problem effects.)

TABLE 5.2 Data Highlights

- Prevalence range for past-year elder mistreatment in the United States: 7.6%–11% (Acierno et al., 2010; Lachs & Berman, 2011; Laumann et al., 2008).

- Annual incident range of self-neglect among older Americans: 0.5–7 per 1,000 older adults (Dyer & Reyes-Ortiz, 2017).

- Prevalence of past-year elder fraud and scams in the United States: 5.4% (Burnes et al., 2017).

- Rate range of elder abuse reporting to authorities: 4%–20% (Lachs & Berman, 2011; National Center on Elder Abuse & Westat, Inc., 1998).

- Prevalence range for substance abuse among older Americans: 2%–20% alcohol, 50%–75% potentially dangerous drug-drug interactions, <2% illicit drugs (Cohen & Eisdorfer, 2011).

- Percentage range of elder abuse perpetrators with substance abuse as a characteristic: 20%–50% (Jackson, 2016).

- Mortality of elder abuse: compared to non-victims, victims of elder mistreatment 2–3 times and victims of self-neglect 2–3 times more likely to die sooner (Lachs et al., 1998; Dong et al., 2009).

- Annual loss range due to elder financial exploitation in the United States: $2.9 billion–$36.48 billion (MetLife Mature Market Institute, 2011; True Link Financial, 2015).

Prevention and Intervention

Mabel, age 80, lives alone in a small house located near Appalachian foothills, with family close by to help as needed. Although she has some health problems, none are so severe that she cannot pretty much manage on her own. Mabel's only concerns are her two grandsons, who show up periodically and unexpectedly, taking cash from her purse and household items to sell in order to support the opioid addiction that dominates their lives. Mabel is reluctant to call the police or even shut off contact with her grandsons. She says, "After all, we're family, and family has to stay together. It's all any of us has." In addition, what happened to her neighbor, Sarah, serves as a kind of warning to Mabel. Sarah was murdered when she called the police on her nephew and his girlfriend for similar thefts. "That could happen to me, too," laments Mabel to herself.

Public Policy

Mabel represents one of the latest trends in elder abuse victimization—financial exploitation (often combined with other forms of elder mistreatment) by a family member or neighbor dependent on opioids or other drugs and seeking to support the addiction through stolen money or medications. This trend has been little studied, but represents growing numbers of reports to APS and law enforcement in states like West Virginia and Ohio, ravished by the crisis (Lusheck et al., 2018).

Responding to Mabel's situation, or those of other elder abuse victims, requires multiple service professionals and agencies working together, because the problems revealed are simply too complex and challenging for any single discipline or system. This section introduces the key public policies and service systems that respond to elder abuse. Although some specialized initiatives exist, to date none have been developed to address the dual concerns of elder abuse and substance abuse, although that is greatly needed, as evident from the chapter's previous sections. Even discussions on clinical strategies for treating substance abusing self-neglecters generally replicate strategies found in the separate literatures on older adult substance abuse and self-neglect, offering little unique to treating the problems when they present together (Blondell, 1999; Dyer, 1992).

Perhaps most beneficial for Mabel and others are multidisciplinary (M) teams, long seen as critical in elder abuse work nationwide. These, too, will be described, including their application in situations like Mabel's, where both elder abuse and substance abuse are evident. Beforehand, however, it is important to note that one of the ways the field of elder abuse lags behind the other major aspects of family violence is in determination of what works and what does not work for responding to the problem (Connolly et al., 2014; National Research Council, 2003). Until recently, little priority was placed on the evaluation of elder abuse prevention and intervention strategies, especially service system approaches. Moreover, when assessed, strategies and approaches typically were found to have inconsistent or inconclusive effectiveness, and occasionally were even deemed detrimental to those targeted (Ernst et al., 2014; Moore & Browne, 2016; Ploeg et al., 2009). Efforts are underway to fill this research gap, but it will require considerable time, effort, and support before this is accomplished. In the meanwhile, what can be and is presented in this section more reflects existing or established practice than best or evidence-based practice.

There are three federal public policies of primary importance to the field of elder abuse. They are the Older Americans Act (OAA), Title XX of the Social Security Act, and Elder Justice Act (EJA). Each law will be discussed in the paragraphs which follow, with an emphasis on their history, purpose, and elder abuse response provisions.

In 1965 the OAA was signed into law as the first federal initiative aimed at providing services for older adults. It emerged during the Great Society and reflected political commitments of those attending the first White House Conference on Aging in 1961 to expand community services for this population. The OAA also was the earliest federal law to explicitly reference elder abuse, doing so through amendments in 1987, where the problem was divided into domestic abuse and institutional abuse, and various forms were named. These and subsequent amendments have infused concern about elder abuse throughout the OAA and most of its titles. The following provisions illustrate this:

- State units on aging are required to assess the need for elder abuse prevention services locally and then develop plans for addressing the needs.
- The NCEA is established to provide information, training, and technical assistance as well as to support research and demonstration projects on the problem and responding to it.
- Title VII in particular targets elder abuse through such provisions as requiring state legal assistance development and Long-Term Care Ombudsman (LTCO) protection of resident rights in facilities, including handling complaints of abuse or neglect.

- Assistance is given to states to improve APS, recently including creation of Voluntary Consensus Guidelines for State APS systems, design of the National Adult Maltreatment Reporting System, and funding of a National APS Resource Center.

Title XX of the Social Security Act became law in 1974, representing the first federal commitment to fund various social services targeting low-income persons. In 1981, during an era marked by federalism, the law was consolidated along with other small funding streams into the Social Services Block Grant. Among its five goals is one that promotes prevention or remedying neglect, abuse, or exploitation of adults unable to protect their own interests. Title XX funding enabled the development and spread of APS nationwide. After block granting, states had more discretion on services offered. Although most continued to use this source to support APS, federal funding levels declined over time, and often faced threatened elimination.

State and local resources have helped fill the gap. Still, most APS programs are under-funded, the situation further aggravated by steady increases in elder abuse reporting and greater complexity of issues evident in cases investigated and served (Quinn & Benson, 2012).

The EJA became federal law in 2010, as an amendment to the Patient Protection and Affordable Care Act. In a sense, the EJA represents the culmination of federal elder abuse policy efforts that began more than 30 years before, with the first legislation introduced into Congress to address elder abuse, in this case specifically to establish the NCEA and provide funding for states to offer services for victims. Later revisions to the OAA realized the intent of the earliest legislation. The EJA, however, goes further. First, unlike the OAA and Title XX, all provisions of the EJA represent responses to elder abuse. Second, the overall aims of the EJA are wide-ranging, including national coordination of elder justice activities and research, APS and LTCO program enhancements, forensic centers establishment, and training improvements toward better elder abuse detecting and intervention. Achieving these aims has been hampered by insufficient funding and political will. To date, the EJA has received only around 10% of the $577 million authorized, and it required reauthorization in 2014, which still has not happened. Nonetheless, the EJA represents milestone federal public policy in responding to elder abuse, and it is a focus for advocacy by the Elder Justice Coalition, a non-partisan group with 3,000 members, founded around the time of the EJA's original introduction in 2002, and active since then across a broad array of elder abuse–related legislation considered by Congress.

Other federal public policies support an elder abuse response, even if that is not their primary purpose. These include the Violence Against Women Act and Family Violence Prevention and Services Act. In addition, other enacted legislation is likely to be beneficial in such areas as expanded reporting of financial exploitation and fraud (Senior Safe Act) and improved criminal prosecution (Elder Abuse Prevention and Prosecution Act). Likewise, states have enacted laws to affect the elder abuse response. Examples include mandatory reporting and APS laws, enhanced penalties in criminal convictions involving older adult victims, improvements in guardianship and other probate codes providing surrogate decision-making for adults whose mental disabilities inhibit their capacity to protect themselves or their interests, and laws establishing local multidisciplinary teams for coordinated elder abuse case assessments and interventions across service systems.

Key Service Systems

There are six service systems that offer essential response to situations of elder abuse. Each is briefly described below with respect to its purpose, functions, and practitioners.

- APS, which typically operates out of public departments of social services or state units on aging, is authorized by law to receive and investigate reports of abuse, neglect, or exploitation affecting older adults (and usually vulnerable younger adults); evaluate client status and service needs; provide or arrange services to address harm; and seek legal interventions, if indicated, usually in the form of surrogate decision-making for incapacitated victims or criminal penalty for perpetrators.
- Aging Network represents various clinical or supportive services arising from OAA implementation that can (1) address elder abuse risk factors and thereby help prevent problem occurrence or reoccurrence, or (2) enable victims to better manage without an abusive caregiver. Such services include congregate and home-delivered meals, transportation, legal services, and adult day care, typically available through area agencies on aging, municipal offices on aging, senior centers, or other community service organizations.
- Law enforcement (including that found with municipal police, sheriff's departments, or prosecutor's offices) functions to address violations in the legal code (like assault, domestic violence, theft, or fraud) and therefore has the authority to arrest and prosecute perpetrators and enforce protective or restraining orders. Law enforcement

also may be the first responder in crisis situations (like the severe battering of an older adult), may sometimes provide safety checks when an older adult's endangerment is a concern, and occasionally may accompany APS in conducting investigations or carrying out involuntary interventions.

- Victim assistance programs work in cooperation with law enforcement and the courts to provide older adult victims of crime with counseling, advocacy, court accompaniment, and victim compensation information. Their importance in elder abuse situations lies in helping victims navigate the justice system, often seen as confusing and daunting.
- Health care (including hospitals, clinics, practitioner offices, and mental health and substance abuse treatment centers) is vital to elder abuse detection and service referral. It also provides treatment for the effects of inflicted harm and for risk factors that contribute to the occurrence of harm.
- Domestic violence and sexual assault programs offer an array of victim services (such as hotlines, emergency shelters, legal advocacy and support groups) aimed at insuring the safety of abuse victims and holding their perpetrators accountable. Some, but not all, programs have made special accommodations to address the particular needs of older adult victims.

Because no service system singularly can respond to every problem in all elder abuse situations, M-teams have emerged as the preferred response (e.g., Anetzberger, 2011; Breckman et al., 2015; Teaster et al., 2003). Essentially M-teams are groups of people representing different professional disciplines or service systems that come together for the purpose of problem identification and treatment recommendation in complex elder abuse situations (Anetzberger, 2017). Their focus tends to be on the victim, but the concerns and problems of others (especially perpetrators and caregivers) may be considered as well. This is important in cases involving substance abuse, since, as noted earlier in this chapter, often alcohol or drug misuse or addiction is characteristic of the perpetrator. There are numerous types of M-teams, such as geriatric assessment, adult protection, fatality review, and forensic center teams. There also are various structures and operations used by M-teams. Critical to their usefulness in addressing elder abuse and substance abuse as interfacing problems is M-team membership that includes representation from the six key service systems, with those from mental health and substance abuse treatment centers present and actively participating. Unfortunately, this does not always happen. A frequently identified obstacle to M-team effectiveness is lack of involvement by key disciplines or agencies, with mental health and substance abuse treatment centers not infrequently named (e.g., Brandl et al., 2007; Twomey et al., 2010). Finally, M-teams engage in assorted activities, including member training and information sharing. However, their core functions are case selection, presentation, intervention recommendation or plan development, and follow-up. It is in fulfilling these core functions that a meaningful elder abuse response perhaps is most likely to be revealed. As stated by one M-team participant, "Whereas professionals working in isolation would be hampered by the limits of their own expertise and authority, as a team they can address each case holistically, which leads to better outcomes for victims" (Breckman et al., 2015, p. 4).

Beyond the above identified service systems, most of which were developed for purposes other than elder abuse response, there are few elder abuse–specific interventions (Pillemer et al., 2015). Those that exist are more likely to address the needs of victims (e.g., shelter within long-term care facilities; Solomon & Reingold, 2012) or caregiving perpetrators (e,g., respite services to relieve caregiver stress; Ayalon et al., 2016), rather than the needs of non-caregiving perpetrators. Although there is both historic and recent recognition of elder abuse perpetrator needs (Anetzberger, 1987; Pillemer et al., 2015), minimal efforts have gone into developing related services, perhaps in part because APS laws target victims and tend to ignore perpetrators and with the criminalization of elder abuse beginning in the 1980s, perpetrators became increasingly stigmatized. Even the rare service that exists for perpetrators (e.g., Stop Elder Abuse and Mistreatment Programs; NYC Elder Abuse Center, 2018) may exclude those with substance abuse problems. This is unfortunate, since there is some evidence that although perpetrators are seldom offered services, when they are, perpetrators are more likely to accept and benefit from the services (Vinton, 1992; Nahmiash & Reis, 2000).

It seems appropriate to end this chapter where it began, with older adults illustrating what it means to experience elder abuse at least in part due to substance abuse. Despite the long-recognized association between these problems, little has been undertaken to address them in combination. This intervention gap deserves to be filled, and as articulated at the conclusion of the Elder Justice Roadmap (Connolly et al., 2014, p. 32), "The time to act is now."

Conclusion

Elder abuse is a problem that affects older adults nearly everywhere. Its prevalence is thought to be high. Among community-dwellers, annually more than 1 in 10 older Americans and 3 in 20 older people worldwide are victimized. There are three broad categories of elder abuse (mistreatment, self-neglect, and fraud), each with various forms. Despite laws that require elder abuse reporting and screening tools that promote detection, relatively few situations come to the attention of systems charged to assist. This is unfortunate, because the consequences of elder abuse can be wide ranging and severe, from loss of money to physical or emotional harm, institutionalization, and death.

Substance abuse is regarded as the dominant predictor for elder abuse occurrence. Early recognition of this correlate surrounded self-neglect, where older adults who lived in squalor and unsafe conditions were found often to drink heavily or misuse drugs. Later attention on mistreatment revealed that perpetrators frequently had substance abuse disorders, with alcoholism particularly common. Subsequent research has firmly established these links.

Policy exists that creates and supports various response systems to elder abuse. Key federal policies include the Older Americans Act, Social Services Block Grant, and Elder Justice Act, and critical systems are adult protective services, Aging Network, law enforcement, victim assistance programs, health care, and domestic violence and sexual assault programs. Except for the Elder Justice Act and adult protective services, each of these policies and systems has a broad purpose, only part of which relates to elder abuse intervention. Nationwide, there are few specific elder abuse interventions. Particularly lacking are those targeting perpetrators, and no interventions are known to focus exclusively on the link between elder abuse and substance abuse. System and service representatives often come together at the local level in multidisciplinary teams for better problem identification and treatment recommendations of complex elder abuse situations, thus enabling more holistic and resource efficient case handling. Cases involving substance abuse are among those commonly reviewed.

Discussion Questions

1. How might a situation involving both substance abuse and elder abuse come to your professional attention?
2. What information would you need to better understand the situation in order to decide whether or not to make a report to adult protective services, law enforcement, or some other legally charged response system?

3. What are some local services that may be helpful in addressing the substance abuse and elder abuse evident in the situation?

Key Terms

Abandonment: Desertion of a vulnerable older adult by anyone with a duty of care.

Caregiver: Someone who assumes responsibility for providing daily living assistance to an older adult who requires it because of health conditions or other circumstances.

Community-dwelling: Residence in a private home, apartment, or other non-institutional setting.

Elder abuse: Infliction of harm, suffering, or loss upon an older adult.

Emotional abuse: Behaviors or words that cause mental anguish or distress to an older adult.

Exploitation: Improper or illegal use of an older adult's money or property for someone else's profit or benefit.

Neglect: Refusal or failure of a caregiver to meet the basic needs of a vulnerable older adult or assure that person's safety and well-being.

Perpetrator: Person who inflicts elder abuse on an older adult.

Physical abuse: Threatening or causing pain, injury, or impairment to an older adult through force.

Scams: Illegal or deceptive acts of trickery inflicted on an older adult by individuals, groups, or companies to obtain that person's money or property.

Sexual abuse: Any kind of non-consensual contact with an older adult or forcing an older adult to witness sexual acts.

Victim: The older adult recipient of elder abuse.

Vulnerability: Physical, mental, or social conditions that compromise the ability of older adults to function on their own or protect themselves from harm or loss.

References

Acierno, R., Hernandez, M. A., Amstadter, A. B., Resnick, H. S., Steve, K., Muzzy, W., & Kilpatrick, D. G. (2010). Prevalence and correlates of emotional, physical, sexual, and financial abuse and potential neglect in the United States: The National Elder Mistreatment Study. *American Journal of Public Health, 100*(2), 292–297.

Almogue, A., Weiss, A., Marcus, E.-L., & Beloosesky, Y. (2010). Attitudes and knowledge of medical and nursing staff toward elder abuse. *Archives of Gerontology and Geriatrics, 51*(1), 86–91.

American Psychiatric Association. (2013). *Diagnostic and Statistical Manual of Mental Disorders* (5th ed.).

Amstadter, A. B., Cisler, J. M., McCauley, J. L., Hernandez, M. A., Muzzy, W., & Acierno, R. (2010). Do incident and perpetrator characteristics of elder mistreatment differ by gender of the victim? Results from the National Elder Mistreatment Study. *Journal of Elder Abuse & Neglect, 23*(1), 43–57.

Anderson, K. (2012). *Federal Trade Commission, consumer fraud in the United States, 2011: The third FTC survey.* https://www.ftc.gov/reports/consumer-fraud-united-states-2011-third-ftc-survey

Anetzberger, G. J. (1987). *The etiology of elder abuse by adult offspring.* Charles C Thomas Publishers.

Anetzberger, G. J. (2000). Caregiving: Primary cause of elder abuse. *Generations, 24*(11), 46–51.

Anetzberger, G. J. (2001). Elder abuse identification and referral: The importance of screening tools and referral protocols. *Journal of Elder Abuse & Neglect, 13*(2), 3–22.

Anetzberger, G. J. (2011). The evolution of a multidisciplinary response to elder abuse. *Marquette Elder's Advisor, 13*(1), 107–128.

Anetzberger, G. J. (2012). An update on the nature and scope of elder abuse. *Generations, 36*(3), 12–20.

Anetzberger, G. J. (2013). Elder abuse: Risk. In A. Jamieson & A. A. Moenssens (Eds.), *Wiley encyclopedia of forensic science.* John Wiley & Sons.

Anetzberger, G. J. (2017). Elder abuse multidisciplinary teams. In X. Dong (Ed.), *Elder abuse: Research, practice and policy.* (pp. 417–432). Springer International Publishing.

Anetzberger, G. J., Dayton, C., Miller, C. A., McGreevey, Jr., J. F., & Schimer, M. (2005). Multidisciplinary teams in the clinical management of elder abuse. *Clinical Gerontologist, 28*(1/2), 157–171.

Anetzberger, G. J., Korbin, J. E., & Austin, C. (1994). Alcoholism and elder abuse. *Journal of Interpersonal Violence, 9*(2), 183–193.

Aurelien, G., Beatrice, M., Cannizzo, J., Capehart, A., Gassoumis, Z., & Green, M. (2018a). *National adult maltreatment reporting system 2018, September 17, NAMRS FFY 2017, Report 2: Key indicators.* Administration for Community Living.

Aurelien, G., Beatrice, M., Cannizzo, J., Capehart, A., Gassoumis, Z., & Green, M. (2018b). *National adult maltreatment reporting system 2018, September 17, NAMRS FFY 2017, Report 3: Case components.* Administration for Community Living.

Ayalon, L., Lev, S., Green, O., & Nevo, U. (2016). A systematic review and meta-analysis of interventions designed to prevent or stop elder maltreatment. *Age & Aging, 45,* 216–227.

Beals, M. E., Carr, D. C., Mottola, G. R., Deevy, M. J., & Carstensen, L. L. (2017). How does survey context impact self-reported fraud victimization? *The Gerontologist, 57*(2), 329–340.

Beckman, K. (2016, November 30). *Elder financial fraud may be worse than thought, study says.* Think Advisor. https://www.thinkadvisor.com/2016/11/30/elder-financial-fraud-may-be-worse-than-thought-st/

Begle, A. M., Strachan, M., Cisler, J. M., Amstadter, A. B., Hernandez, M., & Acierno, R. (2011). Elder mistreatment and emotional symptoms among older adults in a largely rural population: The South Carolina Elder Mistreatment Study. *Journal of Interpersonal Violence, 26,* 2321–2332.

Blondell, R. (1999). Alcohol abuse and self-neglect in the elderly. *Journal of Elder Abuse & Neglect, 11*(2), 55–75.

Brandl, B., Dyer, C. B., Heisler, C. J., Otto, J. M., Stiegel, L. A., & Thomas, R. W. (2007). *Elder abuse detection and intervention: A collaborative approach.* Springer Publishing Company.

Breckman, R., Callahan, J., & Solomon, J. (2015). *Elder abuse multidisciplinary teams: Planning for the future.* NYC Elder Abuse Center, Brookdale Center for Healthy Aging at Hunter College of the City University of New York, and The Harry and Jeanette Weinberg Center for Elder abuse Prevention at The Hebrew House at Riverdale.

Brownell, P., Berman, J., & Salamone, A. (1999). Mental health and criminal justice issues among perpetrators of elder abuse. *Journal of Elder Abuse & Neglect, 11*(4), 81–94.

Burnes, D., Henderson, Jr., C. R., Sheppard, C., Zhao, R., Pillemer, K., & Lachs, M. S. (2017). Prevalence of financial fraud and scams among older adults in the United States: A systematic review and meta-analysis. *American Journal of Public Health, 107*(8), e13–e21.

Burnett, J., Dyer, C. B., Halphen, J. M., Achenbaum, W. A., Green, C. E., Booker, J. G., & Diamond, P. M. (2014). Four subtypes of self-neglect in older adults: Results of a latent class analysis. *Journal of the American Geriatrics Society, 62,* 1127–1132.

Burnight, K., & Mosqueda, L. (2011). *Theoretical model development in elder mistreatment.* National Institute of Justice.

Burr, J. J. (1982). *Protective services for adults.* Administration on Aging.

Butler, R. N. (1975). *Why survive? Being old in America.* Harper & Row.

Centers for Disease Control and Prevention. (2019). *Elder abuse: Definitions.* Retrieved January 2, 2019, from www.cdc.gov/violenceprevention/elderabuse/definitions.html

Chen, R., & Dong, X. (2017). Risk factors of elder abuse. In X. Dong (Ed.), *Elder abuse: Research, practice and policy* (pp. 93–107). Springer International Publishing.

Cisler, J. M., Begle, A. M., Amstadter, A. B., & Acierno, R. (2012). Mistreatment and self-reported emotional symptoms: Results from the National Elder Mistreatment Study. *Journal of Elder Abuse & Neglect, 24*(3), 216–230.

Cohen, D., & Eisdorfer, C. (2011). *Integrated textbook of geriatric mental health.* The Johns Hopkins University Press.

Cole, H. B. (1962, October 22). *Older persons in need of protective services.* Unpublished manuscript.

Connolly, M. R., Brandl, B., & Breckman, R. (2014). *The Elder Justice Roadmap: A stakeholder initiative to respond to an emerging health, justice, financial and social crisis.* U.S. Department of Justice.

Conrad, K. J., Iris, M., Ridings, J. W., Langley, K., & Wilbur, K. H. (2010). Self-report measure of financial exploitation of older adults. *The Gerontologist, 50*(6), 758–773.

Conrad, K. J., Liu, P-J., & Iris, M. (2016). Examining the role of substance abuse in elder mistreatment: Results from mistreatment investigations. *Journal of Interpersonal Violence, 34*(2), 366–391.

Daly, J. M. (2017). *Elder abuse prevention.* The University of Iowa College of Nursing.

Daly, J. M., Schmeidel Kein, A. N., & Jogerst, G. J. (2012). Critical care nurses' perspectives on elder abuse. *Nursing in Critical Care, 17*(4), 172–179.

Day, M. R., & Leahy-Warren, P. (2008). Self-neglect 1: Recognizing features and risk factors. *Nursing Times, 104*(24), 26–27.

DeLiema, M. Fraud vs. financial abuse: The etiology of two types of elder financial exploitation. Paper presented at the Annual Scientific Meeting of the Gerontological Society of America, Orlando, Florida, November 18–22, 2015. Abstract retrieved from https://gsa2015.abstractcentral.com

DeLiema, M. (2018). Elder fraud and financial exploitation: Application of routine activity theory. *The Gerontologist, 58*(4), 706–718.

Dong, X. (2017). Prologue. In X. Dong (Ed.), *Elder abuse: Research, practice and policy* (pp. vii–xiv). Springer International Publishing.

Dong, X., & Simon, M. A. (2013a). Elder abuse as a risk factor for hospitalization in older persons. *Journal of the American Medical Association, Internal Medicine, 173*, 911–917.

Dong, X., & Simon, M. A. (2013b). Association between elder self-neglect and hospice utilization in a community population. *Archives of Gerontology and Geriatrics, 56*, 192–198.

Dong, X., Simon, M., Beck, T., & Evans, D. (2010). A cross-sectional population-based study of elder self-neglect and psychological, health, and social factors in a biracial community. *Aging and Mental Health, 14*(1), 74–84.

Dong, X., Simon, M., deLeon, C. M., Fulmer, T., Beck, T., Hebert, L., … Evans, D. (2009). Elder self-neglect and abuse and mortality in a community-dwelling population. *Journal of the American Medical Association, 302*(5), 517–526.

Douglass, R. L., Hickey, T., & Noel, C. (1980). *A study of maltreatment of the elderly and other vulnerable adults.* University of Michigan, Institute of Gerontology.

Dyer, C. B., Goodwin, J. S., Pickens-Pace, S., Burnett, J., & Kelly, P. A. (2007). Self-neglect among the elderly: A model based on more than 500 patients seen by a geriatric medicine team. *American Journal of Public Health, 97*(9), 1671–1676.

Dyer, C. B., & Reyes-Ortiz, C. A. (2017). Epidemiology of elder self-neglect. In X. Dong (Ed.), *Elder abuse: Research, practice and policy* (pp. 125–139). Springer International Publishing.

Dyer, L. (1992). Geriatric alcoholism and self-neglect. In E. Rathbone-McCuan & D. R. Fabian (Eds.), *Self-neglecting elders: A clinical dilemma* (pp. 127–143). Auburn House.

Erlingsson, C. L., Carlson, S. L., & Saveman, B-I. (2003). Elder abuse risk indicators and screening questions: Results from a literature search and a panel of experts from developed and developing countries. *Journal of Elder Abuse & Neglect, 15*(3/4), 185–203.

Ernst, J. S., Ramsey-Klawsnik, H., Schillerstrom, J. E., Dayton, C., Mixson, P., & Counihan, M. (2014). Informing evidence-based practice: A review of research analyzing adult protective services data. *Journal of Elder Abuse & Neglect, 26*(5), 458–494.

Franzini, L., & Dyer, C. B. (2008). Healthcare costs and utilization of vulnerable elderly people reported to adult protective services for self-neglect. *Journal of the American Geriatrics Society, 56*, 667–676.

Friedman, L. S., Avila, S., Tanouye, K., & Joseph, K. (2011). A case-control study of severe physical abuse of elder adults. *Journal of the American Geriatrics Society, 59*(3), 417–422.

Fulmer, T. T., & O'Malley, T. A. (1987). *Inadequate care of the elderly: A health care perspective on abuse and neglect.* Springer Publishing Company.

Greenberg, J. R., McKibben, M., & Raymond, J. A. (1990). Dependent adult children and elder abuse. *Journal of Elder Abuse & Neglect, 2*(1/2), 73–86.

Griffin, E., McGuire, C., & Snow, K. I. (2017). *Financial exploitation of Maine's older adults: An analysis of Maine Adult Protective Services and Legal Services for the Elderly case records, state fiscal years 2010–2016.* University of Southern Maine, Cutler Institute of Health and Social Policy.

Gunther, J. (2010). *The Utah cost of financial exploitation.* Utah Division of Aging and Adult Services and Bank of American Fork.

Hess, S. (2011). The role of health care providers in recognizing and reporting elder abuse. *Journal of Gerontological Nursing, 37*(11), 28–34.

Holtfreter, K., Reisig, M., Mears, D., & Wolfe, S. (2014). *Financial exploitation of the elderly in a consumer context.* U.S. Department of Justice, National Institute of Justice.

Innovative Research Group. (2007). *2007 CSA investor study: Understanding the social impart of investment fraud.*

Jackson, S. L. (2016). All elder abuse perpetrators are not alike: The heterogeneity of elder abuse perpetrators and implications for intervention. *International Journal of Offender Therapy and Comparative Criminology, 60,* 265–285.

Jackson, S. L. (2018). *Understanding elder abuse: A clinician's guide.* American Psychological Association.

Jackson, S. L., & Hafemeister, T. L. (2010). *Financial abuse of elderly people vs. other forms of elder abuse: Assessing their dynamics, risk factors, and society's response.* Final report to the National Institute of Justice, supported under award no. 2006-WG-BX-0010.

Jackson, S. L., & Hafemeister, T. L. (2013). *Research in brief: Understanding elder abuse: New directions for developing theories of elder abuse occurring in domestic settings.* National Institute of Justice.

Jackson, S. L., & Hafemeister, T. L. (2014). How case characteristics differ across four types of elder maltreatment: Implications for tailoring interventions to increase victim safety. *Journal of Applied Gerontology, 38,* 982–997.

Jogerst, G. J., Daly, J. M., Galloway, L. J., & Zheng, S. (2011). Substance abuse associated with elder abuse in the United States. *The American Journal of Drug and Alcohol Abuse, 38*(1), 63–69.

Johannesen, M., & LoGiudice, D. (2013). Elder abuse: A systematic review of risk factors in community-dwelling elders. *Age and Ageing, 42*(3), 292–298.

Kapp, M. B. (1995). Elder mistreatment: Legal interventions and policy uncertainties. *Behavioral Sciences & the Law, 13,* 365–380.

Kelly, P., Dyer, C., Pavlik, V., Doody, R., & Jogerst, G. (2008). Exploring self-neglect in older adults: Preliminary findings of the Self-Neglect Severity Scale and next steps. *Journal of the American Geriatrics Society, 56,* S253–S260.

Kuerbis, A., Sacco, P., Blazer, D. G., & Moore, A. A. (2014). Substance abuse among older adults. *Clinics in Geriatric Medicine, 30*(3), 629–654.

Labrum, T. (2017). Factors related to abuse of older persons by relatives with psychiatric disorders. *Archives of Gerontology and Geriatrics, 68,* 126–134. https://doi.org/10.1016/j.archger.2016.09.007

Labrum, T., & Solomon, P. L. (2018). Elder mistreatment perpetrators with substance abuse and/or mental health conditions: Results from the National Elder Mistreatment Study. *Psychiatric Quarterly, 89*(1), 117–128.

Lachs, M., & Berman, J. (2011, May). *Under the radar: New York state elder abuse prevalence study, self-reported prevalence and documented case surveys, final report.* Lifespan of Greater Rochester Inc., Weill Cornell Medical Center at Cornell University, and New York City Department of Aging.

Lachs, M. S., Williams, C. S., O'Brien, S., Pillemer, K. A., & Charlson, M. E. (1998). The mortality of elder mistreatment. *Journal of the American Medical Association, 280*(5), 428–432.

Lau, E. E., & Kosberg, J. I. Abuse of the elderly by informal care providers: Practice and research issues. Paper presented at the Annual Scientific Meeting of the Gerontological Society of America, Dallas, Texas, November 20, 1978.

Laumann, E. O., Leitsch, S. A., & Waite, L. J. (2008). Elder mistreatment in the United States: Prevalence estimates from a nationally representative study. *Journal of Gerontology, Social Sciences, 63B*(4), S248–S254.

Longres, F. (1994). Self-neglect and social control: A modest test of an issue. *Journal of Gerontological Social Work, 22*, 3–20.

Lusheck, B., Muttillo, E., & Tarter, W. (2018). Adult protective services: Case study of seven counties. *Center for Community Solutions, State Budgeting Matters, 14*(2).

MacMillan, D., & Shaw, P. (1966). Senile breakdown in standards of personal and environmental cleanliness. *British Medical Journal, 2*, 1032–1037.

MetLife Mature Market Institute. (2011). *The MetLife study of elder financial abuse: Crimes of occasion, desperation, and predation against American elders.* Metropolitan Life Insurance Company.

Mosqueda, L., Burnight, K., & Liao, S. (2005). The life cycle of bruises in older adults. *Journal of the American Geriatrics Society, 53*(8), 1339–1343.

Moyer, V. A. (2013). Screening for intimate partner violence and abuse of elderly and vulnerable adults: U.S. Preventive Services Task Force Recommendation Statement. *Annals of Internal Medicine, 158*, 478–486.

Nahmiash, D., & Reis, M. (2000). Most successful intervention strategies for abused older adults. *Journal of Elder Abuse & Neglect, 12*(3/4), 53–70.

National Adult Protective Services Association. (2019). What is abuse? Retrieved January 2, 2019, from www.napsa-now.org/get-informed/what-is-abuse/

National Center on Elder Abuse (2019a). What is elder abuse? Retrieved January 2, 2019, from https://ncea.acl.gov/faq/index.html

National Center on Elder Abuse (2019b). Types of abuse. Retrieved January 2, 2019, from https://ncea.acl.gov/faq/abusetypes.html

National Center on Elder Abuse (2019c). What we do: Research. Retrieved January 14, 2019, from https://ncea.acl.gov/whatwedo/research/statistics.html

National Center on Elder Abuse & Westat, Inc. (1998). *The National Elder Abuse Incidence Study: Final report.*

National Clearinghouse on Abuse in Later Life. (2019). Defining abuse in later life & elder abuse. Retrieved January 2, 2019, from www.ncall.us/defining-abuse-in-later-life-and-elder-abuse

National Committee for the Prevention of Elder Abuse & National Adult Protective Services Association. (2005). *The 2004 survey of state adult protective services abuse of adults 60 years of age and older.*

National Institute of Justice. (2014). *Elder mistreatment: Using theory in research.*

National Research Council. (2003). Elder mistreatment: Abuse, neglect, and exploitation in an aging America. In R. J. Bonnie & R. B. Wallace (Eds.), *Panel to review risk and prevalence of elder abuse and neglect.* The National Academies Press.

Neale, A. V., Hwalek, M. A., Scott, R. O., & Stahl, C. (1991). Validation of the Hwalek-Senstock Elder Abuse Screening Test. *Journal of Applied Gerontology, 10*(4), 406–415.

NYC Elder Abuse Center. (2018, November 12). Spotlight on the Stop Elder Abuse Mistreatment (S.E.A.M.) program. *Elder Justice Dispatch.*

O'Brien, J. G., Thibault, J. M., Turner, L. C., & Laird-Fick, H. S. (1999). Self-neglect: An overview. *Journal of Elder Abuse & Neglect, 11*(2), 1–19.

O'Keeffe, M., Hills, A., Doyle, M., McCreadie, C., Scholes, S. Y., Constaine, R., … Erens, B. (2007). *UK study of abuse and neglect of older people: Prevalence study report.* National Centre for Social Research, King's College London.

O'Malley, H., Segars, H., Perez, R., Mitchell, V., & Knuepfel, A. (1979). *Elder abuse in Massachusetts: A study of professionals and paraprofessionals.* Legal Research and Services for the Elderly.

Pak, D., & Shadel, D. (2011). *National fraud victim study*. AARP Foundation. https://assets. aarp.org/rgcenter/econ/fraud-victims-11.pdf

Pavlou, M. P., & Lachs, M. S. (2008). Self-neglect in older adults: A primer for clinicians. *Journal of General Internal Medicine, 23*, 1841–1846.

Payne, B., & Gainey, R. (2005). Differentiating self-neglect as a type of elder mistreatment: How do these cases compare to traditional types of elder mistreatment? *Journal of Elder Abuse & Neglect, 17*(1), 21–36.

Perez-Carceles, M. D., Rubio, L., Pereniguez, J. E., Perez-Flores, D., Osuna, E., & Luna, A. (2009). Suspicion of elder abuse in South Eastern Spain: The extent and risk factors. *Archives of Gerontology and Geriatrics, 49*(1), 132–137.

Pillemer, K. (1985). The dangers of dependency: New findings on domestic violence against the elderly. *Social Problems, 33*, 146–158.

Pillemer, K., Connolly, M. T., Breckman, R., Spreng, N., & Lachs, M. S. (2015). Elder mistreatment: Priorities for consideration by the White House Conference on Aging. *The Gerontologist, 55*, 320–327.

Pillemer, K., & Finkelhor, D. (1988). The prevalence of elder abuse: A random sample survey. *The Gerontologist, 28*(1), 51–57.

Ploeg, J., Fear, J., Hutchison, B., MacMillan, H., & Bolan, G. (2009). A systematic review of interventions for elder abuse. *Journal of Elder Abuse & Neglect, 27*(3), 187–210.

Podnieks, E., & Thomas, C. (2017). The consequences of elder abuse. In X. Dong (Ed.), *Elder abuse: Research, practice and policy* (pp. 109–123). Springer International Publishing.

Quinn, K. M., & Benson, W. F. (2012). The states' elder abuse victim services: A system still in search of support. *Generations, 36*(3), 66–72.

Ramsey-Klawsnik, H. (2006). Dynamics of self-neglect, Part 1. *Victimization of the Elderly and Disabled, 8*(5), 69–70, 76.

Rathbone-McCuan, E. Intergenerational family violence and neglect: The aged as victims of reactivated and reverse neglect. Paper presented at the 11th International Congress of Gerontology, Tokyo, Japan, August 20–25, 1978.

Rennison, C., & Rand, M. (2003). Nonlethal intimate partner violence: A comparison of three age groups. *Violence Against Women, 9*(12), 1417–1428.

Ritter, J. (2017, April). Frauds, scams, rip-offs: The ultimate guide to beating the crooks. *AARP Bulletin*, pp.14–16, 18, 20, 22, 24.

Roberto, K. A. (2016). The complexities of elder abuse. *American Psychologist, 71*, 302–311.

Roberto, K. A., & Teaster, P. B. (2017). Theorizing elder abuse. In X. Dong (Ed.), *Elder abuse: Research, practice and policy* (pp.21–41). Springer International Publishing.

Schofield, M. J. (2017). Screening for elder abuse: Tools and effectiveness. In X. Dong (Ed.), *Elder abuse: Research, practice and policy* (pp. 161–199). Springer International Publishing.

Schofield, M. J., Mishra, G. D., Powers, J. R., & Dobson, A. J. (2002). Screening for vulnerability to abuse among older women: Women's Health Australia study. *Journal of Applied Gerontology, 21*(1), 24–39.

Snowdon, J. (1987). Uncleanliness among persons seen by community health workers. *Hospital and Community Psychiatry, 38*, 491–494.

Snowden, J., Shah, A., & Halliday, G. (2007). Severe domestic squalor: A review. *International Psychogeriatrics, 19*(1), 37–51.

Solomon, J., & Reingold, D. A. (2012). Creating an elder abuse shelter: A best-practice model for nonprofit nursing homes. *Generations, 36*(3), 64–65.

Stahl, S. M. (2015, July). *Building consensus on research priorities in elder mistreatment*. U.S. Department of Justice.

Steinmetz, S. K. (1977). *The cycle of violence: Assertive, aggressive, and abusive family interaction*. Praeger.

Substance Abuse and Mental Health Services Administration (SAMHSA). (2017). *Key substance use and mental health indicators in the United States: Results from the 2016 National Survey on Drug Use and Health* (HHS Publication No. SMA 17-5044, NSDUH Series H-52). Center for Behavioral Health Statistics and Quality, SAMHSA.

Substance Abuse and Mental Health Services Administration. (2019). *Substance use disorders.* Retrieved January 2, 2019, from https://www.samhsa.gov/disorders/substance-use

Teaster, P. B. (2011). *Examining the costs of elder abuse: Three case studies.* National Committee for the Prevention of Elder Abuse.

Teaster, P. B., Nerenberg, L., & Stansbury, K. L. (2003). A national look at elder abuse multidisciplinary teams. *Journal of Elder Abuse & Neglect, 15*(3/4), 91–107.

Titus, R. M., Heinzelmann, F., & Boyle, J. M. (1995). Victimization of persons by fraud. *Crime & Delinquency, 41,* 54–72.

Tredal, I., Soares, J. J. F., Sundin, O., Viitasara, E., Melchiorre, M. G., Torres-Gonzales, F., ... Barros, H. (2013). Alcohol use among abused and non-abused older persons, aged 60–84 years: A European study. *Drugs: Education, Prevention and Policy, 20*(2), 96–109.

True Link Financial. (2015). *The True Link report on elder financial abuse 2015.* https://www.truelinkfinancial.com/research

Twomey, M. S., Jackson, G., Li, H., Marino, T., Melchior, L. A., Randolph, J. F., & Wysong, J. (2010). The successes and challenges of seven multidisciplinary teams. *Journal of Elder Abuse & Neglect, 22*(3/4), 291–305.

U.S. Government Accountability Office. (2011). *Stronger federal leadership could enhance the response to elder abuse* (GAO-11-208).

U.S. Office of Disease Prevention and Health Promotion. (2019). *Healthy People 2020: Substance abuse.* Retrieved January 2, 2019, from https://www.healthypeople.gov/2020/topics-objectives/topic/substance-abuse

U.S. Preventive Services Task Force. (2018). *Intimate partner violence, elder abuse, and abuse of vulnerable adults: Screening* (Published final recommendations). Retrieved January 19, 2019, from https://www.uspreventiveservicestaskforce.org/Page/Document/UpdateSummaryFinal/intimate-partner-violence-and-abuse-of-elderly-and-vulnerable-adults

U.S. Senate Special Committee on Aging. (2018). *Fighting fraud: Senate Aging Committee identifies top 10 scams targeting our nation's seniors.* https://www.aging.senate.gov/imo/media/doc/Fraud%20Book%202018%20FINAL.pdf

Vinton, L. (1992). Services planned in abusive elder care situations. *Journal of Elder Abuse & Neglect, 4*(3), 85–99.

Wallace, R. B., & Crabb, V. L. (2017). Toward definitions of elder mistreatment. In X. Dong (Ed.), *Elder abuse: Research, practice and policy.* (pp. 3–20). Springer International Publishing.

Wang, J. J., Tseng, H. F., & Chen, K. M. (2007). Development and testing of screening indicators for psychological abuse of older people. *Archives in Psychiatric Nursing, 21*(1), 40–47.

Wiglesworth, A., Austin, R., Corona, M., Schneider, D., Liao, S., Gibbs, L., & Mosqueda, L. (2009). Bruising as a marker of physical elder abuse. *Journal of the American Geriatrics Society, 57*(7), 1191–1196.

Wolf, R. S., Godkin, M. A., & Pillemer, K. A. (1986). Maltreatment of the elderly: A comparative analysis. *Pride Institute Journal of Long Term Home Health Care, 5*(4), 10–17.

World Health Organization (2002). *Missing voices.*

World Health Organization. (2006). *Elder abuse and alcohol.* Retrieved December 10, 2018, from www.who.int/.../violence/world_report/factsheets/fs_elder.pdf

World Health Organization. (2019). *Elder abuse.* Retrieved January 2, 2019, from https://www.who.int/en/news-room/fact-sheets/detail/elder-abuse

Yaffe, M. J., Wolfson, C., Lithwick, M., & Weiss, D. (2008). Development and validation of a tool to improve physician identification of elder abuse: The Elder Abuse Suspicion Index (EASI). *Journal of Elder Abuse & Neglect, 20*(3), 276–300.

Yon, Y., Mikton, C., Gassoumis, Z. D., & Wilber, K. H. (2019). The prevalence of self-reported elder abuse among older women in community settings: A systematic review and meta-analysis. *Trauma, Violence, & Abuse, 20*(2), 245–259. https://doi.org/10.1177/1524838017697308

Ziminski Pickering, C. E., & Rempusheski, V. F. (2014). Examining barriers to self-reporting of elder physical abuse in community-dwelling older-adults. *Geriatric Nursing, 35*(2), 120–125.

Spotlight on Special Issues

Elder Abuse, Substance Use, and Public Health Crises

Margaret I. Campe, PhD, and Holly Harden-Ramella, MA

Risk factors, including substance use and social isolation, for elder abuse have been well established in the literature (Jogerst et al., 2012). In recent years public health emergencies that disproportionately negatively affect marginalized populations, including often already isolated older adults, have become increasingly common (Raker et al., 2020; Wingate, 2007). The term public health emergency varies in definition from state to state, but most definitions refer to "occurrence or imminent threat of widespread or severe damage, injury, or loss of life or property resulting from a natural phenomenon or human act" (Haffajee et al., 2014, p. 986). Natural disasters, including events like flooding, wildfires, or tornadoes, as well as disease outbreak can all be categorized as public health emergencies. Often one of the consequences of a public health crisis is displacement due to hazardous or life-threatening conditions or, as the COVID-19 pandemic highlighted, a loss of housing due to economic insecurity (Jones & Grigsby-Toussaint, 2020; Raker et al., 2020). For older populations, this may result in the older adult having to move in with a family member, or family members having to move in with them, and could also result in homelessness or unsafe housing with inadequate access to resources such as mental health and medical care (Li & Mutchler, 2020).

A trend toward technology utilization in health and mental health services may be a double-edged sword, creating increased convenience and access for some, while exacerbating disparate access for older populations who may be particularly at risk of experiencing violence or substance use disorders (Kruse et al., 2020). Add to this a public health crisis that causes displacement or upends a stable living situation, and the disproportionate risk some older populations face in terms of violent victimization by a caregiver, family member, or increased propensity for substance use as a coping mechanism will be exacerbated. For example, social distancing and quarantining related to the COVID-19 pandemic has upset the way a multitude of services are accessed and has increased reliance on technology such as videoconferencing (Ellison-Barnes et al., 2021). Elderly populations living independently, with caregivers, or in care facilities, already face increased isolation from family, friends, and social endeavors (Dury, 2014). Some studies have indicated that increased connectedness through technology such as social media and email may help ease some of the isolation (Bradley & Poppen 2003; Chen & Shultz, 2016). But, with the growing reliance on technology for more than social connectedness, including a shift to virtual or telehealth services, avenues for health care and mental health care that may help identify and intervene with elderly people who are being abused or who are at risk for substance use disorders have been diminished (Ellison-Barnes, 2021; Wosik et al., 2020). Those who live independently and have access to the internet, and capable devices (computers, tablets, and smartphones) may have limited assistance that they are able to obtain when trying to navigate care through telehealth appointments. Those who live with a caregiver or in a care facility may have the assistance required to successfully engage in telehealth, however they may also have limited ability to engage in private discussion with their health care providers, thereby limiting the opportunity to disclose abuse or feel comfortable talking about substance use disorder (Ellison-Barnes, 2021; Hargittai et al., 2019).

Recovery communities also suffer greatly with reduced or altogether cancelled in-person services during public health crises. For elderly populations that may have reduced access to technology, or whose meetings or treatment programs have been suspended due to factors outside of their control, there will be higher risk for relapse (Melamed et al., 2020). Substance use is known to increase risk for elder abuse, thus the stressors of a public health emergency creates something of a perfect storm in terms of risk for elder abuse in conjunction with substance use (Jogerst et al., 2012). The COVID-19 pandemic provides a whole host of chilling examples. Rates of family violence have increased or intensified with more stressors from families cohabitating or experiencing economic instability and being in an isolated environment due to quarantine and social distancing (Han & Mosqueda, 2020). Rates of substance use have also increased dramatically with the COVID-19 pandemic (Panchal et al., 2021; Wei & Shah, 2020). The confluence of increased reliance on technology for communication and service provision and the isolation many older adults experience has underscored the need to examine the access to resources and continuum of care for older adults at higher risk of experiencing elder abuse, or substance use disorders.

Despite barriers to access made more pervasive during public health emergencies, health care providers may still be more likely to have interaction with elderly populations during these times than others. Therefore, health care practitioners that provide regular or intermittent care to older populations may be the best possible avenue to implement measures that diminish risk for substance use disorders as well as elder abuse. This is doubly important during times where other physical and social contact with friends and family is limited, such as during a global pandemic or natural disaster, which differentially negatively impact the elderly. Health care providers working with elderly populations, or those that serve wide-ranging age groups, should implement consistent screening measures for both substance use disorders and elder abuse. They should also familiarize themselves with community resources available to intervene, such as adult protective services, AA and NA meetings that are specific to older adults, or substance use disorder treatment available in the community. Beyond awareness and providing referrals, health care practitioners should stay attuned to the rapidly changing availability of or access to community resources that address elder abuse and substance use disorders, such that they can prepare for or educate older populations of potential changes, and in so doing reduce the likelihood of a prolonged disruption in continuum of care. Both researchers and practitioners should examine more thoroughly the numerous negative implications of public health emergencies on older populations and develop robust public health preparedness measures for these populations in an effort to prevent increased rates of elder abuse and substance use during times of turbulence caused by public health emergencies.

References

Bradley, N., & Poppen, W. (2003). Assistive technology, computers and Internet may decrease sense of isolation for homebound elderly and disabled persons. *Technology and Disability, 15*(1), 19–25. https://doi.org/10.3233/TAD-2003-15104

Chen, Y.-R. R., & Schulz, P. J. (2016). The effect of information communication technology interventions on reducing social isolation in the elderly: A systematic review. *Journal of Medical Internet Research, 18*(1), e18. https://doi.org/10.2196/jmir.4596

Dury, R. (2014). Social isolation and loneliness in the elderly: An exploration of some of the issues. *British Journal of Community Nursing, 19*(3), 125–128. https://doi.org/10.12968/bjcn.2014.19.3.125

Ellison-Barnes, A., Moran, A., Linton, S., Chaubal, M., Missler, M., & Evan Pollack, C. (2021). Limited technology access among residents of affordable senior housing during the COVID-19 pandemic. *Journal of Applied Gerontology, 40*(9), 958–962. https://doi.org/10.1177/07334648211013634

Han, S. D., & Mosqueda, L. (2020). Elder abuse in the COVID-19 era. *Journal of the American Geriatrics Society.* https://doi.org/10.1111/jgs.16496

Hargittai, E., Piper, A. M., & Morris, M. R. (2019). From internet access to internet skills: Digital inequality among older adults. *Universal Access in the Information Society, 18*(4), 881–890. https://doi.org/10.1007/s10209-018-0617-5

Jogerst, G. J., Daly, J. M., Galloway, L. J., Zheng, S., & Xu, Y. (2012). Substance abuse associated with elder abuse in the United States. *The American Journal of Drug and Alcohol Abuse, 38*(1), 63–69. https://doi.org/10.3109/00952990.2011.600390

Jones, A., & Grigsby-Toussaint, D. S. (2020). Housing stability and the residential context of the COVID-19 pandemic. *Cities & Health.* https://doi.org/10.1080/23748834.2020.1785164

Kruse, C., Fohn, J., Wilson, N., Patlan, E. N., Zipp, S., & Mileski, M. (2020). Utilization barriers and medical outcomes commensurate with the use of telehealth among older adults: Systematic review. *JMIR Medical Informatics, 8*(8). https://doi.org/10.2196/20359

Li, Y., & Mutchler, J. E. (2020). Older adults and the economic impact of the COVID-19 pandemic. *Journal of Aging & Social Policy, 32*(4–5), 477–487. https://doi.org/10.1080/08959420.2020.1773191

Melamed, O. C., Hauck, T. S., Buckley, L., Selby, P., & Mulsant, B. H. (2020). COVID-19 and persons with substance use disorders: Inequities and mitigation strategies. *Substance Abuse, 41*(3), 286–291. https://doi.org/10.1080/08897077.2020.1784363

Namkee. G. C., & Mayer, J. (2000). Elder abuse, neglect, and exploitation. *Journal of Gerontological Social Work, 33*(2), 5–25. https://doi.org/10.1300/J083v33n02_02

Panchal, N., Kamal, R., Cox, C., & Garfield, R. (2021). *The implications of COVID-19 for mental health and substance use. Kaiser Family Foundation.* https://www.kff.org/coronavirus-covid-19/issue-brief/the-implications-of-covid-19-for-mental-health-and-substance-use/

Raker, E. J., Arcaya, M. C., Lowe, S. R., Zacher, M., Rhodes, J., & Waters, M. C. (2020). Mitigating health disparities after natural disasters: Lessons from The RISK Project. *Health Affairs, 39*(12), 2128–2135. https://doi.org/10.1377/hlthaff.2020.01161

Wei, Y., & Shah, R. (2020). Substance use disorder in the COVID-19 pandemic: A systematic review of vulnerabilities and complications. *Pharmaceuticals, 13*(7), 155. https://doi.org/10.3390/ph13070155

Wingate, M. S., Perry, E. C., Campbell, P. H., David, P., & Weist, E. M. (2007). Identifying and protecting vulnerable populations in public health emergencies: Addressing gaps in education and training. *Public Health Reports, 122*(3), 422–426.

Wosik, J., Fudim, M., Cameron, B., Gellad, Z. F., Cho, A., Phinney, D., Curtis, S., Roman, M., Poon, E. G., Ferranti, J., Katz, J. N., & Tcheng, J. (2020). Telehealth transformation: COVID-19 and the rise of virtual care. *Journal of the American Medical Informatics Association, 27*(6), 957–962. https://doi.org/10.1093/jamia/ocaa067

Index

About the Authors

Margaret Campe, Ph.D. has experience that spans multiple sectors related to family violence and substance use, having held positions in the prevention and intervention of violence; government response policy evaluation; academic research and teaching focused on violence, substance use, and intersectional methodology; and both community-based and governmental program performance evaluation. Margaret's work focuses on the ways in which social problems such as violence and substance use disorders, and the corresponding response systems, disparately affect marginalized populations.

Kathi Harp, Ph.D. is an assistant professor in the College of Public Health at the University of Kentucky. Dr. Harp, a sociologist, is an addiction health services and health disparities researcher. Her work investigates the substance use disorder (SUD) treatment needs of mothers and treatment-related outcomes of mothers with SUD and their children, with a specific focus on those from underserved populations.

Dr. Carrie Oser, DiSilvestro Endowed Professor in the Sociology Department, is the associate director of the Center for Health Equity Transformation and faculty affiliate in the Center on Drug and Alcohol Research at the University of Kentucky. As a health criminologist, she leads interdisciplinary teams in conducting rigorous high-impact research to improve the lives of individuals with substance use disorders and promote health equity. Dr. Oser has been continuously funded as a principal investigator for over 15 years by the National Institutes of Health and has published over 100 peer-reviewed papers.